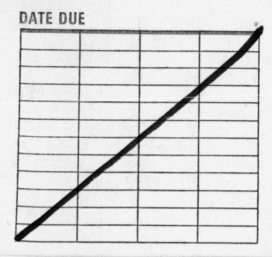

Cyril O. Houle

THE
DESIGN
OF
EDUCATION

Jossey-Bass Publishers
San Francisco · Washington · London · 1976

THE DESIGN OF EDUCATION
by Cyril O. Houle

Copyright © 1972 by Jossey-Bass, Inc., Publishers
615 Montgomery Street
San Francisco, California 94111
&
Jossey-Bass Limited
44 Hatton Garden
London EC1N 8ER

Library of Congress Catalogue Card Number LC 76-186573

International Standard Book Number ISBN 0-87589-125-X

Manufactured in the United States of America

JACKET DESIGN BY WILLI BAUM

FIRST EDITION
First printing: April 1972
Second printing: March 1973
Third printing: March 1974
Fourth printing: August 1976

Code 7207

The Jossey-Bass
Series in Higher Education

CYRIL O. HOULE, *University of Chicago*
Special Advisor, Adult and Continuing Education

To the community of scholars
who study the nature and processes
of education at
The University of Chicago

Preface

The three parts of this book have been developed simultaneously and are intended to provide an integrated whole. (1) The text is written in as straightforward a fashion as I can contrive in order to make its meaning clear to widely varied groups of people interested in adult education. (2) The glossary defines the important terms for the use of analytical readers. It is presented in two different ways: in the customary alphabetical form and in an exposition which uses the key words in context and thereby provides a brief statement of the whole argument of the book. (3) The bibliographic essay identifies some of the major published sources on which that argument relies and suggests additional readings on the topics with which it deals. Thus the second and third part free the text from the elaborate definition of terms and the documentation which would otherwise be necessary.

The system presented here has evolved over a quarter century of practice, teaching, discussion, reading, and reflection. During much of this time, the W. K. Kellogg Foundation supported my research and writing activities and I am grateful to it for doing so.

My obligation to many people for the ideas in the book is so great that I cannot acknowledge it without providing a list of tedious length. My chief debt—both emotional and intellectual—is to one who needs no special acknowledgement since everybody who knows me has long been aware of my reliance on her. My other chief source of help and inspiration has been my colleagues and students at The University of Chicago, and it is to them that the book is dedicated.

Chicago   CYRIL O. HOULE
February 1972

Contents

The Design
of Education

~~~~~~

CHAPTER I

Credos and Systems

~~~~~~

*There are nine and sixty ways
of constructing tribal lays, And
every single one of them is right.*
Rudyard Kipling,
In the Neolithic Age

1

When an episode of learning or teaching is analyzed, either while it is occurring or afterward, it is seen to be an intricate meshing of countless aims and actions. The teacher, if there is one, has general purposes, specific ends, and personal reasons for undertaking his work. Similarly, each learner has broad aspirations, immediate goals, and private motives. Some evidence of objectives may be made manifest by formal statements, but beneath this visible tip of the iceberg lie all the desires and dreams unexpressed by either teacher or learner and sometimes hidden deep in their subconsciousnesses.

The efforts made to achieve desired ends are also diverse and complexly interwoven. If a class is discussing Plato's *Republic,* for example, any thoughtful person can readily identify such customary components of education as leadership, teaching technique, content, social interaction, and evaluation. However, the full reality of what occurs in the mind, emotions, and body of each participant and the nature of its effect on him are so intricate that they defy complete analysis, particularly since close scrutiny makes both teacher and learners self-conscious, thereby altering the nature of the educative experience.

Yet the process of education can be neither understood nor improved unless the realities of learning and teaching are examined in either a natural setting where an individual or group embarks on a personally guided quest for knowledge or in some managed setting, such as a formal classroom. One approach to studying the learning process focuses on a specific component of instruction which is separated from the others for detailed analysis. While every such investigator is likely to overestimate the significance of his topic, he usually understands very well that it is but one part of a total educational process. Another approach is to focus on the learning process as a whole and try to combine its components into an overall system which can serve both as a tool of analysis for understanding what happens in an educational activity and as an instrument of program planning to guide future actions. This second approach is the one used in this book.

The central purpose of this book is to present a system of educational design which may have relevance to education at any age of life, but one which has grown specifically out of an analysis of the

2

organized and purposeful learning activities of men and women. In one way or another, adult education has been a continuing aspect of man's history from the time he emerged from the darkness of prehistory, but the first effective expression of the term adult education did not appear until after World War I. Since then many people have sought to identify its essence as a field of endeavor and perhaps eventually as a profession. The system proposed here owes much to the growth of thought in adult education and the credos and systems which have been widely espoused as guides to practice.[1] Against this background, the rest of the book describes and illustrates the system of educational design suggested here.

Growth of Systematic Thought in Adult Education

Adult education has emerged as a distinctive field of study and application, giving coherence to many activities which formerly were not thought to be related to one another. As has been true in such other comprehensive areas of human aspiration as health, welfare, safety, and recreation, those who first perceived the vast scope of adult education did so with a spirit of exaltation. They believed that men and women who understood the limitlessness of learning as a way of developing human potential would seize every educational opportunity offered them to advance both themselves and society. The early period of the field, therefore, was a time of defining goals and exhorting everyone to achieve them.

But after a first surge of growth and interest, which occurred in the United States in the 1920's it became clear to the leaders of the emerging field that enunciation by writers and lecturers of the values of adult education is not sufficient to make most men and women seek to achieve them. Learning experiences which embody those values must be so organized and conducted that a gradually increasing number of learners can discover the rewards of greater skill, understanding, and sensitiveness. The experiences must then be analyzed to discover their principles of success which can be applied creatively in other situations. As these truths were realized, there began a period of preoccupation with process, either as a generalized

[1] The analysis of these topics rests on an elaborate documentary study which is summarized in the bibliographic essay at the end of the book, thereby relieving the text of a heavy burden of quotations and citations.

technique (such as discussion, demonstration, or sensitivity training) or as a form of service performed by such institutions as a university, an industry, or a voluntary association. The field itself, as a synthesis of many such processes, developed slowly as methods and activities were perfected and their use broadened and as the leaders of various programs established and maintained contact with one another.

As time went on, it became increasingly evident that no substantial unity could be built upon such casual approaches and fortuitous contacts. The people involved in what was essentially a field of practical operation rather than of abstract thought had no deep sense that they were all engaged in the same fundamental activity. An evening school, a public library, and a settlement house might be located in the same neighborhood, they might all serve adults, their directors might be good friends, they might occasionally use one another's facilities and services, and they might be guided by the same aims of community improvement. Yet the staff members of each agency would regard themselves as representatives of a distinctive institution employing a way of work essentially different from that of the others.

Their view was reinforced by the traditional conception that education is an institution-centered activity. Adult education emerged late on the scene at a time when egalitarian influences were reinforcing the rapid advancement of schools, colleges, and universities. Both analysts and administrators of education for children and youth centered their attention almost entirely on the classroom setting with only occasional glances at other learning and teaching activities undertaken in individual, group, or institutional settings.

But the points of service and the areas of application of adult education are multiform. Its practice is more like that of the engineer, social worker, architect, or therapist—indeed, like that of most professions—than it is like that of the school or college teacher or administrator. Since adulthood stretches out for many years and the diversity of life styles is great, the education of men and women occurs in many different settings and takes countless forms. Any effort to build a system of educational process on the work of a specific goal, method of practice, or institution is limited. For example, the attempt to make universal generalizations on the basis of community development, group discussion, or the procedures of an evening school are repudiated by many educators of adults because those generalizations do not conform to the reality they experience.

Some theorists have therefore sought to make a sharp cleavage between the education of children and youth, which they see as institution centered, and that of adults, which they see as process centered. In the United States in the 1920s and 1930s many theorists distinguished between "formal" and "informal" learning or other similar pairs of terms. In continental Europe, where the word *pedagogy* is widely applied to the study of the education of children, the parallel term *andragogy* is often used to refer to the study of the education of adults.

This cleavage of practice into two wholly different parts based on age is denied by those who believe that education is fundamentally the same wherever and whenever it occurs. They assert that it deals always with such basic concerns as the nature of the learner, the goals sought, the social and physical milieu in which instruction occurs, and the techniques of learning or teaching used. These and other components may be combined in infinite ways as, throughout life, the individual embarks on self-directed inquiry either alone or with others, as he benefits from the individual guidance of a tutor, or as he takes part in formally structured group or institutional activity, but, it is argued, the essentials of the educative process remain the same for all ages of life and the basic design of learning is identical whenever or wherever it occurs.

Consequently, beginning in the 1930s, efforts were made to find better and deeper ways of conceptualizing programs. Generalized plans and methodologies, such as group dynamics, change theory, community development, and systems analysis, were proposed. Each was accepted by some people and rejected by others. At least a few of the latter, restive at being called conservative or traditional because they would not espouse the new techniques, looked more deeply than before at their work and developed theories of process which made explicit what had hitherto been implicit in, for example, independent study, tutorial teaching, and the creative use of the classroom. As a result of the advancement of new systems and the better understanding of old ones, the level of discussion deepened and a more mature, thoughtful sense of common identity began to emerge.

As yet, however, it cannot be said that most of the work in the field is guided by any of these systems or even by the desire to follow a systematic theory. The typical career worker in adult education is still concerned only with an institutional pattern of service or a methodology, seldom or never catching a glimpse of the total terrain of which he is cultivating one corner, and content to be, for example, a farm or home advisor, museum curator, public librarian, or industrial trainer. While such people are adult educators, they do not know or do not wish to believe that they are. The winning of their attention and support must be a major aim of anyone who hopes to enlarge and strengthen the field.

Those who do identify themselves with adult education hold widely varying views about its essential nature. Most such people have worked out a guiding credo[2]—a simple statement of belief which channels and directs their ordinary practices. Others have put forward organized systems to achieve a basic coherence of process which the field does not at present possess. A few such model builders are doctrinaire and even evangelistic, but the field has not been polarized by rigid and opposing systems of belief. Instead, much fluidity and even inconsistency of opinion exist. A healthy safeguard against dogmatism is the fact that most people who build careers in the field must constantly meet the test of the market; they must attract and retain the attention of men and women who are free to do things other than learn.

The following review of credos and systems is therefore not a way of sorting everybody in the field into neat categories based on dominant conceptions of practice but a summary of widely held and used views from which a given individual may shift back and forth as necessity dictates. About each credo or system only enough is said here to identify it, but the bibliographical essay refers the reader to much fuller statements of it, by those who believe in it profoundly.

[2] The key terms used in this book either are defined when they make their first substantial appearance or are clear in the context in which they are used. All such terms are formally defined in the Glossary.

One credo which has been consistently avowed since the earliest days of the organized field and is still staunchly supported by many people is the belief that adult education should be a movement unified by a common effort to achieve a single all-encompassing goal. The first major definition of the field was published in 1919 by the Adult Education Committee of the British Ministry of Reconstruction in a document which had a powerful impact on both English and American thought. Its authors were almost wholly oriented to what they variously called general, humanistic, nonutilitarian, or liberal education. The force and persuasiveness with which they expressed its values consolidated a point of view which has affected English adult education ever since and which has in the 1920s and the 1950s served as a model for heavily financed efforts to influence American practice. Other examples of mission-oriented adult education are abundant in the cultural histories of various nations, where efforts have been centered on such objectives as national economic advancement, religious evangelism, the winning of a war, or the conversion of a people to a political or economic theory. In any such case, it has been argued that if all people who consider themselves adult educators believe deeply in the same broad mission, they will create a movement built upon its achievement.

A second credo is based on the belief that since men and women know what they need to learn, the task of the educator of adults is to discover what it is and provide it for them. Among those who hold this view, the public librarian wants a balanced collection to meet any request for a book, the evening school director offers to provide any course desired by ten or more people, and the community college dean uses advisory committees and surveys to discover the desires of his constituency. The educator's methodological task is to devise, perfect, and use the techniques and instruments which reveal the apparent interests and the felt or ascribed needs of the individuals or groups he serves. The field gains coherence from a common concern with this task, a sharing of the ways by which it is undertaken, and a collective use of its results.

A third credo is centered on the idea that the educator of adults should adapt the aims and methods of other forms of schooling to fit the requirements of men and women. Sometimes this adaptation is merely one of time or place as when a high school equivalency program is offered in the evening or a university extension course is given off campus. Sometimes it is creative in approach as when the elementary school curriculum is redesigned to suit the needs of adult illiterates or a special program is created to lead to the baccalaureate degree. The central idea in any such case is that certain standards for mastery of content or skill have already been established, and it is the task of the educator of adults to achieve them with his own clientele. This common concern gives unity of approach to the whole field and elevates its stature since the central focus of effort is upon the achievement of goals which are already well established in any literate society.

A fourth credo emphasizes the importance of powerful and creative leaders in various roles. The teacher should be a master operating in an individualistic fashion, his teaching an expression of basic character tempered by thought, study, and experience; he transforms abstract knowledge by the use of what the Danes call the living word. The creator of an institution or a movement—such as Bishop Grundtvig, Jane Addams, or Seaman Knapp—uses the force of personality to achieve the ends sought. The administrator infuses the program with his own ideas and policies; the head of a Danish folk high school is called a *vorstander,* a particularly apt term since such a man usually stands very much at the forefront of his institution. The field of adult education may be given unity by this conception in three general ways. First, all those concerned chiefly with leadership find community in discussing and fostering it. Second, the leaders of various institutions interact with one another in dealing with their common interests and concerns; in the United States, this activity has provided most of the unity achieved. Third, the idea of adult education itself may become the central concern of a leader— such as Albert Mansbridge, Fredrick Keppel, or E. A. Corbett— who uses the resources of his personality to knit its several components together.

A fifth credo is based on the improvement of generalized institutional processes. The most evident fact about adult education is its multiple sponsorship, and all who administer programs have common concerns arising from an effort to master the fundamentals of management but also from a desire to know how to handle such specifics of adult learning as the provision of learning resources, the charging of fees, the scheduling of activities, and the recruitment and compensation of teachers. Much of the shoptalk of adult educators and much of the training in the field deal with such matters as these. Also, efforts are constantly being made to define the proper roles and interrelationships of institutions. For example, what service should the industrial training department offer on its own and what service should it request of tax-supported organizations? Should the museum be concerned solely with displaying its own resources or should it also lend them to other institutions? What is the level of subject matter appropriate to the public school, the community college, and the university? The effort expended in dealing with such questions tends to knit the field together.

A sixth credo, not widely held, perhaps, but expressed often enough to deserve mention, is given its impetus by a desire to subvert formalism so that energies may be creatively released. Those who hold this view do not seek to replace present structures with others more personally desirable. They argue only that institutionalization of either structure or thought creates undesirable rigidity and that adult educators should stress informality, improvisation and new and unconventional ways of thought. The goal of adult education should be the freeing of the human spirit; the means used should be unusual, provocative, and challenging to those who take part. This view can range all the way from a mild posture of independence to a determined nihilism and from a general impatience with the status quo to a dedicated seeking of the avant-garde. The field itself is defined in personal terms as a communion of fellow spirits.

While the thoughts of at least a few people seem to be wholly encompassed by each of these credos or others like them, most educators of adults are not thus confined. They may express one belief at one time, another at another. They may accept one credo as dominant, subordinating one or more of the others to it. They may even espouse several at the same time. But some of the credos directly contradict one another; for example, the first is inconsistent with the second and the fifth with the sixth. Therefore while each credo has provided some unifying force in the field, none of them is stable or profound enough to synthesize all practice.

The need for a deeper conception of the field than could be provided by any of these credos has been the chief reason why so many systems of thought have been proposed, each of them designed to provide a theoretical basis for educational programing. Some were simple. Their proponents announced, often in an exalted fashion, that some such learning method as discussion or the creative use of problem solving or some teaching technique such as programed or computerized instruction was so important or so suited to the requirements of adults that it reduced all other approaches to insignificance. Other systems provided undergirding for one of the credos, pushing its analysis to a deeper level of thought. For example, the work of Richard Livingstone was powerfully influential in reinforcing the all-encompassing goal of liberal adult education, and many books have dealt with group behavior or institutional theory in terms which suggested they were universal to all adult education. Broader and more systematic approaches to programing than these have also had some acceptance. Some of these approaches overlap each other, but each has a distinct thrust of its own, and each is considered separately in the following account of them.

Systems based on Dewey's thought. The early major development of adult education in the United States in the 1920s and 1930s occurred at the same time the educational theories of John Dewey were finding their fullest expression in practice. His thought was centered on the child in the school, but, perhaps as a result of his experiences in such institutions as Hull House and the extension programs of The University of Chicago, his theories of teaching and learning had a universal quality which strongly appealed to the founding fathers of adult education. Many of them felt that their own work was a protest against what they regarded as the rigid, formal, and involuntary servitude of the schools and therefore they applauded Dewey's attacks on traditionalism and made enthusiastic common cause with the leaders of the progressive education movement, which carried out his ideas in schools and colleges.

In a summary of his educational thought made late in his career, Dewey established the dichotomies which contrasted his own approach to that of "educational reactionaries, who are now gaining force." He said, "To imposition from above is opposed expression and cultivation of individuality; to external discipline is opposed free activity; to learning from tests and teachers, learning through experience; to acquisition of isolated skills and techniques by drill is opposed acquisition of them as means of attaining ends which make direct vital appeal; to preparation for a more or less remote future is opposed making the most of the opportunities of present life; to static aims and materials is opposed acquaintance with a changing world."[3] While such language as this has relevance to learning at any age, some educators of adults took it as almost a direct message to themselves since it expressed so clearly their own feelings about the nature of their field and the mission it was called upon to perform.

More important, they found underpinning for programing in the pragmatic approach which Dewey suggested. His insistence that education be related to all experience made it possible to consider the work not merely of established institutions of formal schooling but also of such other organizations as libraries and museums and of such forms of activity as community development, independent study, supervision, and travel. The specific goals of learning, he argued, are constantly changing and evolving, the sole principles of process are the continuity of experience and the interaction of the learner with his environment, and the central distinction between education and miseducation is that the former enlarges the capacity of the individual or society for richer experiences in the future while the latter arrests, diminishes, or distorts it. The very openness of the system of programing thus suggested gave a sense of exhilarating progressiveness and forward motion to many people as they set about the reconstruction of the learning or teaching experiences with which they were concerned.

While their method rested fundamentally on Dewey's conception of the nature of education, it was reinforced by the breadth of his thought on other topics and issues of concern to the early leaders of adult education. The very act of thinking, he argued, was a process of solving problems: a difficulty arises, the specific nature of the problem is defined, possible solutions are formulated and tested, and finally the most adequate one is chosen. When this

[3] J. Dewey, *Experience and Education* (New York: Macmillan, 1938), pp. 5–6, 22.

process is used to guide education, it becomes a constant quest for competence and enlightenment as an individual or group seeks continuously to solve problems encountered in the effort to reach defined goals. Such an approach is equally applicable in the classroom and in the world outside it and can therefore provide unity for the great array of structured experiences which make up the field of adult education. This sense of coherence was also fostered by other aspects of Dewey's thought as he turned his attention to the advancement of democracy, to ethics, to art, to creation of groups and communities, to growth of the individual, and to countless other matters.

Articulate exponents of his method and thought soon interpreted them to educators of adults. As early as 1926, Eduard C. Lindeman published a series of essays which applied Dewey's approach in various ways, suggesting, for example:

> The approach to adult education will be via the route of *situations,* not subjects Our academic system has grown in reverse order: subjects and teachers constitute the starting point, students are secondary. In conventional education the student is required to adjust himself to an established curriculum; in adult education the curriculum is built around the student's needs and interests. Every adult person finds himself in specific situations with respect to his work, his recreation, his family life, his community life, et cetera—situations which call for adjustments. Adult education begins at this point. Subject matter is brought into the situation, is put to work, when needed. Texts and teachers play a new and secondary role in this type of education; they must give way to the primary importance of the learner.[4]

An even more systematic exposition of Dewey's thought as it applied to adult education was published by Ruth Kotinsky in 1933.[5] Such books were supplemented by countless essays dealing firsthand or derivatively with Dewey's approach. Gradually his influence came to permeate the methodological thought of the emerging field.

In a broad sense, it still does, for some of its central ideas are embedded in the subsequent systems which are described later. Each sets forth a more explicit process of program-development than that

[4] E. C. Lindeman, *The Meaning of Adult Education* (New York: New Republic, 1926), pp. 8–9.

[5] R. Kotinsky, *Adult Education and the Social Scene* (New York: Appleton-Century-Crofts, 1933).

which Dewey formulated and has thereby in some measure violated the openness and fluidity of approach characteristic of his work. His thought was a point of departure for all of them, however, a fact which can be demonstrated by both analytical comparison and study of historical relationships. Even those theorists who depart radically from his views in some respects (holding, for example, that the central aims of education are enduring and universal and do not grow out of the interaction of the individual with his environment) tend to follow program-development systems based on Dewey's theories. When some of the detailed conceptualizations of process (such as change theory and systems analysis) grow tedious and mechanical, it is refreshing to return to their wellsprings in Dewey's writing to gain the vast perspective it provides.

Systems based on Tyler's thought. The educational reactionaries of whom Dewey spoke did not give way readily before the onslaught of the new forms of education based upon his work. The major lines of battle were drawn within the schools themselves as conservatives confronted progressives. Conflict also arose at the points where one level of institution intersected with another. For example, universities required entering students to have completed an established pattern of courses based on the mastery of prescribed subject matter. Secondary school staffs who wished to be innovative found themselves unable to make very many changes without penalizing their college-bound students. In cases of direct confrontation between defenders of traditional values and proponents of radical change, victory went now to one side, now to another, but it soon became clear that some new conception of curriculum building would have to be devised to serve as a synthesis between old and new. Many leaders of education turned their attention to this task, but the major contribution proved to be that made by Ralph W. Tyler.

His work was essentially comparative and collaborative. He directed major national studies of secondary schools and colleges, undertook countless surveys of institutions and areas of work, and became a continuing consultant to the staffs of many agencies. He accepted adult education as an essential part of the instructional establishment, paying particular attention to the Cooperative Extension Service and to continuing occupational and professional training. Thus he examined, led in establishing, or guided many forms of educational innovation and derived his fundamental methodology from the study and comparison of a large and broadly based variety of cases. He involved in this work not only members of the staffs of the programs he aided but also many colleagues who shared in his leadership, some of whom became outstanding leaders of American educational thought. While he wrote several seminal works, his major impact was felt directly on the field itself as institutions put into effect his ideas on the fundamental strategy of program building.

That strategy is now so well understood and established that it undergirds most modern educational theory and practice. Its essence can be summarized briefly. In any program, the first task is to define purposes by considering studies of the learners, of contemporary life, and of the suggestions of subject specialists. Such data as may be derived from these studies should be screened by the educational and social philosophy of the curriculum builder and by the findings of the psychology of learning in order to produce specific objectives which should guide instruction. These objectives should be stated in a fashion which makes them useful in selecting learning experiences and guiding teaching. Such experiences are then chosen according to certain principles and to conform to various categories of goals and are organized in such a way as to produce desired results. The processes of evaluation should be so designed as to measure the degree to which identified objectives have been achieved, and that knowledge should be used in future planning.

This brief summary suggests only the bare outline of the Tyler rationale as first presented in 1950.[6] Since then, its various aspects have been enormously enlarged and enriched. The sources and nature of objectives have been extensively and variously analyzed and taxonomized. The application of the strategy of program building in countless situations has vastly increased knowledge of how that process should be used even as central reliance on a single fundamental rationale has given coherence to work undertaken at every level of education. As scientific knowledge has grown concerning the sources and screens (such as the nature of the learner, the

---

[6] R. W. Tyler, *Basic Principles of Curriculum and Instruction* (Chicago: University of Chicago Press, 1950).

suggestions of subject specialists, or the psychology of learning), it has been put to use within the established system. Expertise in the evaluation of learning has been carried to a high degree of competence.

Even as Tyler's thought has evolved through the years, so has that of his followers. A number of variant program-development systems have been proposed, and sharp disagreements exist over the proper way to consider various components of the rationale, most particularly the sources or method of statement of objectives and the validity of various forms of evaluation. But even with all this amplification and disagreement, the fundamental way of thought which Tyler suggested still remains intact, underlying the discussion and practice of most education today. In this process, the old debates between the progressives and the reactionaries have been lessened as both parties have found an acceptable method of designing and conducting education.

The reinforcement of the rationale in the field of adult education has come about in three major ways. First, many institutions have found it necessary to reconstruct their programs and have used all or part of Tyler's rationale in doing so, often with his direct guidance or that of one of his followers. Thus the staff members involved have come to have first-hand experience with the application of his ideas. Second, almost all of those who hold advanced degrees in adult education have secured them in graduate departments or schools of education where they have been extensively exposed to Tyler's ideas. Finally, many of the program-planning models devised by theoreticians of adult education have flowed directly or indirectly from his rationale. Certainly that fact is true of the framework suggested in this book.

Systems based on Lewin's thought. The educational ideas of both Dewey and Tyler grew out of their observation of the processes of education, and while both were aware of learning as a universal and lifelong activity, they tended to center their attention on its most highly developed form, the work of schools and colleges for children and young people. The two clusters of systems which are now to be considered reversed that emphasis since they were first used extensively in program building for adults and were only later applied in the schooling of youth. Moreover, both clusters were borrowed from social psychology, not education. They were inspired by the conceptions of many people but, most significantly, of Kurt Lewin, a European who migrated to the United States in the 1930s and whose early death prevented him from working out the program patterns suggested by his ideas. A group of his students and followers, however, found in the burgeoning growth of adult education an opportunity to develop and systematize his thought.

The first set of systems was originally known by the umbrella term *group dynamics*. This designation was always inappropriate, for if the term had a literal meaning at all, it referred to that subfield of social psychology which deals with the objective study of the nature of small groups and their influence on the actions of their members. To those who engaged in such study, however, it soon became clear that the theoretical knowledge they discovered could have major practical consequences. Many new concepts and techniques were devised (among them feedback, role playing, buzz groups, hidden agenda, special forms of nondirective leadership, reactor panels, listening teams, problem census, and involvement) which were to become part of the colloquial speech of educators of adults. Somehow the term *group dynamics* came to be used as a collective term to describe such practices and their theoretical foundations.

Back of this language lay the deeply serious belief of those who identified themselves with the group dynamics movement that the group and the larger human associations of which it is the cellular unit have a powerfully educative potential for man and society. Since several leaders of the movement were also key figures in adult education, it was natural that that field should be used to explore means for channeling and using the power inherent in the group. It seemed likely that the central methodological purpose of adult education could be found in group dynamics. Leland Bradford suggested as much in 1947:

> Perhaps the basic problem of adult education is that of educating adults for group work. We have educated people as individuals and expected them to perform successfully in a society that is primarily one of group complexity. . . . The most difficult problems we face today are essentially group problems. They are major problems primarily because we have not been taught the skills of working as groups toward the solution of group problems. . . . The education of adults demands different methods than do other

educational fields. . . . The basic method of adult education is rapidly becoming the discussion method. . . . It is obviously incumbent upon those in adult education to strengthen discussion method and group work as the process of democracy. . . . We must, in adult education, go deeply into an exploration into methods and technics of group discussion and group growth. Only as we become really skilled in these areas will we be of important service to others.[7]

As these ideas were worked out in the late 1940s and the 1950s, group dynamics came to have a powerful impact on adult education. People who believed strongly in the group approach served as officers, executives, or editors for national associations and journals and used their positions to put forward their ideas in publications and speeches and to structure meetings according to their theories. Strong opposition to this alleged effort to capture the field quickly grew up, with the result that opinion became polarized. Some of the wounds inflicted in ensuing battles have still not healed.

As time went on, however, efforts to study or enhance the educativeness of the group began to change. Attention shifted from means to ends, to finding out what people could learn about themselves and their relationships with others and how they could use that knowledge creatively in primary social associations. Instead of being called the group dynamics approach, the movement began to be known as sensitivity training or human relations education. Methods of analysis also grew more subtle and applications more profound. The formalized training group (T-group) and the encounter group were devised and began to take many different forms, some elaborate, some bizarre. These complex formulations could not be as readily transplanted to all fields of practice as could such simple techniques as feedback and nondirective leadership. Sensitivity training gradually became a special program area of adult education, cutting across all institutional lines in its application but no longer being advocated as a universal system of planning and analysis.

But group dynamics did make a significant positive contribution to adult education by stressing the importance of treating every

[7] L. Bradford, "Report of the Division of Adult Education Services of the National Education Association," *Adult Education Bulletin,* 1947, *11,* 167–70.

socialized learning situation as a group. Teachers, leaders, and administrators of even the most formal kinds of activities strive much harder than they did in earlier days to take advantage of the important reinforcement which fellow learners can offer one another. And learners themselves are likely to suggest or even insist upon a group approach, for an awareness of sensitivity training in one or another of its countless forms has now entered into the common culture and become an accepted part of human association.

The second cluster of program-design theories which grew out of Lewin's ideas came to be called change theory. While highly complex in its formulations and applications, it rests on the idea that in any defined social situation, the present level of accomplishment is supported by some forces and held back by others. The amount of goods produced in a factory, the incidence of disease in a community, the ability of a woman to read and write her mother tongue, the stability and social integrity of a nation—all such conceptualized levels of practice can be analyzed in the same basic way by asking two questions: What forces are at work to increase the level of performance? What forces operate to keep it from rising higher?

Anyone seeking to improve practice in any situation must begin by answering these questions and then go on to ask two others. How can the positive forces be reinforced? How can the negative ones be weakened? The operative task becomes one of identifying a present performance level, "unfreezing" it by strengthening positive influences and weakening negative ones, establishing as high a new level of operation as desirable, and then "refreezing" it so that it will not slip back again. In this process, two major roles are involved: the client or client system, who is helped to improve and who may be an individual, group, institution, community, or society; and the change agent, a single person or group who uses both technical expertise and skill in human interaction to bring about the desired change by entering into a helping relationship. For example, if increased production in a factory is desired, its supervisory group is the client system and a specialist in industrial management is the change agent. To be fully effective the agent must be an expert in both production techniques and the handling of human relationships.

This concept of method has been widely used in many fields of social action and is not distinctive to adult education. Indeed, the analysis of forces in a situation usually reveals that they take complex forms, some unrelated to education. Industrial production, for example, may be held back by a low level of work skills but also by poor wage incentive systems, weak management, bad working conditions, and ineffective collective bargaining practices. The change agent must take account of all such conditions or he is effective neither as an analyst nor as an instrument of reform. But in the search for an integrative theory of program design, some educators of adults have been so attracted by the change theory concept that they have adopted it as their central strategy. Its influence is clearly seen, for example, in Coolie Verner's definition of adult education as "a relationship between an educational agent and a learner in which the agent selects, arranges, and continuously directs a sequence of progressive tasks that provide systematic experiences to achieve learning for those whose participation in such activities is subsidiary and supplemental to a primary productive role in society."[8]

The processes through which a change agent and client interact are infinitely complex, but the bare outlines of at least one strategy may be sketched. A sequence begins when a client becomes aware of the existence of a problem; sometimes this awareness appears independently, sometimes it results from stimulation by the agent. The agent assesses the motivation and capacity of the client to change, thereby diagnosing the forces which either favor or resist growth. The agent also assesses his own motivations and resources in helping the client. As a result, appropriate change objectives and targets are worked out, and the helping role of the change agent is more precisely defined than it was before. Suitable strategies are identified and applied. Throughout this process but particularly at its conclusion, attention is devoted to the ways changes will be stabilized and maintained. Finally, the helping relationship is terminated.

Many alternate strategies of application of change theory have been devised, growing out of both theoretical considerations

[8] C. Verner, "Definition of Terms," in G. Jensen, A. A. Liveright, and W. Hallenbeck (Ed.), *Adult Education, Outlines of an Emerging Field of University Study* (Washington, D.C.: Adult Education Association, 1964), p. 32. Italicized in original.

and applications to special types of situations. Also, several terms, particularly *change agent*, have proved to be attractive and are used either by themselves or as parts of strategies which have different theoretical bases. The term *change* has itself been given many interpretations. To some people, it signifies broad social advance toward new conceptions of personal or social order; it is progressive, liberal, or radical in connotation. But other people adopt a less value-laden approach. Desired change may equally as well, they say, be directed toward the strengthening of conservative or reactionary values.

Change theory is particularly useful when education must be undertaken in natural situations, not those formally established for the sake of learning. Its milieu is the factory, the community, the labor union, or some similar setting, particularly one in which changes must be brought about by the use of several kinds of activity. For example, a safety specialist acting as a change agent may reduce the highway accident rate by better law enforcement, improved engineering, and more effective education. He may apply this third remedy in many ways: mass campaigns to inform drivers of the rules of the road, stringent training programs for those who want drivers' licenses, instruction of engineers on appropriate standards of highway construction and of law enforcement officers on how to carry out their duties, and special courses required of habitual breakers of traffic laws. For him, education is not a separate approach but is intimately intertwined with enforcement and engineering.

The application of change theory is less useful in other situations. Its reliance upon the distinction between the change agent and the client means that it cannot serve very well to guide the self-educative activities of the individual. Verner recognizes this difficulty and eliminates such activities from consderation.[9] Other theorists suggest that the same individual can play the roles of change agent and client simultaneously, but in practice this conception is hard to apply. Nor does change theory easily fit other categories of situations such as the voluntary group, the classroom, or the educative use of the mass media. And its general design has to do with the handling

[9] Verner, pp. 31–32.

of a specific act or episode and therefore does not provide for either a series or an aggregate of episodes.

Systems based on community development. The attempt to use community improvement as a basic strategy of program design in adult education has had many different starting points. The focal idea is that residents in a community (which may be variously defined in geographic or social terms) should be helped to act collectively to solve some problem which affects the lives of all of them. In planning and undertaking this task they achieve tangible results, but if the process is skillfully handled, they also learn how to attack other problems and are motivated to do so by their feeling of success in their initial efforts. Thus a community may be transformed from a traditional way of life which has few satisfactions for any of its members to one which offers tangible rewards and hopes for all of them. The system initiates and provides the mobilizing force for many activities, as Richard Poston suggests:

> It is a process of education by which people of all ages and all interests in the community learn to share their thoughts, their ideals, their aspirations, their joys, and their sorrows, and in large measure to mold and shape their communal destiny for themselves. It is a process of self-discovery by which the people of a community learn to identify and solve their community problems. These problems may vary from the need for a new sewage disposal system to a need for becoming better informed on world affairs or on the contents of the great books.[10]

The strategy of community development follows Dewey's problem-solving approach and is in a sense an application of his method. The people of a locality become aware of its imperfections either gradually or as a result of some galvanizing event. They mobilize their forces to cope with their difficulties. Either by themselves or with specialist help, they define their problem, collect and analyze the data relevant to it, examine various possible solutions, choose one, put it into effect, and subsequently evaluate their progress. The habits of association or organizational structure which they have developed to cope with this problem then continue in

[10] R. W. Poston, "The Relation of Community Development to Adult Education," *Adult Education*, 1954, *4*, 194.

being, and the leaders choose another problem on which to work. In dealing with it they use both the knowledge of themselves and of their community and the method of attack which they have learned in dealing with the first problem.

This strategy is also like that used in change theory and has often been powerfully reinforced by it. But the two strategies have separate histories and can be distinguished from one another in important ways. In community development there may or may not be an independent change agent. When there is, he may be the central preexisting feature; thus the staff member of a university-based community development bureau may go in search of localities to help. And, perhaps most important, the central idea in community development is not to bring about planned change in some concrete specific aspect but to use the initiating episode in which such change occurs as a way of achieving sequence and continuity of a self-renewing sort.

In North America, community development has traditionally been part of the outreach service of an established educational institution. One of the most important of these is the public school, which has been suggested again and again as the proper place for mounting a unified attack on the social ills of the area it serves. This idea came to prominence in the 1930s, when a number of model programs began to appear and has continued ever since, particularly after the activities of the Mott Foundation in Flint, Michigan, received national attention and support. Colleges and universities have also been centers for such work. The best-known program was that initiated by St. Francis Xavier University in Nova Scotia, which has served as a prototype for many other ventures. A number of universities provide expert consultants for localities which seek help, and in some cases community development bureaus have been established to carry out this function. In some places, too, the work of the Cooperative Extension Service has been conceptualized as a process of community development with the farm or home advisor serving as a resident specialist.

In other countries, community development has sometimes evolved as a separate function of government. Nations with few economic resources feel the need to mobilize the energies of people in programs of self-help which are immediately rewarding in terms of such tangible accomplishments as roads, schoolhouses, or latrines, and which also give the people involved a sense of progressive effort and accomplishment. Striking successes have been achieved in both respects in many communities throughout the world, and, in some nations, developmental programs have been institutionalized to provide widespread coverage of the country.

While the concept of community development is exciting and its broad strategy of operation is not hard to grasp, the application of its principles in specific situations is made difficult by two pervasive aspects of community life. The first is the habit pattern of the people themselves, a pattern which holds them in established ways of action reinforced by mores and folkways as well as by traditional systems of authority. An African chief is likely to regard as a threat any effort to change the nature of the community he rules, particularly when the source of that effort is a national government which he knows can grow in authority only at the expense of his own. The second difficulty arises in accomplishing the essential second phase of community development, when people who have been carefully guided through a first venture should presumably be able and eager to undertake a second task on their own using the principles they have learned. Practical people have difficulty abstracting and using theoretical principles. To build a road is one thing, to build a schoolhouse another. How can anyone learn from doing one how to do the other? The community development specialist constantly confronts this question, and unless he can answer it— and put his answer into successful practice—he perpetuates the dependence of the community on him and therefore fails as an educator.

Systems analysis systems. All of the foregoing ways of planning or analyzing educational activities can be fully understood only in terms of the contexts in which they have been developed and applied. But each could also be viewed abstractly and theoretically as a system, a set of interrelated ideas, principles, or practices which forms a collective entity. It is in such fashion that a systems analyst would view each one, for his concern begins with a way of thinking and then proceeds to its application. He is interested in how a process can be conceptualized, usually in a diagram, so that its essential components are identified and put into a proper sequential order to facilitate action and decision making. He therefore works at a higher level of abstraction than do the theorists dealt with earlier in this chapter, for his system building has to do with the nature of systems themselves.

This approach has ancient antecedents but it became highly visible in the 1960s. An earlier concern with such instruments of analysis as flow charts and tables of organization gradually grew into a much more sophisticated approach. Some social scientists became preoccupied with model building. Educators developed programed learning with its linear, branching, and recycling concepts. Industrial managers developed complex ways of charting the flow of work. The concept of program budgeting was developed and spread through industry, commerce, government, and private nonprofit organizational work. The definition of systems and their analysis in terms of input, throughput, and output became common. Many different systems of system building have now been proposed. By mid-1969, Hartley was able to identify sixty different generalized code names or acronyms, such as operations research, PERT, PPBS, cost-benefit analysis, and modular scheduling.[11]

Systems analysis has been extensively used in education, particularly in the administration of institutions and in the structuring of learning sequences for computer-assisted or other forms of programed instruction.[12] While this approach might theoretically be used in any educational situation, its sophisticated complexity has caused its major application to be made in large-scale and expensive enterprises. It is well suited to the direction of a national adult literacy campaign but less useful as a guide to handling a single literacy class. Meanwhile the opponents of the practice of systems

[11] H. J. Hartley, "Limitations of Systems Analysis," *Phi Delta Kappan*, May 1969, 516.

[12] Each such system is highly complex and requires elaborate explanation. Moreover, a comparison of several approaches is required to understand the general theory of systems analysis. Anyone wishing to make such a study might begin with the following references: D. L. Cook, *Program Evaluation and Review Technique*, Cooperative Research Monograph 17 (Washington, D.C.: Office of Education, 1966); B. W. Kreitlow and T. MacNeil, *An Evaluation of the Model for Educational Improvement as an Analytical Tool for Describing the Change Process* (Madison: Center for Cognitive Learning, The University of Wisconsin, 1969); and M. Toye, "Training Design Algorithm," *Training in Business and Industry*, October 1970.

analysis, as distinguished from its theory, have charged that it is too rigid, too centralized, too prone to a simplistic treatment of complex problems and practices, and too likely to treat the individual teacher or learner as a faceless unit in a system.[13] While defenders of systems analysis maintain that such objections can be overcome, no way has yet been devised for adapting its highly sophisticated approach so that it can be used as a daily guide by the learner or the educator.

Misapplied systems. As the descriptions of change theory, community development, and systems analysis have all made clear, adult education is often complexly related to the achievement of purposes which are different from learning or teaching. In each of these three cases, a well-developed theory of operation guides practice and helps to make clear the relationship between education and other purposes. In many situations, however, adult education is accepted as being subordinate or identical to some related function, and a way of work which is appropriate to it is accepted as being the fundamental system to be used to guide learning or teaching.

One such function is *public relations.* When well conducted, programs of adult education can have important favorable consequences for the institutions which sponsor them, a truth which is not lost upon university presidents, school superintendents, industrial executives, or labor union officials. In any such case, there is a strong temptation to design and conduct a program so that it will win support among opinion makers, achieve favorable attitudes for the parent institution, or reinforce another activity, such as the K-12 program of the public schools, the "regular" offering of the university, or the point of view of industry, commerce, or labor. (In bygone days, the educational committee of a local union was sometimes composed of muscular gentlemen chosen because of their ability to persuade their fellow members of the wisdom of certain policies.) When used only as a public relations endeavor, adult education can be successful, at least in the short run. But men and women are not likely to be fooled very long, particulary in this sophisticated age, by any program which, under the guise of helping them in one way, covertly seeks to win their support for something else. In the long run, the best public relations is produced by a program which is

[13] For a review of such criticisms, see Hartley.

centered on the desire to achieve educational goals and is successful
in doing so.

Service can be distinguished from adult education by the
fact that the aim of those who offer it is not to impart skill, knowledge, or sensitiveness, but to give direct assistance to their clients.
In practice, the two purposes are often confused, particularly if
service is elevated to the loftiness of an all-pervasive goal, as it is,
for example, in a university whose officers declare that its three purposes are research, teaching, and service. In such a case, a county
agricultural agent of that university may have a difficult time deciding what duties are appropriate. When should he test soils, order
seeds, administer a cooperative, or grade farm produce? If he is an
offerer of service, he does all these things as needed, and his method
is appropriate to the task he is performing. If he is an educator, he
undertakes them only for demonstration or guidance purposes and
as they fit whatever system of educational design he believes appropriate. As thus stated, the difference is straightforward, but in the
realities of community life, the distinction may be hard to draw. For
example, should the county agent give service to influential farmers
so that they help support his educational program? If he does not,
he may not be able to maintain it. If he does, he may discover, almost before he knows it, that his educational program is dominated
by his provision of service. While such a result is not necessarily
bad, it does blur the two purposes and may keep either of them from
being effectively achieved.

Recreation may or may not be pursued in an educative
fashion. Pleasurable activities may be undertaken simply because of
the satisfaction inherent in them, but many people do want to
deepen their enjoyment by learning and therefore embark upon a
program of study. In many cases, recreation and education are
linked together so intimately that it is hard to separate them. However, a failure to recognize that they are essentially different purposes may lead to unfortunate consequences. Someone who wants to
increase his competence may think that practice alone makes perfect
and therefore may fail to seek the instruction he needs. Someone
who wants only to enjoy himself may have the idea of improvement
thrust upon him, thereby ruining his sense of satisfaction. An evening school may maintain activities and facilites (such as choruses,

drama groups, arts and crafts shops, and hobby clubs) which offer little or no instruction but use public funds supposed to be devoted to education. Such practices lead to a blurring of purpose and program design which is harmful for both functions.

Closely related to recreation is *esthetic appreciation.* The enjoyment of the beautiful in any of its varied forms can be experienced directly with no thought of improvement, but satisfaction can also be deepened by education. The two purposes differ from one another as every museum director knows. He can arrange the objects on display so that each can be seen to fullest advantage by those who want to admire it or he can put them in some instructive order and add guides to their understanding. Usually some balance is struck, but the achievement of a harmony of the two functions requires that both of them be considered.

When *fraternization* occurs naturally in life, it is usually not influenced by the desire to learn or to teach. Comradeship is its own excuse for being. If it turns into a mutually shared inquiry or a master-disciple relationship, it becomes more complex than before precisely because a new dimension has been added. This difference is sometimes not recognized when fraternization is structured, as it is in interest groups or voluntary associations. In such cases, conviviality is accepted as the equivalent of education, and a sense of enjoyment or satisfaction in being with other people is taken as the measure of accomplishment of learning. For instance, the participants in a residential conference may give it a high rating simply because they enjoyed it so much. Alternatively, sociability may be lessened or ruined by the introduction of didactic elements. The members of a club attend because they want to enjoy the fellowship, but the program committe requires them to hear a lecture. In group or institutional settings, fraternization and education may be combined and may well reinforce one another, but if so, the relationship must be conceived as a complex one which combines two inherently different purposes.

The promotion of *welfare,* defined as a social effort to provide minimum standards of acceptable life for all members of a society, subtly pervades much adult educational thought and practice. Many people seem to believe that learning in adulthood is essentially the effort to give a second chance for basic education to those who missed their first chance or that it is concerned solely with such goals as occupational competence for the unemployed, family life improvement for threatened homes, or consumer skills for poor people. This conception of adult education as solely an activity of a welfare state or of private charity limits its scope and narrows its range of designs. Many programs are excluded which are educative in a broader sense and which could be improved if subjected to program analysis and planning. For example, either a learned society or a literary club can become stultified and ineffective because none of its members realize that what they are doing falls within the scope of adult education. Also much needed nonwelfare learning or teaching may never be undertaken. A public school system may offer literacy and vocational courses but never try to educate those community leaders who determine the major social policies of the city. Most damaging of all is the separation of educators from learners along class or income lines and the consequent introduction of an overt or covert condescension into the very heart of the educative process.

Therapy is the hardest function to distinguish from education, in both practice and concept. Therapy implies the treatment of illness or disability in order to achieve a normal state of being, whereas education implies the realization in countless ways of an infinite human potential. But this obvious distinction is often blurred by those who relate the two functions in any one of three essentially different ways.

Some people take therapy and education to be virtually identical. Such a view is held, for example, by anyone who argues that people study only because they have needs, identified either by themselves or by others. It follows that any form of unfulfilled potential is equated with deficiency and any measure taken to remedy it is essentially therapy. A similar view is held by those who conceive certain methods of psychotherapy (such as nondirective counseling or psychoanalysis) to be ways of helping a client examine his beliefs so that he can construct a system of values to guide his life. Thus defined, such techniques may begin by being therapeutic but are essentially educative in character and, their adherents would claim, are the profoundest methods of learning now available.

Some people subordinate education to therapy, viewing it as

a methodological resource, as it is used, for example, by a physical therapist or a dietitian. In this sense, it parallels such other forms of treatment as surgery and chemotherapy.

Some people consider therapy to be merely one approach to education. While it is true that some learning and teaching endeavors arise out of and are guided by a sense of need or deprivation, others grow out of a positive zest, interest, and desire to improve. Education has at least as much to do with the achievement of outstanding excellence as it does with bringing deficient people up to some kind of norm. Paralleling the therapy or needs approach, therefore, should be one which is based on interest, a feeling of curiosity, fascination, or absorption in the achievement of some goal whose accomplishment is intended to give rise to satisfaction and enjoyment.

All three approaches so clearly identify education and therapy with each other that the two functions seem virtually inseparable. Much of the literature of education is, in fact, influenced more or less directly by this view. But this linkage, in any of its forms, does damage to the independence of education as a distinctive process worthy of being considered on its own terms, as it has been by those who have built most of the systems previously described.

Many other functions or activities have also been misapplied as systems for educational program planning or analysis. Among them are communication, the performing arts, religion, participation, creativeness, and health. An analysis of these functions and of the seven mentioned previously reveals that they are closely related to education in three ways. Some (such as service, recreation, and religion) have purposes which are similar to education but essentially different from it. Some (such as esthetic appreciation and health) delineate broad clusters of educational goals. Some deal with one component of educational design; thus fraternization is a form of social reinforcement and public relations of interpretation. Functions can also intersect with education in more than one of these ways. For example, welfare, recreation, or esthetic appreciation may be perceived either as a parallel purpose or as a goal cluster. Therapy is both of these and, in addition, provides theories of methodology which have been influential in some programs of adult education.

Since these differences and distinctions are complex and sometimes hard to understand, the occasional domination of adult education by systems or ways of thought derived from other functions (or even by special applications of the credos mentioned earlier) is not surprising. As Cardinal Newman pointed out in distinguishing recreation from education, "All I say is call things by their right names, and do not confuse together ideas which are essentially different."[14] The best corrective against confusing other functions with adult education is to develop and use a system of practice based wholly on learning and with sufficient strength not to be overwhelmed by systems used in allied but essentially different fields of human activity.

A New System

All the credos and systems described above have been considered in developing the system proposed in this book. The field of adult education is even at this time old enough to make possible not merely an analysis of the theoretical bases of these credos and systems but also an assessment of their several values and limitations as they have been used in many situations. Even misapplied systems can be useful. For example, some of the people who have believed that fraternization is the chief end of learning have now developed procedures of social reinforcement which can be widely applied.

But the system that *The Design of Education* describes is not an eclectic one. Some concepts and components of other systems have been used in constructing it but have been integrated into a pattern essentially different from earlier models, one which it is hoped is sufficiently broad to accommodate the conceptions and guide the actions of a wide range of educators. The system itself is sketched in the second chapter and illustrated and described in detail in the subsequent ones.

[14] J. H. Newman, *The Idea of a University* (New York: Longmans, Green, 1910), p. 144.

CHAPTER II

The Fundamental System

> Science is an allegory that asserts that the relations between the parts of reality are similar to the relations between terms of discourse.
>
> Scott Buchanan,
> *Poetry and Mathematics*

31

Adult education is the process by which men and women (alone, in groups, or in institutional settings) seek to improve themselves or their society by increasing their skill, knowledge, or sensitiveness; or it is any process by which individuals, groups, or institutions try to help men and women improve in these ways. The fundamental system of practice of the field, if it has one, must be discerned by probing beneath many different surface realities to identify a basic unity of process.

Some Assumptions

The system proposed rests on seven assumptions: *Any episode of learning occurs in a specific situation and is profoundly influenced by that fact.* Every human being lives in a complex personal and social milieu which is unique to him, which constantly changes, and which influences all his experience. Any segment of that experience devoted to learning occurs in a distinctive and specific situation which can be separated out for analysis but which is inherently part of his total milieu. The purposes, pattern, and results of that learning are all profoundly affected by the situation in which it occurs. Every activity he undertakes is unlike any other; for example, every class he attends is unique. If he participates in more than one educational situation such as independent study, tutorial instruction, group participation, or membership in a voluntary association, each kind is different from the others.

The uniqueness of situations applies equally to each person who shares in them and to the social settings in which the instruction occurs. Each learner in a group and each educator who guides its members lives within his own milieu and is influenced in a distinctive way by the situation in which he finds himself. If attention is shifted away from individuals toward the social entities in which they learn—groups, classes, or institutions—the same distinctiveness of milieu and situation also applies.

The analysis or planning of educational activities must be based on the realities of human experience and upon their constant change. Since every situation is unique, the effort to understand or to plan educational activities must be centered as far as possible upon realities, not upon forms or abstractions. An objective is a purpose which guides a learner or an educator, not the formal statement of that purpose. Anyone who designs an educational activity may make as clear and exact a forecast as possible of what he hopes to achieve, but the words of that forecast do not capture all his ideas, nor are those ideas the sole determinants of what will occur after the activity begins. He must constantly reshape his plans and procedures in order to come to terms with changes brought about by the desires and abilities of other people or the specific instructional resources he finds available. The evolving objectives are different from his initial statement of them. The methods he uses are not exactly like those in his lesson plans. And no predetermined method of evaluating the results of instruction can adequately measure the achievement of goals which do not become evident until the episode is completed or which exist only in the private intentions of the teacher or the learner.

Reality is hard to grasp (as the literature of epistemology demonstrates), but that fact does not mean that the effort to discern it should be abandoned. A continuing effort to perceive the reality of an educational activity must be attempted before the learning begins, while it is occurring, and as it is appraised afterward.

Education is a practical art. As is true in such established professions as law or medicine, success in the process of education is always measured by what occurs in the specific instances of its practice. What is the verdict of the jury, how well and how speedily is the patient returned to health, to what degree does the learner master the knowledge he seeks? As a sophisticated practical art, education draws upon many theoretical disciplines in the humanities and the social and biological sciences. It also uses an extensive and complex body of principles which has emerged from analysis of its own previous practice, and it has a history and lore of its own. But if this abstract and applied knowledge is to prove effective, it must be used in a specific situation to bring about a desired end.

To illustrate the point further, it may be said that any learning or teaching design is similar to plans made by an architect. He has a deep knowledge of esthetics, engineering, economics, and other sciences. He is aware of architectural traditons; of the range of building materials available, the methods of putting them together, and their relative values in various settings; and of the ways by which harmony is achieved between a building and its environment. Yet he knows that he must design each particular building in terms of its immediate terrain and surroundings, using the construction materials and labor available, and staying within the allotted budget. The educator's design has similar imperatives. He may know a great deal about the theory and practice of education but in each case he has a specific learner or group of learners to reach; limited resources of money, time, and materials to use; and a given setting in which to work. His success is judged by himself and others not by how much he knows but by his competence in using that knowledge to deal with the situation at hand.

The entire career of the educator is judged by some balancing out of the relative successes and failures of all the programs he designs and conducts. The variation among these programs may be simple. For example, a literacy teacher may simply repeat her courses over and over again for twenty years, making only changes required by different groups of students or by the appearance of new teaching aids. Usually, however, variations are complex. Just as the architect builds many houses, so the educator deals with many different situations, in each of which he applies his talents and his resources of knowledge to the task at hand. Success in each case may be judged separately, but he and others appraise his career in terms of his capacity to deal with the whole range of his endeavors.

The same generalization applies to the learner. He may design a program of independent study for himself or he may fit into an activity designed by a tutor, group leader, teacher, or institutional staff. In each case, his success is judged, by himself and by others, in terms of his mastery of the goals he seeks. His total learning achievement, however, is not measured by the results of any one act or episode but by the fruits of all the endeavors in which he has engaged.

Education is a cooperative rather than an operative art. The distinction between these two terms is an ancient one. An operative art is one in which the creation of a product or performance is essentially controlled by the person using the art. The painter, sculptor, engineer, actor, shoemaker, and builder are operative artists. A cooperative art, though no less creative than an operative one, works in a facilitative way by guiding and directing a natural entity or process. The farmer, physician, and educator are three classic examples of cooperative artists. The farmer does not create the crops; he helps nature produce them. The physician aids and reinforces the processes by which the patient gets well. ("God heals," said Benjamin Franklin, "but the doctor takes the fee.") The educator does not put ideas into the minds of learners nor does he give them skills or sensitiveness. Instead he helps them learn these things for themselves and, by the use of his art, facilitates the accomplishment of desired goals.

In education the term *cooperative* is used in two major senses. In its profoundest meaning, it signifies action by both learner and educator in accordance with the dictates of nature. The learner must work in terms of his innate individualism as well as in terms of the social stimulation supplied by any learning group of which he may be a part. Also, like all other human beings, he has limitations. Some of them are generic; no hand can span two octaves on the piano. Others are specific; only a relatively few people in any generation can become master pianists. The learner's education is profoundly influenced at every point by his capacities and concerns, and, as they change over time so must his goals and his facility in achieving them. As for the educator, his aims and procedures are always influenced by his abilities and interests. He must work in terms of the opportunities and limitations they make possible.

In its second sense, the term *cooperative* implies voluntary interaction among individuals during learning. Even the solitary student guiding his own program with no fixed instructor seeks the help and encouragement which others can give him. When education occurs in any social setting, those who take part should have some sense of collaboration in both its planning and its conduct. At one extreme, this sharing is so complete that it requires a group to decide everything that it does together. At the other extreme, the sharing may be implicit in the teaching-learning situation, as when many people flock to hear a lecturer. Those who attend vote with their feet, as the saying goes, and one cannot assume from their physical passivity and silence as they sit in the auditorium that they are not cooperating fully in their instruction.

Any individual or group who designs an educational program must take both forms of cooperativeness into account. An educational program must originally be planned in terms of the estimated nature of the learner or learners and of the educator (if there is one) and then revised in the light of the constantly changing reality which appears as the program is put into effect. In some situations, it is possible to involve learners or their representatives in planning and thus foster a collaborative approach. In other situations, the educator must act alone, drawing upon his experience and his knowledge of people to design the program and then being alert to adjust it to meet the realities he encounters when he embarks upon it. Even a lecturer, using what is often thought to be a highly teacher-centered method, can constantly sense his audience's response and shift his approach to deal with it.

The planning or analysis of an educational activity is usually undertaken in terms of some period which the mind abstracts for analytical purposes from complicated reality. Learning can occur in a random fashion or as the unintended byproduct of acts performed for other purposes. Even when knowledge is consciously sought, its pursuits may vary in depth and scope from the simple looking up of a word in a dictionary to the undertaking of a lifelong and intensive inquiry. But the effective planning or analysis of education is aided by the selection of a time dimension which sets boundaries to what is either sought or observed.

Thus an evening college instructor may design a course in introductory chemistry in terms of an eighteen-week semester with two hours of class and four hours of laboratory work per week. He may then plan smaller segments of the course, each built on a unit of content, and may even decide in advance how he will conduct each session. He is aware that his course fits within at least three larger patterns to which thought must be given by himself or by others: the total offering of the evening college, his program of teaching, and the place of his course in the degree sequences taken by his students. All three patterns influence what he does in his own course since they help determine the answers to some important questions. What are the prerequisites for his course? How much time can he devote to it in terms of his other obligations? Is it designed as an introduction for those who plan to specialize in chemistry or as a survey course for those who want to broaden their general education? Or must it fulfill both of these functions because the evening college staff is not able or willing to separate the two groups of students?

Each student in the course also plans in terms of several temporal patterns. He selects the degree program whose successful completion requires that he take chemistry. He has some freedom of choice as to when that subject comes within the sequence of his work. During the semester in which he takes it, he determines what other courses give him as balanced a program as possible. He also plans the use of his time each day in terms of his needs to work, to have time for his family and recreation, to attend classes and laboratory sessions, and to make his preparations for them.

As this example suggests, good program planning or analysis usually requires both educator and learner to have at least four periods in mind, each of which gains meaning by its interaction with the others and all of which are logical abstractions, patterns imposed on reality for the sake of utility. An educational episode is a related series of learning or teaching events making up a coherent whole. It is more than a single exposure to knowledge but less than a long-sustained series of endeavors. Examples are a course, a residential conference, a workshop, a plan of reading based on a list of books, or a series of meetings by a group studying a topic. Of the four periods, the episode is the one most frequently and most intensively chosen for planning and analysis and is therefore the central time focus used in this book. An educational act is a specific and relatively brief learning or teaching event. It may be part of an episode, it may stand alone (as in an isolated lecture to an audience or an educational program on television), or it may be one event in a chain of otherwise unrelated occurrences (as when a discussion group chooses a different topic each time it meets). An educational series is a succession of related episodes, as in a curriculum for a degree, a progression of annual conferences, or a linking of courses of graduated difficulty. An aggregate of simultaneous episodes is a pattern of educational activities occurring in the same span of time in the life of an individual, group, or institution. The episodes may be linked together, may include one or more courses in a series, or may be unrelated except for the common period during which they occur.

Sometimes a learner or an educator does not set any time

limitation on his educational planning. Through choice or necessity, he embarks on an activity with no clear idea of how long it will sustain his interest or attention. For example, he joins or accepts the leadership of a group, starts out to visit cultural institutions, or enters into a tutorial relationship which may be broken off at any point. In such a case, his planning occurs one act at a time with only a very general idea of continuity beyond it. Later, in retrospect, the sum of his actions may be seen to have been an episode, a series, or an aggregate, but such was not his original intent.

   The planning or analysis of an educational activity may be undertaken by an educator, a learner, an independent analyst, or some combination of the three. In many educational activities, two distinct roles appear: the provider of focus, direction, and content, and the person or persons whose learning is shaped and led. In formal settings, the first of these is usually called a teacher and the second a student or a pupil. But the first may also be called a leader, a counselor, a coordinator, a curator, a supervisor, or any of a number of other terms, and the second may be referred to as a participant, a member, a counselee, a patron, a client, or another similar name. The terms *educator* and *learner* are used generically here to indicate the two roles. A third role sometimes appears when somebody who stands outside the educational activity itself helps to plan or analyze it. An administrator, a curriculum specialist, a consultant, an external examiner, or other people may plan, study, or appraise a program either independently or in collaboration with the educator, the learner, or both. This third role is here designated as that of *analyst.*

   While the usual patterns of collaboration among these three are well understood, it is not always realized each can operate independently of the others. The educator may do the whole job of planning, conducting, and appraising an educative program by himself, as when a public health specialist devises and provides a series of posters to teach the basic principles of nutrition. The learner may work completely on his own, as when he plans, carries out, and appraises a series of visits to Civil War battlefields because he is interested in American history. The analyst can design an activity which never comes to fruition, or he can study the operation of a program for which he has no responsibility and with which he may never come in direct contact.

Any design of education can best be understood as a complex of interacting elements, not as a sequence of events. In theory, the process of education usually goes through the stages of identification and refinement of objectives, selection of means of accomplishing them, conduct of the planned activity, and retrospective evaluation of it. If these various elements are to be identified and understood, they must be recorded in some fashion, and the temporal order is as good as any other for the purpose. But practice usually does not follow this logical pattern. An activity may be initiated because some resource is available or intriguing. For example, the director of an educational television station may begin his planning when a time slot opens up on his schedule, or an experimenter with computerized instruction may develop a course which tests that method. In such cases, the objective is chosen to fit the means, not the reverse.

Even more important, the mind seldom works in a completely logical fashion. The procedure of planning or analyzing an educational program is often very like the process of research. A distinguished group of psychologists once observed:

> [Research] is a rather informal, often illogical, and sometimes messy-looking affair. It includes a great deal of floundering around in the empirical world. . . . Somewhere and somehow in the process of floundering, the research worker will get an idea. In fact, he will get many ideas. On largely intuitive grounds he will reject most of his ideas and will accept others as the basis for extended work. . . . If the idea happens to be a good one, he may make a significant positive contribution to his science— "may" because between the idea and the contribution lies a lot of persistence, originality, intuition, and hard work.[1]

From beginning to end, the design of an educational activity is usually in a constant state of reformulation. It emerges first in at least an embryo form when the possibility of the activity first appears, and it is reconsidered frequently during the time of planning, the time of action, and the time of retrospection. All the component

[1] American Psychological Association, Education and Training Board, "Education for Research in Psychology," *American Psychologist*, 1959, *14*, 169.

parts of the design mesh together at every point at which it is considered. Only when they are separated for formal analysis do they appear to be logical and linear.

When stated baldly as propositions, some of these seven assumptions may sound platitudinous since they underlie so much excellent practice. They are presented here, however, chiefly because they are so often violated in other practice. All too often, abstract systems of teaching, such as textbooks, lesson plans, or course outlines, are worked out on the basis of a generalized conception of content, method, evaluation, and the nature of the "typical" student and are then imposed virtually intact upon many different situations. An institution builds up a generic pattern of service, such as a ten-session course meeting one night a week for ten successive weeks, and then seems unable to vary it, implying that all knowledge relevant to its purpose should be conveyed in this fashion. These and similar rigidities deny in practice the situational approach to educaton expressed in the foregoing assumptions.

Practically speaking, the learner or the educator may use this approach in either of two ways. He may work wholly within the situation in which he finds himself, building up a design of activity which is determined entirely by its dictates. Or he may begin with a generalized program but adapt it, profoundly if necessary, to fit the requirements of the situation. The failure to use this second approach creatively leads to excessive formality of education.

Two-Part System

These assumptions might undergird many different systems of program planning or analysis. The one proposed here requires two complementary actions: the examination of the situation in which the learning activity occurs to determine the basic category to which it belongs and the application to that situation, in ways which are profoundly influenced by its category of a basic framework or model in order to produce a design or program. These two actions must be described separately here, but in practice they are closely interrelated.

Categories of Educational Programs. The most familiar category of educational programs is instruction in a classroom, where a group of students learns from a teacher, usually under institutional sponsorship. Classroom instruction is, in fact, so commonly used in the schooling of young people from kindergarten through graduate instruction that many people carry over into their adulthood the belief that it is virtually the only possible learning situation. This view is shared by many educators of adults. An extension dean may believe that the only university-level instruction which is intellectually respectable is one in which an acknowledged master of a field of content teaches it to a group of well-prepared students. The dominance of classroom instruction is further reinforced by both professional and lay discussions of education, most of which imply that it is the only form of learning and teaching which is worth consideration.

But as earlier parts of this chapter suggest, both processes also occur in countless situations which do not fit the classroom form. Among the most popular of these are the small self-directed group, the residential conference or institute, the voluntary association, and the tutorial relationship. Each of these has sufficient clarity of form to be widely understood, but each has its own protagonists. To some people, for example, the small self-directed group is the only valid form of adult learning; to others, the residential conference is supreme. An advocate of a "new" category often helps make his case for it by disparaging the classroom, thus unintentionally accentuating the dominance of that form.

If overall harmony of process is to be achieved in adult education, it is apparently necessary to have some typology of the categories into which learning and teaching situations can be fitted. Five such categories have already been roughly identified. When they are arrayed side by side, they can be looked at dispassionately as being alternative ways to undertake the educative process. Some people may still like one form better than others, may wish to work wholly within it, and may try to establish their personal preference as a panacea. However, those who seek to make sense of the field as a whole (as it is and not merely as they wish it to be) or who hope to broaden their range of personal competence to include a mastery of various categories of process, will find it useful to look speculatively at each of them, understanding its form and assessing its relative utility. The central question is not "Is Category A better than Category B?" but "In what circumstances is Category A better than Category B?"

Anyone who tries to answer this question must look beneath the surface of the formal settings in which learning and teaching occur. The essential distinction among categories is not to be found in their outward form. On that basis, it is often hard to distinguish a class from a group or either of them from a conference. The inner reality lies in the source of authority and direction so far as planning and control are concerned. In the class, it is the teacher; in the group, its own members; and in the conference, a committee. Each of these forms can use a great variety of methods and resources. For example, a teacher can lecture, hold recitations, lead discussions, provide demonstrations, use role playing, arrange field trips and work experiences, require readings, invite visiting speakers, show films, or ask that the students write themes. In every case, however, the teacher, though he may use all the arts of cooperation, is the chief designer of the program, thus distinguishing it from either the group or the conference.

Eleven educational planning categories are suggested here as those most common in current practice. Each is somewhat broader in scope and more exact in definition than the five popularly designated categories to which reference has just been made; thus "classroom instruction" becomes "a teacher or group of teachers designs an activity for, and often with, a group of students." These eleven are classified into four sets in terms of their central foci, and are usually referred to subsequently by their numerical designations as C-1, C-2, and so on. While the reader may find this method of reference to be initially awkward, it has the advantage of brevity as contrasted with the relatively lengthy description in words which would otherwise be repeatedly required. Each category will be described in detail in Chapter Four but is identified and illustrated here (in Table 1 and the following paragraphs) in order to establish the nature of the first of the two essentials in the system.

One set of situational categories is centered on individual learning.

C-1. An individual designs an activity for himself. Examples: A women decides to broaden her knowledge of music by reading about it, systematically listening to it, and attending courses in it. The educational director of a prison undertakes to improve his performance by reading the literature on the rehabilitation of criminals and by visiting other prisons and detention centers.

C-2. An individual or a group designs an activity for another individual. Examples: A supervisor in a department store tries systematically to help one of his staff to become a better salesman. A librarian in the natural sciences collection of a large public library works out a bibliography of readings to suit the special needs of a patron. A group of specialists in the State Department in Washington briefs a newly appointed ambassador on various aspects of life in the country to which he is being sent.

A second set of situational categories is centered on the learning which occurs in a group activity.

C-3. A group (with or without a continuing leader) designs an activity for itself. Examples: A club of faculty members drawn from the various departments of a university meets regularly to keep its members abreast of new scholarly developments. The pastor of a liberal church organizes a group of men to read and discuss the writings of Paul Tillich.

C-4. A teacher or group of teachers designs an activity for, and often with, a group of students. Examples: A home economist teaches a group of low-income mothers how to select and prepare inexpensive foods that provide a balanced diet for the family. A team of heart specialists conducts a course for the nurses in a hospital teaching them new techniques of caring for cardiac patients.

C-5. A committee designs an activity for a larger group. Examples: A committee works out the program for the annual conference of a professional society. The officers of a study club plan its activities for the next year.

C-6. Two or more groups design an activity which enhances their combined program of service. Examples: The presidents of a number of voluntary groups in a city neighborhood form a council to identify common problems and study ways to deal with them. Delegates from all the clubs in a settlement house meet together to develop a combined program for it.

A third set of situational categories centers on the learning which occurs under the auspices of an institution.

Table 1. MAJOR CATEGORIES OF EDUCATIONAL
DESIGN SITUATIONS

INDIVIDUAL

C-1 An individual designs an activity for himself

C-2 An individual or a group designs an activity for another individual

GROUP

C-3 A group (with or without a continuing leader) designs an activity for itself

C-4 A teacher or group of teachers designs an activity for, and often with, a group of students

C-5 A committee designs an activity for a larger group

C-6 Two or more groups design an activity which will enhance their combined programs of service

INSTITUTION

C-7 A new institution is designed

C-8 An institution designs an activity in a new format

C-9 An institution designs a new activity in an established format

C-10 Two or more institutions design an activity which will enhance their combined programs of service

MASS

C-11 An individual, group, or institution designs an activity for a mass audience

C-7. A new institution is designed. Examples: A businessman starts a private correspondence school. Congress establishes and funds a program to provide basic vocational education for the persistently unemployed. A national association is formed to educate its members on foreign affairs.

C-8. An institution designs an activity in a new format. Examples: A university extension division creates a new curriculum which prepares adults for a special baccalaureate degree. A museum staff designs a new exhibit. A local YMCA sets up a program to help its members learn new recreational skills.

C-9. An institution designs new activities in an established format. Examples: The staff of an educational television station selects and develops the broadcasts which will highlight its program for the coming season. The director of a community college adult educational program chooses the new courses he will offer. A conservation association plans its program emphasis for the year.

C-10. Two or more institutions design an activity which enhances their combined program of service. Examples: The heads of the major agencies of adult education in a city develop a program of collaborative action to deal with the common needs on which their institutions should be working. A county extension director and a regional public librarian develop a number of systematic ways by which each can foster the other's program.

A final situational category is centered on the provision of education to a mass audience. The learners can be identified only in terms of very general characteristics and not as specific groups or individuals.

C-11. An individual, group, or institution designs an activity for a mass audience. Examples: A professor presents a course by television. A publisher issues a set of books intended to educate readers on various subjects. A voters' league holds a series of mass meetings to inform the public on current political issues. A state department of agriculture issues a number of farmers' bulletins, each written to tell readers how to cope with some practical problem.

Central and subordinate categories. The process of education is strongly influenced by the nature of the category in which it is conducted. This fact is considered at length in Chapter Four, but it may be useful to illustrate it at this point. If the pastor of the liberal church referred to as an illustration of C-3 leads a discussion on the writings of Tillich at the request of the group, using the books themselves as the fundamental sources of content and accepting any interpretation of them which seems reasonable to the churchmen involved, he is acting in C-3. If he treats the writings as a text which he uses as a base for expressing his own knowledge of the matters with which they deal and presents his own interpretation of Tillich's ideas, he is acting in C-4. Neither category is inherently superior to the other, but the two are different from one another in establishing both the ends and the means of the learning process. That difference is particularly sharply felt when a group believes itself to be in one situation and its leader believes himself to be in the other. The churchmen may feel frustrated if they seek instruction from their pastor (C-4) but find that he constantly throws them back on their own resources (C-3). Learning is hampered until the difference in viewpoint has been resolved.

Once a planner or analyst has identified the basic category or categories with which he is concerned, he may want to shift focus from time to time. Thus the pastor may view the course on Tillich as being essentially a C-4 situation but want to have some sessions in C-3. In such a case he may need to make the shift in category dramatically clear, perhaps by having a member of the group lead the C-3 sessions and remaining away from them himself in order to symbolize the temporary abdication of his authority as a C-4 teacher. The use of central and subordinate categories may become very complex. For example, the evening college professor of introductory chemistry to whom reference was made earlier knows that the central focus of his course is on C-4, but he also knows that when one of his students is considering his total program of educational activities, he is working in C-1. Within his course, the teacher may need to design subcomponents in C-2 (if he finds it necessary to work with individual students), C-3 (if he makes provision for group-directed discussions), and C-5 (if he encourages a group of students to prepare and present a demonstration on some special topic). He also knows that his course is but one episode in a series of courses, most of which are also C-4 but which may include a number of other categories as well.

Framework and components. Even as central and subordinate categories are being identified, the planner or analyst is performing the complementary task of fitting together a framework of interrelated components which compose the design of the activity. These components and the process of harmonizing them are detailed in Chapters Five and Six. At this point, the overall framework is merely sketched to make the outline of the model clear. Two parallel presentations of the same material are given, one in Figure 1 and one in the textual analysis.

In conformity with an assumption identified earlier, these components are to be understood as a complex of interacting elements, not as a logical sequence of steps. In applying the model to a

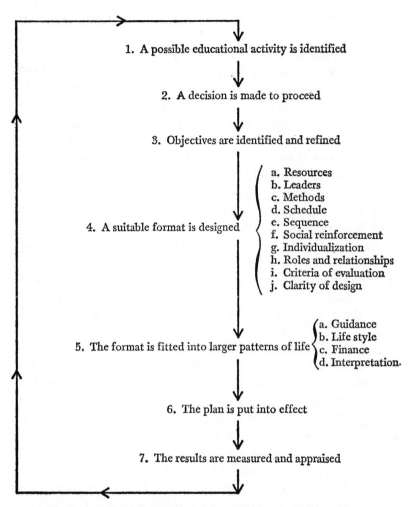

1. A possible educational activity is identified

2. A decision is made to proceed

3. Objectives are identified and refined

4. A suitable format is designed

   a. Resources
   b. Leaders
   c. Methods
   d. Schedule
   e. Sequence
   f. Social reinforcement
   g. Individualization
   h. Roles and relationships
   i. Criteria of evaluation
   j. Clarity of design

5. The format is fitted into larger patterns of life

   a. Guidance
   b. Life style
   c. Finance
   d. Interpretation.

6. The plan is put into effect

7. The results are measured and appraised

FIGURE 1. Decision points and components of an adult educational framework.

situation, one may begin with any component and proceed to the others in any order, and in many cases the program needs to be reviewed many times during the course of the activity. But the general framework must be introduced to the reader by presenting the components one after the other in some rational fashion, and long experience with various overall designs has shown that the series of decision points used in Figure 1 and in the text is the one which brings about the most rapid understanding and the firmest eventual grasp of essentials.

1. A possible educational activity is identified. The impulse to learn or to teach may arise from almost any source within or without the life pattern of an individual, a group, or an institution, and it may be created either by a sense of need or deprivation or by a sense of desire or opportunity. In C-1, an individual may contemplate a learning activity because he becomes dissatisfied with the routineness of his existence, because he gets a different job, because a branch library opens in his neighborhood, because he must learn to live with a disease or a handicap, because he has come to the end of one activity and is casting about for a new one, or because he grows interested in a new avocation. In C-10, a program may appear desirable because a major social need is identified, because the institutions involved are not achieving maximum results, because a new source of financing becomes available, because influential figures in a community think it wise to imitate a similar program elsewhere, or because the appearance of a major new organization threatens the work of existing institutions.

2. A decision is made to proceed. This decision may be taken for granted, it may be rapidly reached, or it may emerge slowly as judgment is brought to bear on the relevant factors in the situation. It is usually helpful to think through the possible program trying to conceptualize how the various components will be dealt with. In this way, a preparatory design of a possible future activity is built. It can then be examined to see whether it is worthwhile in terms of available resources and probable accomplishments. Sometimes (as is often the case in C-9) some choice must be made among various possible alternative programs. If the decision to go ahead with an activity is negative, the process of program building ends. If it is positive, the next steps are taken.

3. Objectives are identified and refined. Every educational activity is based on some conception of the ends it should achieve. Out of the complex array of complementary or conflicting possibilities present in the situation, dominant and guiding purposes emerge to give shape to the educational program. A class in art (C-4) may be based on the desire to improve its students' painting skills or on the attempt to increase their understanding and apprecia-

tion of mankind's great art treasures. Every aspect of the course is influenced by the decision as to which of these two purposes is dominant. Often several objectives must be sought simultaneously, as when a cluster of groups (C-6) seeks by collaborative effort to improve existing separate programs, to find and remedy gaps in service, and to discover new activities which its members can jointly sponsor. These three goals may be pursued separately, but in the total setting they are intimately interrelated, and that fact influences every component of the design.

Usually some hierarchy of objectives, in which broad purposes comprehend limited ones, must be developed. Sometimes this ordering is based on a logical analysis of content; a tutor teaching introductory Spanish to a student (C-2) knows that to convey a basic capacity in the language, he must teach vocabulary, pronunciation, and grammar. Sometimes the hierarchy is based on a balancing out of complementary goals; a course designed to train secretarial workers must provide occupational skills, a knowledge of office procedures, and an awareness of the need for good personal grooming. Hierarchical analysis is particularly significant when several educational periods are considered simultaneously. If the staff of a public school adult education program decides to introduce a complete curriculum leading to the high school diploma (C-8), a broad objective is required for the series and more specific ones for the episodes. Meanwhile the educator in charge of each episode must identify its general purpose but also define specific goals for each of its acts.

4. A suitable format is designed. Any educational activity, however brief or extended, has a distinctive shape or pattern which gives unity to its various elements. Each of them may be considered or planned separately and in any order, but a successful program requires a fusion of all such elements in terms of the situation in which the education occurs.

4a. Learning resources are selected. Such resources include any persons, facilities, or materials which can be used to achieve the purposes identified. In some situations, a program planner must try to provide resources where they do not currently exist. Most of the people of the world have no access to books; where this fact is true, a first step in an educational program may be to create a library or other materials center (C-7). In other cases, the task is one of selection. A group wishing to study modern art (C-3) in an American city can choose from many possibilities, among which are a packaged course provided by a publisher, a self-selected list of books or pamphlets, films, slides, and collections of works of art.

4b. A leader or group of leaders is chosen. In one sense, a leader is a learning resource since he often possesses some knowledge or competence which the learner must master, and as is often true in C-4, this knowledge or competence may go far in determining the whole course of the learning activity. But the leader also plays a dynamic role. He takes the initiative to guide, direct, instruct, question, demand, or interact in other ways, and by taking any of these actions he becomes more than a resource.

4c. Methods are selected and used. They are often automatically established as soon as learning resources or leadership are determined. If a computerized game is to be played, the group involved must use the method required by the game it chooses. If the leader is viewed as the chief source of content, the lecture method may be required. Methods set limits to both resources and leadership. In mass programs (C-11), the very nature of the medium (publishing, television, radio) helps to define both the content and the human resources which present it. But despite the close relationship of method to other elements, it should usually be considered independently since in most situations several methods could be used and it is important to choose the best one for the immediate setting. Also variety is often important; the planners of a weekend residential conference (C-5) may decide to use several methods so that none of them becomes dull or fatiguing.

4d. A time schedule is made. Often the schedule is inherent in the situation, for many educational institutions operate in terms of fixed allocations of time. An educational television station may offer one-hour programs on a subject once a week for thirteen weeks, and an evening school may have classes on Monday and Thursday evenings for ten weeks. Such established patterns as these define the boundaries of time available and the overall schedule is accepted as it stands. However, if a program is being newly planned by an independent learner (C-1), a group (C-3), an institution (C-8), or in any other category, it is necessary to decide how long the activity should last and when it should occur.

4e. A sequence of events is devised. Even within a single learning act, progression occurs; for example, a lecturer develops his theme according to some ordering of his ideas. The arrangement of events so they will be maximally educative grows in importance as activities increase in complexity and length. Sequence may occur in terms of a logical principle, such as early to late, simple to complex, easy to difficult, specific to general, or general to specific. Sometimes several such approaches must be designed, as when a course in history proceeds in terms of successive chronological periods but, in each one, certain basic themes are considered. The sequence of events may also be wholly psychological, growing out of the developing interests and interactions of learners and educators, as happens in T-groups or other forms of sensitivity training.

4f. Social reinforcement of learning is provided. Whenever two or more people are involved in an educational activity, they have feelings about one another, and these feelings can either aid or limit the learning which occurs. In a tutorial situation (C-2), for example, a nondirective counselor may play a wholly supportive and reinforcing role, while an athletic coach may develop a pattern of challenge, demand, and reward. The emotional aspects of interpersonal relationships are always keenly felt by groups of learners; in most cases when they are asked to appraise an educational activity, they begin by expressing their feelings toward its leader or their fellow students.

4g. The nature of each individual learner is taken into account. Each person is unique and learns in a distinctive way, a fact which should never be forgotten by the planner or the analyst. The task of taking this element into account grows more difficult as groups or institutions increase in size, but even in mass learning programs (C-11), efforts may be made to reach a few individuals. Thus a poster in a public health campaign may urge its viewers to consult a physician or dentist, an educational radio station may give close consideration to letters of inquiry, and a lecturer may focus his attention on several individuals in his audience to observe their reactions to his words.

4h. Roles and relationships are made clear. When people are related to one another in an educational activity, as in any other, each person develops both expectations toward the others and beliefs about what they expect of him. When a supervisor is instructing a staff member (C-2), for example, their superior-subordinate position is important to the learning relationship. Ambiguities are always present in social interaction but it is usually helpful to the learning process to have duties and responsibilities as clearly understood as the situation allows. When the voluntary groups in an underprivileged neighborhood work together to inform their members and the whole community of the need for urban reform (C-6), attention must be paid to the allocation of functions, the definition of authority of the officers and members of each group, and the manner in which both existing power structures and emerging leaders can be duly recognized.

4i. Criteria for evaluating progress are identified. An educational activity should bring about those changes in the learners which are indicated by its objectives. If goals are stated in behavioral terms ("to be able to demonstrate the proof of any Euclidean theorem"), they suggest both a form of measurement and a criterion for the judgment of success. If goals do not establish such criteria, the planner or analyst must identify them if he is to make an appraisal. Thus a conference on industrial management offered to executives may set three standards for itself: satisfactory completion by all members of a multiple-choice test on the content, expression of a personal sense of heightened competence by all members on a form provided for the purpose, and active participation by all members from beginning to end as observed by the staff. At least some of the criteria of appraisal and methods of measurement should be clear from the very beginning of an activity, though they may be altered and others added as time goes on.

4j. The design is made clear to all concerned. A perennial complaint in every kind of educational activity is "I didn't know what I was supposed to do" or "nobody told us what was expected of us." Many a beautifully planned convention (C-5) has failed because its organizers understood it so well that they forgot that the other people involved (speakers, panel members, discussion leaders, chairmen, and participants) did not know how they were to carry out the plans made for them. At the start of an activity, therefore, its design should be made clear to all concerned, and any changes in it should be fully communicated as they occur.

5. The format is fitted into larger patterns of life. The learning activities of men and women must ordinarily be introduced with some care into a complex milieu which includes work, home, civic, and other responsibilities. At least four kinds of adjustments must usually be considered.

5a. Learners are guided into or out of the activity both at the beginning and subsequently. Since any given program is appropriate for some people but not for others, some means must often be found for including the first and excluding the second. Much of this differentiation occurs by self-selection; courses in the calculus or in gourmet cooking have such clear purposes that student choice may provide adequate guidance. But special planning and procedures may also be required; the staff of a university extension center considering its courses for the following year (C-9) may devote a good deal of attention to identifying present and potential clienteles and to finding ways by which individuals and groups can discover which of the varied activities are most rewarding for them.

5b. Life styles are modified to allow time and resources for the new activity. In most cases, educational activities cannot simply be added to whatever the learner or educator is doing. Something else—work, home, or leisure—must be changed. An individual (C-1) or group (C-3) planning a program of study must give up some other existing or potential pursuit, and that relinquishment requires alteration of a total plan of life. If several evening colleges in the same city develop a coordinated program of offerings (C-10), each institution may have to drop some courses and add others, thus changing the shape of its previous independent offering.

5c. Financing is arranged. The cost of adult education includes not only the outlay for instruction and such allied expenses as travel, meals, and child care, but also, in at least some cases, the loss of income which might be derived from an alternative use of the time. Other goods and services which might be bought with the money spent on education are denied. In the long run, expenditures for education build human resources and thereby often produce increased income, but for many people the funds required to make the initial expenditures are either lacking or are so limited that their use requires a sacrifice or the choice of a low-cost pattern of learning rather than an expensive one. The problem of finance is also often crucial to the educator, particularly when new institutions (C-7) or major new formats (C-8) are created. The high death rate among them is chiefly because they have inadequate funds to keep alive.

5d. The activity is interpreted to related publics. This step usually requires that those who belong to any such public both understand it and assent to it. Since participation in adult education usually depends heavily on voluntary choice by the learners, interpretation plays an important part in most situations. A man needs to make it clear to his wife and family why he wants to be away from home one evening a week. The relationship between tutor and student needs to be understood by those who observe it. Participants need to be recruited for groups, courses, conferences, and institutions. Collaborative arrangements among associations or organizations need to be explained to their memberships or constituencies. Sometimes proper interpretation is crucial to the success of learning activities; sometimes it is merely facilitative or tension reducing; but it must always be actively considered as part of a design.

6. The program is carried out. In this process what was abstract is made concrete; education becomes, in the fullest sense, a cooperative art. Much of the direction and content of the activity may be determined only after it begins, particularly in learning which is centrally concerned with problem solving or human interaction. In other cases, constant adaptation is needed to adjust to problems or opportunities. Often it is wise to have a periodic reinspection of purpose and format to see whether they need to be adjusted to changing situations. Thus a conference or convention may retain its original planners (C-5) or choose a new steering committee to make decisions about such developments as an unexpectedly large attendance, a missing lecturer, or a demand from a group of participants that the program be revised to meet its needs.

7. The results of the activity are measured and appraised. Measurement is based on quantitative data, and appraisal is an estimate of success based in part upon the results of measurement. Taken together they make up evaluation. Both processes go on simul-

taneously during an educational activity but are culminated at its conclusion. While the two are intimately related, they need to be considered separately. It is important to gather all of the evidence which can be economically collected both by the means originally devised in the program and by any other means which may appear subsequently. To use a very simple example, a typing teacher may plan to measure the speed and accuracy of her students by giving them timed tests. During the term, she may also note an unusually high repair bill and frequently jammed machines. When she appraises her own accomplishments and those of the members of her class, she takes into account both the factual data and her subjective observation. Was the students' progress as good as expected? If not, why not? Was it better? If so, why? Were they careless with their machines or did the mechanical difficulties arise from other causes? The answers to such questions as these provide the bases for the judgment of success. In educational activities it is never possible to measure every outcome—a fact particularly true when goals are less tangible than are typing speed and accuracy. The learner or educator must always supply some appraisal which goes beyond the data if he is to arrive at a final judgment concerning the degree of success of the activity and to probe into the causes of that success.

8. The situation is examined in terms of the possibility of a new educational activity. Here the cycle of program planning recommences, and if the decision to proceed is made, a new design must be created. In some cases that decision is virtually automatic regardless of either measurement or appraisal and may even be made before they can occur. Thus teachers often take it for granted that they will repeat their courses again the next year—an assumption which leads at least a few of them to forget the continuing need to be creative, cooperative artists. Similarly a group or an institution may cling to a continuing existence long after it retains only a shadow of its original substance. Rejection can be as automatic as acceptance; many a student ends a course or a program with the belief that it completes his education or the judgment that learning has been so distaseful or profitless that he will never undertake it again. But the completion of an activity also often leads, either immediately or subsequently, to a reexamination of the situation to see

whether a new act, episode, or series would be desirable. The consideration of this question requires as critical an examination as does the decision to undertake an initial activity.

Using the System

This two-part system is proposed in a spirit of pragmatic utilitarianism. If it works effectively and economically in either explaining or improving educational practice, it can be used. If it does not work, some other system should be tried. In every case, the learner or the educator should be the master since only he can comprehend the situation which he chooses or in which he is placed by circumstance. Anyone who becomes inflexibly attached to the following of a process rather than to the achievement of ends is, by definition, doctrinaire.

The system suggested is a natural one, using familiar terms and components which have a common sense foundation, requiring neither special terminology nor elaborately intricate exposition. It can be used with some success even by those who have little knowledge of educational theory and practice. Figure 1 and Table 1 can, in fact, be readily grasped by volunteer lay leaders in a single training session. The great body of educational research of the past fifty years has been focused on the several components of design, so that no matter how sophisticated the educator may become, he can still fit his knowledge about these components within these categories and frameworks. Unless he does use some such systematic plan to provide order to his approach to the designing of educational activities, he cannot work effectively as a practical artist. The more knowledge he has, the less efficient he is.

All the components of the system must be kept in balance. Each depends upon all the others; the change of one influences the rest. For example, effective social reinforcement should be considered separately, but it is also a product of decisions made about leadership, resources, individualization, clarity of design, and other elements. If any is given undue stress, it negatively influences all the others. When any component, such as finance, schedule, or measurement, is fixed, all the others must be considered in terms of it. Otherwise the system loses its equilibrium and therefore its fullest effectiveness.

The scarcity or misuse of time often limits or destroys the balance essential to an effective design. A planner may have too short a notice or too many programs to allow him to pay attention to separate components or to their blending. In other cases, so much time is devoted to particular aspects of the system that other aspects suffer. A group may spend so many hours on refining objectives that it has no time left to fulfill them or a teacher may become so obsessed with evaluative procedures that finally he teaches only what he knows he can measure. In the practical world, overplanning is as bad a habit as underplanning.

As the copious earlier illustrations suggest, the framework is fundamentally the same in all categories of situations, though its applications vary from one to another. Anyone who wishes to think through these applications systematically might find it useful to guide his thought by a two-way grid in which the eleven situational categories are listed on one coordinate and the components of program design are listed on the other. Such an examination shows a few places where format elements are inapplicable or have only limited relevance. A self-guided learner (C-1) does not need to think about creating social reinforcement within the activity itself, though he may need to find ways to maintain a positive attitude of his own. In a mass educational activity (C-11), instruction cannot be individualized, but, as noted earlier, an effort may be made to personalize it in some fashion. In most cases, however, the components apply in all categories, though in different ways.

The mastery of this system of planning and analysis, like that of any other complex process, is initially tedious since it requires close attention and application. One must examine many cases, looking beneath the specifics of each activity to discover the basic structure which gives a common design to all of them. Chapter Three presents and interprets a few cases in order to introduce the practical use of the system, and sources of additional cases for study and discussion are suggested at the end of the book. But the major way by which anyone can learn the system is by the analysis of his own practice. In time, the ability to identify categories and construct designs is greatly facilitated. Experience provides not only skill but speed, particularly in the delicate art of balancing components.

Chapters Four and Five return to the categories and the

components respectively to give a somewhat fuller account of each of them than was possible in this overview chapter. The primary effort in both cases is to convey an understanding of how the system works in the creation of an activity or in the process of revision which occurs as the cycle of planning is repeated.

But occasionally something more than normal change is required. Circumstances demand a complete reconstruction of program. An individual or a group feels the need of a thoroughgoing change of educational activity, or an institution is required by choice or necessity to alter the whole design of its work. Such a reconstruction is a form of program planning or analysis, using the same components as does creation or normal revision, but it requires that they be used in a special way which is described and illustrated in Chapter Six.

The final brief chapter is no more than a coda, reexamining certain themes which have earlier been fully expressed and looking toward the adult education of the future.

CHAPTER III

Four Cases

> Studies themselves do give
> forth directions too much at
> large, except they be bounded
> in by experience.
> Francis Bacon, *Of Studies*

In this chapter, four unique programs of adult education are described and analyzed in terms of the model sketched in Chapter Two. The processes of learning and teaching are presented as they occurred when learners or educators coped with the situations they encountered. The programs were designed or conducted by people who had no knowledge of the system proposed in this book, and the men involved in the fourth case were not even aware that theirs was a venture in adult education. Following each case is an analysis of how it exemplifies the model, but the reader may wish in each instance to make his own interpretation before reading that of the author.

A Hobo School

In the matter of barging about the world, I've had a bit of experience.[1] During the World War I was in France and Mesopotamia with the British, and after that I followed the sea, until the depression put me high and dry on the beach.

Shanghai, Hong Kong, and Rio are spots that I can look at with sated eyes. In my time I've been shipwrecked off the Great Barrier reef and, all in all, I've lived what the lady reporters call "an eventful life."

Nevertheless, looking backward, I can think of no episode that can hold a candle to my recent adventure in pedogogy.

But to start at the beginning, when I was a youngster in school I would study nothing but geography. The pictures in the big geography book seemed to hypnotize me and, using the pictures as a starting point, I would dream of far-off places—green seas, dense jungles, and snow-capped mountains. So zealously did I concentrate on geography, to the detriment of all other studies, that in the fourth grade the teacher set me down as the class dunce and told my parents that it was no use to send me to school. After the war, I endeavored to recapture the romance of my childhood days, only to find myself approaching the two-score mark, with a fringe of gray-

---

[1] By W. D. Griffith, reprinted by permission from: *Adult Education in Action,* Mary L. Ely, editor (New York: American Association for Adult Education, 1936). Here and in subsequent quoted cases, quotation marks have been omitted.

ing hair, a past resplendent with bizarre episodes, and a future black as a wailing wall in the Holy Land.

In fact, last year I found myself shuffling along day after day in a Seattle breadline and wondering if, after all, the big adventure did not lie under the turbulent waves over which I'd sailed so many years.

However, I found a haven in the reference room of the public library. At first the place was just four walls and a ceiling to protect me from the rains that usually prevail in the Pacific Northwest. But with every passing day the association grew dearer, life took on a purpose, and I looked forward to the hours of study.

I was staying in a shelter for homeless men down on Second Avenue when purpose began to shape my life. There were over a hundred and fifty of us derelicts—eager-faced youngsters, tottering lumberjacks, rheumatic sailormen, and frost-bitten prospectors. Most of them had played a part in building the Pacific Empire, and the same reckless vagabond spirit that had urged these fellows to the Orient, to Alaska, and into the tall timber had also landed them in that municipal flop-house.

Every night at nine o'clock, after the public library closed, I would rush to these quarters with a book and a pad of paper under my arm. This accouterment of erudition earned for me the title of a knowledge tramp, or library bum, and on the strength of these credentials I was able to horn into any bunkhouse arguments in progress.

One night when I came in, Milsudski, a Slav who slept in the deck above me, eyed the textbook under my arm, I thought, somewhat enviously. "You read 'em book?" he asked.

"Sure," I answered, "I read 'em all but the big words."

"I like t' read 'em," he said, "not big book, but fonny paper."

"There's nothing to stop you." I waxed into quite an enthusiastic oration on what a man could do with his spare time. "You're on the bum, walkin' the pavement twelve hours a day. If you would use an hour of that time every day for three months, you'd be able to read Moon Mullins and Boob McNutt."

"You t'ink so?" he asked.

"I don't think so. I know so. A guy can do anything with his spare time. Look what Lincoln did!"

"Dat's good car: I ride one time; go like hell!"

"Not a Lincoln car—Abe Lincoln, the President of the United States."

"Roosevelt, him President."

Finally the talk veered back to adult education, and Milsudski pinned me down as to what book he should read in order to get the full import of the comic section. I was quite vague, I admit, but in a generous moment I promised to help Milsudski in his quest for knowledge, and with that promise I inadvertently founded Dumbbell University, a school that weeks later was to become a joke along the "Skid Road," the waterfront district of Seattle.

The next day I went to the children's department of the Seattle Public Library and asked the lady in charge for some material on a method of teaching a "Bohunk" to read the funny papers. And did she supply me with material! That women stacked books and magazines in front of me in huge piles. I muddled through this maze of knowledge but for the life of me I couldn't see where any of it would help me in teaching a dense Slav.

I was discouraged and regretted that I had been so enthusiastic about Milsudski's chances of learning to read. Yet, the next day I took him down to a tie pile along the railroad track and produced a paper and pencil. "Now," I said, drawing a large A, "that's A."

"Yes, I know, that's A."

"And this is B," I said, drawing a generous B.

Then I pointed to the A. "What's that?"

"That's B."

"Nobody but a thick Hunky would say that; at least, not after it was pointed out as an A. See, A. Catch 'em A."

"Sure, I catch 'em A."

Day after day the lessons proceeded, with me goading Milsudski during every lesson.

A Swede lumberjack, Ole, who wished to learn to figure lumber, joined the class. He could add a little, subtract a little, but could neither multiply nor divide. Ole would not respond to goading in the manner of Milsudski; instead of digging into his lessons harder than ever, he would sulk a bit and tell me to jump in the lake. However, when I praised the Scandinavin people, asserting that they were the pure Nordic stock that supplied the world with the explorers who discovered America long before Columbus, the lumberjack would swell his chest and strive his utmost to solve the intricacies of the decimal system.

In contrast to this pair of students, the next fellow to enroll, an Irishman, would work well when his efforts were challenged. I found that by being dubious I could spur him on to greater endeavors. He wanted to learn how to do crossword puzzles, and I shook my head. "You'd better give up the idea; a Laplander might learn to do puzzles, but it's all beyond the ken of an Irishman."

"Is that so?" O'Malley retorted. "I'll show ye that an Irishman can learn to do anything an Eskimo can!"

Excepting a sing-song school I saw in Constantinople—where all the students were reciting the Koran aloud—I think that Dumbbell University was the queerest fountain of knowledge the sun ever shone upon. We had no schoolroom, but in fair weather we congregated on a pile of ties in the Northern Pacific Railroad yards. During rainy days we sought shelter in a convenient box car.

Later, along with the three students I had to goad, to praise, and to challenge, were two Filipinos, a man who had put in years in South America, and a Negro who wished to learn some "big dictionary words."

I think the remarkable thing about this class was that each man achieved his goal: Milsudski learned to read the comic section; the Swede learned to scale lumber, after a fashion; O'Malley solved the mysteries of the easier crossword puzzles; the man from South America brushed up on his Spanish; and the Filipinos learned a patter they fondly believed to be English. As for the colored member of the class, yesterday I met Booker T. Jackson on Pike Street, and he hailed me with a wide, white-toothed grin: "Perfesser, let's me an' you git t'gether on a high-brow confab. I'se got t'talk collo- qualisms t'mah customers."

It's strange, but only I, the teacher, am left on the bread- line. However, the goal that I've set for myself is higher and the road leading to it more rocky than the pathway to the palms of the other students.

Analysis. This memoir of the great depression contains evi- dences of both independent study (C-1) and tutorial teaching (C-2). The first, the effort of Mr. Griffith to use the reference room of the Seattle Public Library as the center of his own self-education, is so briefly mentioned that the program design cannot be analyzed, though he makes it clear at the end of his account that his unstated goal had not been achieved. The six episodes of tutorial teaching are sketched out fairly clearly and suggest—as in the contrasting approaches used with Milsudski, Ole, and O'Malley—how the tutor must adapt his approach to the desires and nature of each student. Milsudski wanted to read the comics, Ole wanted to figure lumber, and O'Malley wanted to do crossword puzzles. Milsudski had to be goaded, Ole's national origin praised, and O'Malley's national origin challenged.

The steps are fairly clear. The possibility of the group of related episodes was raised by Milsudski's interest and Griffith's sense of evangelism, the situation was not tested at all, and "in a generous moment" the decision was made to proceed. The specific objective was unique to each student, but the broad goal of learning to read and write was common to all. In all episodes, the elements in the format were probably similar, though each episode had unique features. In Milsudski's case, for example, the *resources* were the paper and pencil, the open-air classroom, and eventually perhaps the library books. The *leader* was Griffith, the *method* was teaching by rote, the *schedule* was a daily session, the *sequence* was that imposed by the acquisition of literacy, the *social reinforcement* was established by a man to man goading, the *individualization* was inherent in the situation, the *relationship* was that of two equals, one of whom was guiding the other, the proposed *criterion of evaluation* was the ability to read the comics, and the *clarity of design* was established by the facts in the situation itself.

This tutorial teaching was fitted into the overall situation imposed by the shelter for homeless men and the lumberyard where the teaching occurred. Each of the men taught was *guided* into the relationship by his own goals and changed his otherwise rather aimless *lifestyle* to accommodate it. *Finances* were covered by the resources provided by society—library, breadline, shelter, and Griffith's contribution of his time. The *interpretation* required that the activity violate all the folkways of the situation; Dumbbell University became a joke on "Skid Row" and only six men out of one hundred fifty took part. After the plan had been *put into effect* and run its course for an unstated length of time, Griffith *measured* the capacity of each of his students to perform the task he sought to master and *appraised* the program as being a success. The memoir does not say whether there was any further educational sequence in the lives of either Griffith or his students.

Educational Farm Program

Otis R. Griggs is an educator, adviser, purveyor of information, executive, and representative of the United States Department of Agriculture in the conduct of educational farm programs in Reno County, Kansas, where he is the county agent.[2] He is one of the 6,343 county agents in the country. His training, activities, and responsibilities are much like those of the others, whose charter of operations is a memorandum of understanding drawn up in 1955 by the Secretary of the Department of Agriculture and the heads of land-grant colleges and universities. It specified that the Department would refer its educational responsibilities to State Extension Services. The county agent—who sometimes is referred to as agricultural agent, extension agent, and farm adviser—puts the programs into action in his county. He serves all segments of agriculture. In Reno County, for example, are farm-related industries that produce alfalfa meal, margarine, frozen and dried eggs, flour, feeds, grain and elevator equipment, dairy supplies, silos, farm machinery, fertilizer, and meat products.

Reno is the second largest county in Kansas. Its 2,289 farms in 1962 averaged 340 acres. Its population was 59,116. The population of Hutchinson, the county seat, was more than 37,000. Urban residents look to Mr. Griggs and his staff for information about lawn grasses, vegetable varieties, control of insects and diseases, fertilizers, landscaping, sprays for fruit trees, weed control, flowers, and other phases of the broad field of agriculture. Because the county agent is responsible for planning an educational program to meet the changing needs of the rural and urban residents of his area, Mr. Griggs keeps contact with an Extension council of 102 members. Individuals representing agriculture, home economics,

[2] By H. E. Jones and H. Shankland, reprinted by permission from *After a Hundred Years*, the 1962 Yearbook of the United States Department of Agriculture (Washington, D.C.: Government Printing Office, 1962).

and 4-H clubs are elected annually from each township and incorporated city in the county. He works also with the board of county commissioners on the Extension budget and the district agent, who represents the State director. Reno County financed 82 per cent of the 1962 Extension budget. Federal and State funds provided 18 per cent.

In his day-to-day activities, Mr. Griggs informs residents of the county about new research findings, Government programs, such as the emergency feed-grain program, new varieties of crops, and the market outlook. Because Reno is in the center of the Kansas wheat belt, Mr. Griggs joined in a wheat quality improvement program in 1954. By 1961, the farmers had increased their acreage in strong gluten varieties from 4 to 33 per cent. Kansas wheatgrowers increased their acreage in the desired varieties from 17 to 39.1 per cent. Reno County was one of the pilot counties in the Plains States reforestation program of the thirties, and it still is interested in shelterbelts and windbreaks. Helped by the cooperative Forest Service-Kansas State University tree distribution project, started in 1957, farmers of the county ordered nearly 147 thousand trees in 5 years. Another project Mr. Griggs stressed, control of brucellosis in dairy and beef cattle, also was successful. The county became the sixth among the State's 105 counties to be declared a modified-certified brucellosis free area. Calfhood vaccination is emphasized now to limit the buildup of brucellosis in mature livestock. Much of Mr. Grigg's educational work is conducted through cooperating groups. A mid-Kansas swine marketing association, which originated in Reno County, now includes surrounding counties. Fat lambs are marketed on a graded basis through three outlets, which he helped to organize. Farm management long has been a strong point in the Extension program. One of Kansas State University's first district farm management associations, organized in the early thirties, included Reno County, which, in 1961, had more members than any other county in the association.

No day is like any other in a county agent's life, but one day, which we can consider as typical as any, Mr. Griggs began with a radio program at 6:30 a.m. He made another broadcast at 12:30 p.m., when he discussed the importance of deep watering and timely mowing of bluegrass lawns and others topics of particular interest to urban residents. From the radio station, he stopped by the newspaper office to submit material for news releases. His first two or three hours in the office he spent with callers—for example, a businessman on his way to work brought in a twig from a tree affected by a blight. Mr. Griggs suggested the cause and treatment and later mailed the twig to the State Extension plant pathologist for further details. With another caller he discussed aspects of farm financing; those questions Mr. Griggs referred to the representative of the Farmers Home Administration. One man, who asked about soil conservation practices, was referred to the work unit conservationist in the county. Out of the office, the county agent inspected some of the twenty-four field demonstration plots scattered over the county. He checked with the superintendent of the State experiment field concerning tests with supplemental crops. He helped a farmer who was erecting a "hay keeper," in which chopped hay is dried and self-fed to livestock. He stopped to see a family whose farmstead he had helped landscape and wanted to show him how well the planting had done and to get his suggestions on other plantings.

Otis Griggs was born in Brookville, Kansas in 1921. He grew up on a 160-acre farm. He is a graduate in dairy husbandry of Kansas State University. He and his wife, Roselma, have four children. He served 5 years in the Navy. Thereafter he was successively supervisor of the Marion County Dairy Herd Improvement Association, junior assistant county agent in McPherson and Lyon Counties, and county agricultural agent in Stevens County. He became associate county agent in Reno County in 1954 and the county agent in 1960. On his staff are an associate county agent, a home economics agent, an associate home economics agent, and a 4-H Club agent.

Analysis. Mr. Griggs maintains a complex aggregate of simultaneous educational acts, episodes, and sequences and engages in all categories of program-design situations. Presumably he acquires some of his continuing technical competence by self-directed (C-1) and group study with his extension associates (C-3). He has many tutorial contacts (C-2) in his office and on the farms of his clients. Much of the content he conveys must be taught by himself or other professional or volunteer teachers (C-4), and in his work with various cooperating associations, he must often find himself a member of a planning group (C-5).

His Extension Council is an example of C-6. He helps create new institutions which are at least semieducational, such as the mid-Kansas swine marketing association (C-7), and his county represents an important segment of the district farm management association (C-10). In this latter case, it is not completely clear that the ascription to C-10 is correct since the reader is not told whether each county group has a semi-independent status; if not, the farm management association is a second example of C-7. Mr. Griggs regularly takes on new programs of service (C-8) such as those involved with wheat quality improvement, reforestation, and control of brucellosis. He and his staff must also constantly help plan new activities in the established programs (C-9) for clubs and farm commodity groups. He broadcasts over the radio and issues news releases (C-11).

The one aspect of program design stressed in this account is measurement. The accomplishments achieved in Reno County are tangible and substantial, as indicated by the increase in acreage of strong gluten wheat, the number of trees ordered by farmers for reforestation, and the achievement of freedom from brucellosis.

Prevocational Academic Instruction in the Army

In early June, 1956, I was reassigned duty with the US Army Support Detachment, Chicago, as an Education Advisor (Administrative).[8] The reason for this reassignment was to organize an educational development program for Army Antiaircraft Artillery units in the Chicago-Gary Complex. I was to be the first Education Advisor to be assigned full-time duty with non-Post Units in the history of the Army's General Educational Development Program for Military Personnel. Up to that time Education Advisors were rather stationary at a military post. Units not physically located at that Post received educational development services only by personally visiting the Army Educational Center proper. In short, this opportunity (?) promised to be a real challenge and I wasn't convinced in my own thinking that the concept was practical. I was only

[8] Prepared by R. H. Heylin in April, 1964, and with his permission is here being published for the first time in an abbreviated and edited form.

too willing to give my all, sensing the possibility of rapid promotion for myself and the opportunity to lend more than lip service educational development services to deserving Army personnel who through no choice of their own happened to be assigned to Units from five to fifty miles away from our Education Center. To further complicate the implementation of any program, these AAA Units were all in the process of converting from the World War II anti-aircraft guns to the new NIKE Surface-to-Air missile. I was to work with three Battalions of these people, totaling approximately 3,000 officers and men located at fifteen separate sites and scattered over the West, Southwest, and South Suburban areas of Greater Chicago plus Northwest Indiana. I had the full-time use of one enlisted man from the Education Center who would accompany me daily to one of these fifteen installations on a prepublished schedule. All funds for the conduct of educational development services within these three Battalions were to come from the operating budget of the Army Education Center. There was adequate financial support available to cope with any success I might enjoy.

My two-and-one-half years' prior experience in the Army's GED Program—part as an Enlisted Man on Okinawa and part as an Education Advisor in Korea—prompted me to take careful stock of the situation before attempting to promote any program(s). I spent the first full month in just (a) evaluating education level surveys from March, 1956, (b) obtaining such information as was available from my immediate superior, the Post Education Officer, and (c) introducing myself to AAA Unit Commanders, Personnel Officers, and Training Officers, and discussing general Department of the Army educational goals with them.

By mid-July, 1956, it appeared to my thinking that priority consideration should be given to promoting formal classroom instruction for a great number of Enlisted Men who possessed less than high school completion or its equivalency. These men were not of the illiterate category, just below the academic level generally considered necessary to absorb Army technical training and/or meet civilian institutions' admission requirements for further academic study. I felt that classroom instruction should encompass English, arithmetic, geography, history, and basic physical science. The previously mentioned educational level survey of March, 1956, dis-

closed that approximately 50 per cent of all Enlisted Men had
achieved less than high school completion. While this rate was considerably above the United States' average for adults, it was unsatis-
factory for potential career soldiers who were soon to face training
for handling highly technical equipment as a team. I just couldn't
see how this group could possibly absorb any technical training
without first acquiring a proper academic base! To further document my position before approaching each of the three Battalion
Commanders on the problem, I directed a letter of inquiry to the
Antiaircraft and Guided Missile School at Ft. Bliss, Texas, to establish minimum academic requirements for the Electronics Sub-
Course which preceded each of their missile service school courses.
Reply was received before the end of July, 1956, affirming my
hypothesis that a minimum of current 8th grade capability in arithmetic and English were necessary to handle the Electronics Sub-
Course. The Electronics Sub-Course presented algebra and those
areas of high school physics, for example, heat, electricity, levers,
light, which were considered basic to the study of radar operations,
missile launchers, and missiles themselves. I reiterate at this juncture
that we were concerned not with a once-recorded academic level,
rather a current proficiency therein. I must also include the items
that the officers and senior Non-Commissioned Officers in the three
Battalions appeared to be well-qualified for any retraining required
in this missile conversion operation ahead.

Armed with the data on the number of Enlisted Men below
apparent training potential and with the correspondence from the
AA and GMS, I approached each Battalion Commander individually before the end of July, 1956, with a request for a discussion
of the possibility of conducting formal classroom instruction at each
Battalion Headquarters as a means of reducing the number of untrainable Enlisted Men in their respective battalions. Each Battalion
Commander agreed to the proposal. It was agreed that I would
serve as moderator. At each Battalion discussion, the following key
individuals would participate: Battalion Commander, Battalion
Training and Operations Officer, Battalion Personnel Officer, and
the five Battery Commanders. Discussions were scheduled for mid-
August, 1956.

Although I had enjoyed some nominal success in Korea with

advanced elementary/junior high school level pretechnical instruction, I had felt that the predominant Army-wide concept of half-day instruction for two or three days each week left much to be desired. Consequently, at each of these three Battalion discussions on the subject, I pushed for a schedule of half-day instruction each afternoon, Monday thru Friday, once we could administer appropriate diagnostic testing and individually counsel each untrainable Enlisted Man. I also decided to push for formal instruction for only voluntary students, based on undesirable consequences from earlier experience. In summary the following ramifications were agreed upon by majority opinion during each Battalion discussion:

(1) It would be my responsibility to administer the California Achievement Test (Advanced Elementary Form) to all Enlisted Men below high school completion or equivalency prior to October, 1956, but only after preliminary group counseling.

(2) I or I and another Education Advisor as supplied by my Supervisor at the Education Center would individually counsel only Regular Army examinees between October 1 and December 1, ascertaining in writing as to whether or not such instruction before AA and GMS training or High School Equivalency Testing should be considered. I regretted each Committee's decision not to give Drafted Enlisted Men the same opportunity, but felt this group could be reached later on if the program were to be successful.

(3) Between December 1 and January 1, 1957, each of the five Battery Commanders would nominate five students from his Battery for the initial class to start at the Battalion Headquarters the first week of February, 1957. These nominations would come from the list of those who indicated a voluntary interest after counseling. The Battalion Headquarters were situated at Orland Park, Illinois, Skokie, Illinois, and Gary, Indiana.

(4) The curriculum would consist solely of English and arithmetic. This majority decision also disappointed me but I felt I could possibly mediate this prevalent attitude in subsequent classes after the first one.

(5) Class would meet each Monday, Wednesday, and Friday (Federal holidays excluded) for four hours per day in the afternoon. Those students requiring less instruction would be permitted to terminate instruction sooner than those requiring more instruction. A

range of eight to fourteen weeks of classroom activity would be anticipated. This decision also disappointed me but once again I felt I could temper this attitude in the subsequent classes.

(6) Students would be exempt from military duties during the scheduled hours of instruction and each Battery Commander would be responsible for providing transportation to and from each session.

(7) Standardized elementary final examinations would be administered by the instructors upon the completion of each student's time with the group. In addition, the Battalion Personnel Officer would readminister the GT (General Technical) Aptitude Area tests (average of reading and arithmetic) and I or my accompanying Enlisted Education Specialist would administer the High School Equivalency Test upon the completion of each student's time in class.   ·

(8) I would interview, select, and contract part-time teachers from the nearby community(ies). This appeared to present no obstacle since a number of fully qualified mature ladies were registered with local elementary schools for substitute teaching at this level.

As indicated already, several facets of the initial class organization were less than satisfactory to my thinking. I had confronted this difference in opinion in Korea and so I wasn't exactly unprepared for this turn of events. I felt that a half loaf was better than no loaf at all! Certainly, I thought, I could present a better and more convincing position if the initial class in each Battalion proved successful. In short, I felt all future possibility of curriculum expansion, all possibility of consolidating the class hours, and the inclusion of drafted EM into the program rested squarely on the results of our maiden attempt in each Battalion.

During September, 1956, while I was heavily involved with both administering the CAT diagnostic instrument, and group counseling expectant examinees, one of the three Battalions received Reassignment Orders from the Department of the Army. Obviously this sudden announcement forced cancellation of preliminary arrangements for classroom instruction in the Battalion concerned. I have often wondered since what prevocational instruction was afforded the needy EM at their new designation(s). All that I could

do was to insure that a resume of testing and counseling activity—
on individuals already tested and counseled—was made a portion of
their Personnel Records for release to an Education Advisor at the
next Duty Station.

Also during September, 1956, I established contact with—
and interviewed—a number of prospective part-time lady instructors
residing in communities near the remaining two Battalion Headquarters. Local school principals and superintendents were very cooperative in this respect. I was seeking particularly married ladies
who had once—or recently—taught at the upper elementary level
and had sons of high school age or slightly beyond high school age.
I succeeded in locating two very likely ladies for each Battalion class,
one who would present the English portion of the curriculum and
one who would present the arithmetic. I felt these instructors were
the key to our success not only with the initial class but also to my
wishes to expand the curriculum and present a more compact classroom schedule. I immediately supplied each selected instructor with
adult-level advanced elementary materials for preservice training.
It should be noted that I maintained personal contact with each of
these four instructors on a bi-weekly basis during the inclusive period
October 1 to the start of classes during early February, 1957. Each
instructor found a $5.00 hourly fee for instruction satisfactory, with
an oral commitment of an hourly increase of $.50 for each successive
class until a maximum of $7.50 per hour was reached.

By October 1 my Enlisted Education Specialist assistant
and I had administered nearly 500 California Achievement Tests.
The opening phase of the operation had been accomplished. Although
there had been some 900 EM in the two Battalions below high
school completion or equivalency, only these 500 were Regular Army
Enlisted Men.

Between October 1 and December 1, a fellow Education Advisor and I individually counseled each of these 500 examinees at
their ten different Duty Stations. (Frankly, this was a welcome
change of pace. I thought I had administered enough California
Achievement Tests in the previous six weeks to last me a lifetime!)
Some, that is, 30 per cent, indicated possession of adequate academic
background already to qualify for AA and GMS courses and also
for the High School Equivalency Test. (Note: This same Education

Advisor and I were later able to establish that an adult with current eighth grade capability in English and arithmetic, plus an acceptable level of reading interpretation and comprehension skills, would have a nine to one chance of being successful without benefit of formal preparation on the High School Equivalency Test.) Of the remaining 350 individuals whose CAT results reflected the advisability of formal instruction, only some seventy-five, that is, 21 per cent, refused to participate in the voluntary program. Arrangements were made for the 150 passing examinees to be administered High School Equivalency Tests, and encouragement was simultaneously given to make application for AA and GMS course openings. In summary, we had some 275 voluntary EM for prevocational academic instruction lined up on December 1 for future classroom activity. This broke down into something like 145 EM in one Battalion, and 130 EM in the other Battalion. It appeared, even without input of similarly needy individuals in the intervening months ahead, that it would be necessary to conduct six classes in each Battalion to provide the service promised. I felt optimistically that this task could be accomplished within eighteen months from the start of the first classes in February, 1957. I should note at this point that all conferees in attendance at the August, 1956, discussion were provided written resumes of CAT results and brief counseling reports on EM within their respective Battalions. Each separate Battery Commander was furnished a named roster of those EM with his Battery who were to be considered for instruction.

By January 1, 1957, each Battery Commander had submitted his five nominations for the opening class. I promptly furnished the four instructors with a consolidated class roster of those EM with whom they would be working, also a brief academic biographical sketch to enhance initial rapport. Also, instructional contracts were negotiated during January with each teacher. Textbooks and supplementary student aids were requisitioned from the United States Armed Forces Institute, Madison, Wisconsin.

At long last, in early February, 1957, after seven sustained months of preliminary activity, the first class in each Battalion became a reality! Classroom furniture was made available from the Battalion Headquarters in each instance. Respective Battalion Commanders addressed each class on the opening day, emphasizing the

Army's growing need for more specialized training and broader training capability. I was introduced in turn by the Battalion Commander and I in turn introduced the teachers. This opening day format became a tradition with subsequent classes.

Midway during the initial course, it became readily apparent that the schedule of class sessions was posing certain difficulties within each Battalion! Commanders and first Sergeants found the every-other-day schedule quite perplexing to any training schedule and duty roster. Students were confusing "class afternoons" with "nonclass afternoons." Teachers tactfully mentioned to me that excessive class time was required at the start of each presentation in recapping the previous session's accomplishments. In mid-March, 1957, I requested each Battalion Commander to call an urgent meeting of the planning officers. Each Battalion Conference was held prior to April 1! By unanimous agreement, the conferees decided that Class 2 would meet every afternoon (holidays excluded), Monday thru Friday. Also, since the first class would probably be concluded by May 1, Battery Commanders were requested to forward nominations for Class 2 by April 15. I needed adequate time to continue my project of furnishing each instructor with a class roster and biographical sketch of each new student. Also, time must be allowed for negotiating new teacher contracts and procuring additional text materials.

Class 1 concluded the last week of April, 1957, after twelve weeks. Some students had completed in but seven weeks. The eighth grade standardized tests in English and arithmetic had been successfully administered to all 25 graduates. The Battalion Personnel Officer readministered the General Technical Aptitude Test and my Enlisted Education Specialist administered the High School Equivalency Test. Department of the Army Certificates of Training were provided each student and placed in each student's Military Personnel Folder. In brief, no student required more than 144 hours of combined instruction and terminal testing, though some had started at as low as the fifth grade level!

Class 2 started the second week of May, 1957, within each Battalion. The teachers and I projected an eight week term as adequate for the extreme student. Classes were now meeting every weekday afternoon for four hours each day. Students were scheduled for

Battery Duty only in the mornings and initially everyone seemed pleased. During the 4th week of Class 2, one of the two arithmetic teachers suggested that she could eliminate the "grade" concept of placement with slight modification of the material, thus permitting all students to start arithmetic together and to finish together. Consultation by me with the other arithmetic teacher revealed that she, too, thought this innovation workable. Thinking perhaps that the English teachers might be "open" to some suggestion for improvement, I posed the problem of eliminating "grade level" distinction for English. After several days' deliberation, each English teacher expressed a desire to experiment and promised to jointly prepare a modified English curriculum for Class 3 to come. The noble experiment, if successful, could open the door to several very beneficial changes. The more needy students could conceivably enter more freely into classroom recitation and discussion, additional subjects might be introduced into the program with no appreciable—if any—lengthening of the term, and, last but not least, the teachers would have incentive to further upgrade the quality of the instruction by continued curriculum improvement. I was convinced by now that I was blessed with four fine teachers who were going to keep me on the go to keep up with them!

No student in Class 2 required more than seven sustained weeks of instruction and terminal testing to satisfy requirements. Three students completed after four weeks. All in all, it seemed as though the more compact schedule was as beneficial as the planning officers, teachers, and I had hoped it might be. Everyone was swelling with success; I felt it was just a matter of time now until I could "sell" the planning officers on full-day instruction with a curriculum of five subjects. One little misfortune occurred during Class 2 per the Courts Martial Procedure, causing us to have not twenty-five graduates, but only twenty-four!

Class 3 started during the 1st week of August, 1957. During the four-week interval between Classes 2 and 3, I thought it advisable to individually follow-up on a minimum of 50 per cent of the graduates of Classes 1 and 2. My primary purpose was to attempt to establish some further area(s) for suggested improvement in classes beyond upcoming Class 3. Student opinion of the teachers was extremely high (I passed this on to the teachers!) but this was normal for this type of activity. Many students were awaiting action on applications for an AA and GMS course. One suggestion that arose from these graduates—but was expressed in varying degrees of forcefulness—was that a student in this type of class was the target of unkind slurs from other soldiers of his Battery during the time he was in the Battery. Study facilities within an individual Battery were limited and interviewed graduates thought this could be improved somehow. A minority of graduates reported that they seemed to catch more than their fair share of routine housekeeping jobs during the mornings when attending school. I decided to cross-reference these comments during the conduct of Class 3 with the ten Battery 1st Sergeants. Possibly this course of action would be my big opening for full-day resident instruction.

Class 3 was concluded in mid-September in but six weeks' time! This signified a reduction of twenty full class hours of instruction and terminal teaching over Class 2's 140 hours, that is, a 14 per cent time savings. Complete course outlines were introduced by both English and arithmetic teachers and distributed to each student prior to "start of business" on the opening day. I secured a copy of each outline for each planning office· in the two Battalions. Teachers reported appreciable increase of participation by the more needy students throughout the initial days of the course. By sheer coincidence during the conduct of Class 3, a Department of the Army directive placed greater emphasis on broadening this "preparatory" instruction to include study in the social sciences. This provided all the ammunition I felt necessary to press for expansion of the curriculum to include world geography, world history, and basic physical science. Due to the fast-approaching close of Class 3, I decided to broach the matter with the Battalion Commanders *only* after the added benefit of interviewing graduates of Class 3 and upcoming Class 4. I laid plans to interview 50 per cent of the graduates of Classes 3 and 4, after completion of Class 4 in late November, 1957.

Class 4 was very successfully conducted during the six week period of early October to mid-November, 1957. No change in curriculum or materials was introduced during this Class. Had not the misfortune of that Court Martial in Class 2 occurred, this Class 4 would have signified the graduation of exactly 100 students in each Battalion in only slightly over nine months' of parttime activity.

Ninety-four of the 100 graduates in one Battalion, and ninety-two of the ninety-nine graduates in the other Battalion, produced not only successful High School Equivalency Test results but also considerably above average results on the English and arithmetic portions thereof. All 199 students improved their GT Aptitude Area Score appreciably.

In view of the approaching Christmas-New Year Holiday, both Battalion planning committees decided against offering Class 5 until after the holiday period. This met with my personal approval since I did not particularly relish the prospect of interrupting a class of this nature for a full two-week period. During the last week of November and first week of December, 1957, I interviewed 50 per cent of the graduates of Classes 3 and 4, per my previously discussed plan. I limited my interview with each graduate to two questions, namely (a) his opinion on the relative merits of half-day, nonresident instruction or full-day resident instruction, and (b) his sentiments on adding geography, history, and physical science to the curriculum. I must admit I was pleasantly flattered by the results of the interviews, since twenty of the twenty-five strongly favored adding the three subjects, and seventeen of the twenty-five favored full-day resident instruction. One graduate was noncommital on the matter of curriculum expansion, and three were noncommital on the matter of full-day residential instruction.

Encouraged by this favorable response of my interviews, I once again requested each Battalion Commander to convene his Planning Committee. (Note: Some replacements in each Committee had occurred due to Transfers.) I requested this conference in each Battalion be held not later than mid-December to permit any approved changes to be reflected in Class 5. I forthwith proposed that Class #5 be a full-day, resident program and expanded to include world geography, world history, and basic physical science. I supported this dual proposal with interview summaries from graduates of Classes 1 thru 4, comparative statistical summaries of the results achieved by graduates on the English and arithmetic parts of the High School Equivalency Test as contrasted to results attained on the social studies, natural science, and literature parts, and naturally the early September, 1957, change in concept at DA level on the extent of curriculum. I stated that additional teachers, if necessary, could be procured. I also offered to have the 5th Army Printing Plant reproduce the expanded curriculum in booklet form. Visual aids, I explained, were available through local business firms to enhance the presentation of geography, history, and physical science. I assured the Planning Committees that not more than nine weeks would be necessary. I mentioned that each Battalion Headquarters' Battery Commander had stated that living facilities were available at each Battalion Headquarters' site to accommodate the switch from nonresident to resident instruction. The meeting in one Battalion consumed five hours, the same meeting in the other Battalion consumed six hours, on different days in mid-December, 1957. In each meeting, there was much variation in opinion represented. (Note: I had hoped that the bringing up of a wide range of issues would force each Battalion Commander to make the decisions because there was enough in the package to partially please all members of the Planning Committee and make them willing to accept the total platform because of personal interest in a segment of the platform.) Each Battalion Commander decided about the matters at hand. I'm certain, to this very day, that the good Lord and not my approach, turned each Battalion Commander in favor of accepting the program expansion and concept of resident instruction. The first week of February, 1958, was set as the starting date of Class 5.

A personal conversation with each of the tried and true four teachers disclosed that in each Battalion there was sufficient professional training and experience for the present teachers to split the now five subjects among them. By the first week in January, 1958, each teacher was provided materials to handle the expanded curriculum. Each morning and each afternoon was so organized as to provide a suitable blend (we hoped!) of subject matter presentation, study, individual attention, variety of instructional media, and breaktime. The credit for development of the new curriculum was entirely attributable to the joint planning of the four teachers. I merely served to have the end product neatly printed and bound by the 5th Army Headquarters' Printing Plant, and to secure copyright releases from publishers and photographers for certain extracted items. While the majority of course materials were still USAFI stock, approximately 75 per cent of Class 5's materials were USAFI as compared to 100 per cent in the previous four classes. I should note that all teachers were now being compensated at the hourly rate of $7.50 per early agreement.

The first class under the new approach was conducted as scheduled, February to April, 1958. The fondest expectations of myself and the four teachers were realized in this undertaking. The most significant improvement noted was in respect to the significantly positive deviation in the social studies, natural science, and literature parts of the High School Equivalency Test results. As pertains to the personal satisfaction of the students, their egos did not suffer in the resident setting as had happened in the nonresident setting of the ten Batteries. The classroom used during the day was available each evening, Sunday through Thursday, for study purposes. The teachers noticed a greater degree of mutual problem-solving and a closer group relationship. I was so thankful that our projections went as planned that I was breathing a series of sighs of relief! The teachers, the two Battalion Commanders, and I had gambled heavily on a combination of unproven variables. I believe to this very day that it just was Providence that made things happen in our favor.

This same curriculum and full-day resident concept was continued with equal success through Classes 6 and 7, both concluded by mid-November, 1958. It is significant to note that Class 7 in each Battalion was comprised of individuals assigned to the Battalion since February, 1957. All in all, a total of 329 students were graduated by this program within the two Battalions in twenty months' time. The Classes 6 and 7 did not accommodate the capacity of twenty-five students each. The need for sustained, or even additional classes, had been met at a local level.

What happened to the curriculum? I turned this prized product over to the Education Director, Ft. Sheridan, Illinois, for implementation in both On-Post and Off-Post military organizations to which he furnished educational development services. Since early 1959, he has conducted resident instruction at Ft. Sheridan, Illinois, for Enlisted Men from Chicago, Gary, Minneapolis, and Milwaukee on a consolidated basis since there have not existed—nor do exist today—a sufficient number of Army personnel at any one of these metropolitan centers to warrant separate classes nor to attract and hold qualified instructors. One such class is conducted quarterly at

Ft. Sheridan but diagnostic testing, individual counseling and advisement to Unit Commanders is still furnished at the local situation. Draftee Enlisted Men are now accepted and Commanders have been quite cooperative in this regard.

As it turned out, this full-day resident preparatory instruction program was the first such attempt recorded to date in the Army's General Educational Development Program for Military Personnel. The proof of the pudding, so to speak, was the individual and collective success of its graduates in AA and GMS courses (now renamed the US Army Air Defense School), the planting of the seed for further academic and technical self-development, and the broadened perspective gained by the Commanding Officers involved as to the role of continuing education in the modern Army. This undertaking remains yet in my memory as the outstanding example —of which I have direct or relayed knowledge—of how patience, cooperation, and pooling of ideas can ultimately develop a new program of adult education.

Analysis. This case might be analyzed from several points of view: that of the academic instruction program as a whole (C-8), that of each teacher in it (a series of C-4 episodes), that of a particular group taught by a teacher (a single C-4 episode), or even that of a hypothetical student (a single C-4 episode). The first of these alternatives is chosen here since the central point of view of the paper is Mr. Heylin's and since it offers the richest interpretation. It might be argued that the program should be ascribed to C-7, since in a sense Mr. Heylin created a new institution, but his need to fit everything carefully into the dictates of Army procedures and command structures suggests that C-8 is the more relevant ascription.

This account describes a series of seven episodes. In the first, the program design was clearly established, and in each of the following four it was rethought and significantly altered. In the final two episodes, the design had become so well established that it was merely repeated and the novelty of approach was no longer present. At the conclusion of the series, the failure to recruit the desired number of students needed for another episode led to the appraisal that "the need for sustained, or even additional classes, had been met at a local level."

The program was initiated with Mr. Heylin's appointment which was presumably brought about because someone in the Army hierarchy thought that more education was required at the antiaircraft artillery units. Mr. Heylin presumably identified a number of possible educational activities and finally made a decision based on available facts and his own judgment to proceed with an eighth-grade school completion program to prepare students for further vocational instruction. This broad objective was thought by Mr. Heylin to require instruction in English, arithmetic, geography, history, and basic physical science, but the Army officers who controlled the program allowed only the first two subjects to be taught, thereby limiting specific objectives while retaining the broad one.

The format was designed by Mr. Heylin in collaboration with the officers and in several cases he was required to accept decisions he regarded as undesirable. The resources were provided by several Army units; for example, the classroom furniture came from Battalion Headquarters and the textbooks and other materials came from the United States Armed Forces Institute. The leaders were carefully recruited as demonstrated by their retention in the later episodes of the series. Methods were those customarily used in courses of this sort and the teachers were not only provided with preservice training materials but also supervised by Mr. Heylin. The schedule, worked out to fit Army customs, was less than satisfactory to Mr. Heylin. The sequence of presentation of learning units was probably dictated largely by the arrangement of content of the materials available. The provision of social reinforcement, essentially the responsibility of each teacher, was aided by support secured from military authorities and by initial counseling. To some extent, students were permitted to move at their own rates and some finished the program much earlier than did others. The roles and relationships among the students, their teachers, and their army supervisors were worked out as carefully as possible. Success in the program was to be measured by standardized achievement tests. The program design was explained by an opening session addressed by the Battalion Commander, Mr. Heylin, and the teachers.

A great deal of attention was devoted to fitting the program into the established and all-embracing lifestyle of the Army. Mr. Heylin is explicit at many points about his efforts to involve the

collaboration of the various officers whose support was essential to the success of his endeavors. In this process he did much shared decision making and interpretation. He describes in detail the testing and guidance procedures he used in selecting the students and his efforts to fit instructional time into the Army's on-duty schedule. In this last respect, he was not wholly successful at first since the commanders and first sergeants found the every other day scheduling confusing. The direct and indirect costs of the program were borne by the Army.

When the plan was put into effect, various alterations of procedure were required. Presumably some of them were made at once but others were noted as desirable changes to be incorporated in later episodes. At the end of instruction, which required individuals from seven to twelve weeks to complete, all students had achieved the desired eighth-grade standard, though some had started as low as the fifth grade level. The program was judged a success.

The subsequent episodes incorporated many changes in format, both at the start and as instruction proceeded. The program was generally tightened up with the result that completion of required standards consumed less time than before. A follow-up sampling of the graduates of classes 1 and 2 indicated that the interpretation of the program to fellow soldiers and to first sergeants still left something to be desired. Mr. Heylin noted this need and tried to do something about it during the third episode. Other changes of format were made both in it and in the fourth episode.

It was not until the fifth episode, however, that Mr. Heylin was able to broaden the objectives to include the content areas he had always hoped would be in the program. He describes graphically how the change was brought about by a general Army directive, the wishes of graduates whose opinions he sought, the discussion of planning committees, the decision of Battalion Commanders, his own persuasion, and the intervention of "the good Lord." This change in objective made it necessary to revise several elements of the format, most significantly the instructional resources, the schedule, the methods, the sequence, and the criteria of evaluation. Also the perennial problem of program interpretation was removed because the program became full-time and residential, so that the students no longer had to confront nonstudent fellow soldiers and duty-time first sergeants. The social reinforcement within the group was also significantly improved by various other elements in the format.

As Mr. Heylin took leave of his program, he had many evidences of its success. The reader may well share with him some of the enthusiasm expressed in his final sentence.

Adoption of a Master Plan

The 528 Club is the most elite group of men in a city of about one-half million population.[4] The membership is highly selective and includes the chief wielders of the city's financial, industrial, and commercial power, a few patricians, and two or three men whose charisma does much to establish the jovial good fellowship characteristic of the group. It is a luncheon club whose members attend every day if they can and it meets in a private suite of rooms on a secluded floor of what the general public believes to be the best club in town. The group is, in fact, a club within a club, and is known solely by the number on the door of its suite, but it is not widely known and its name is almost never mentioned in the mass media, whose owners are members.

Amid the badinage of the lunch table, many purposes are accomplished, most of them private but some of them for the improvement of the community. For example, a few of the men are on the board of the city's largest private hospital and, when it needs a new wing, they seek the financial backing of other members. Or if, in the general conversation, it becomes evident that several men think the quality of a public service—health, welfare, education, transit, or any other—is falling seriously below acceptable standards, the word goes out through the channels of power that the controlling board and its staff had better strengthen the system or face serious consequences.

One day the conversation took an unusually serious turn. Several community problems were discussed in turn by individuals particularly concerned with them and the conviction gradually grew in the group that the people of the city should stop their piece-

---

[4] This account was written by the author from an oral description provided by several members of the Club. Several details have been altered to preserve the anonymity of the Club and the informants.

meal approach to community improvement and consider what a unified city plan might be like. Some members argued that any total plan would stifle the individual initiative of various campaigns for civic betterment, but gradually these opposing voices were either won over or fell silent. No decision was reached, but the members thought about the matter and perhaps talked it over with some of their associates. The next day the discussion was resumed almost as soon as lunch began. Before long, the members present seemed to have reached a consensus that the Club itself should undertake to guide and direct the growth of a master plan, though some men still argued that the Club's purpose should continue to be good fellowship or that if a total city plan were contemplated, it should be undertaken from the start not by the Club itself but with much wider community involvement.

Perhaps it was this sense of a continuing division within the group that led one of its wiser members to suggest that the Club itself had better know more than he thought it did about the subject of municipal planning. Taking up this idea, the group undertook several informal sessions, at each of which a local or imported expert on urbanism talked and answered questions about the essentials of a city plan, its possible value in the current situation, and the processes by which one should be evolved. Some sharp questions at every session indicated that some of the members still had grave doubts about the feasibility of comprehensive planning, but after the series had run its course, the group reaffirmed its prevailing belief that the city did need some kind of overall blueprint. The president of a large corporation said that his company foundation would make a grant to the local university to guide the development of such a plan, and the chairman of the board of that university, after making the proper telephone inquiries, promptly accepted the grant.

During the next year, the Club retained a proprietary interest in the development of the plan. The university staff members involved needed some help and advice from specialists employed by the banks and by industry and it was quickly provided. A few centers of resistance to the whole idea were encountered in various units of the local government and members of the Club undertook to "reach" the opponents with generally satisfactory results. Various tentative formulations and ideas were brought before the Club and discussed and criticized by its members. Finally the task was completed and a model was developed of the ideal city as it might appear after fifty years' evolution.

Long before this model was prepared, the members of the Club realized that a task of public enlightenment lay before it if it hoped to win acceptance of the plan. Therefore, under the chairmanship of a member who was head of an advertising firm, a public group representing many segments of the community was formed. Most of its members had no idea that they had been hand picked by the Club; many of them, in fact, did not even know of its existence. For its part, this City Planning Association (CPA) sought publicity. A fanfare greeted its formation, its meetings were well covered by the press, and, in a series of well-timed releases, it told the citizens about the various stages of the model as it progressed.

When the final design was prepared, the CPA launched a careful campaign of widespread study and discussion among other voluntary associations and neighborhood groups. In this process, it became apparent that some of the aspects of the plan had to be revised, some compromises had to be worked out, and some interest groups and individuals were permanently alienated. Despite the sharp objections and the necessary modifications, the basic integrity of the overall plan was maintained and when it was finally presented to the city council for adoption all but two members voted in favor of it. The CPA went out of existence with as great a burst of publicity as that which had heralded its inauguration.

There then ensued a series of special discussions. By direction of the mayor and the council, the health, educational, welfare, transit, police, and other public agencies of the city undertook their own approaches, each built around its distinctive requirements. The private institutions in the same fields responded by reexamining their own projections for the future. As this phase evolved, the planners were realistic. While they knew that the overall plan had won city-wide acceptance and had the support of the central local power bloc, they also knew that the design would never be fully achieved in its totality, since changes would be required by unforeseen happenings, new conceptions, social pressures and resistances, changing political alliances, and other events. But what should be done during the year following the adoption of the plan to make it appear that at least one-fiftieth of the way toward the ultimate ideal had been reached while still holding fast to institutional values? The staff and citizen board of each substantive agency studied this question to be able to formulate the results in its program and budget. Since the 528 Club felt a proprietary interest in the plan, various members made sure that it was kept alive by their active participation on the boards to which they belonged and by the use of their influence on other community agencies.

Analysis. This case illustrates adult education as it is often found—learning is intermingled with action and serves to support and reinforce it. The series of episodes is different in several respects from that described in the Army program. There the series involved the repetition of an ever-changing but basically identical course of study for successive groups of students. In the use of education to help establish a master plan, the series was an evolving one, calling for the development of successive activities for different groups.

Three distinct categories were involved. In the first, the 528 Club planned its own activities (C-3), which, educationally speaking, took place in two episodes—the use of a series of experts to inform the group about the essentials of city planning, and the study of successive phases while the plan was being evolved. The subsequent support of the plan was essentially action, not education. The CPA program was an example of the creation of a new educational institution (C-7). Most of its successive campaigns were based on C-11, the provision of a program by the mass media. As for the separate substantive agencies and associations who took up the task of studying their programs after the city plan was improved, their program development situations might take any of a number of forms depending on the distinctive nature and operation of each. C-6, C-8, C-9, and C-10 would be prominently represented, though perhaps the latter two would be most common.

The most obviously educational episode in the whole inter-related sequence was that in which the 528 Club informed itself about the essentials of city planning. Here the program design proceeded in a fairly straightforward fashion, though the beginning point in the actual process was social reinforcement, as it is with many groups. The Club's values and patterns of behavior which exemplify them were so firmly established that they dominated any educational program which might be undertaken. The design components were not carefully thought through but were all either inherent in the situation or emerged naturally out of the Club's customary ways of proceeding. For example, individualization was particularly important, since each member of the Club is powerful in some sector of community life and the rule of the group is to act collectively only by consensus. At various places, therefore, one might observe some of the members trying to convince the others, using in each case the arguments which might prove to be most appealing to him.

The measurement of educational results was not undertaken directly. Each member of the Club, of the CPA and of the specialized planning groups learned what he thought he needed to know. However, action based on education was substantial. At the end of its first learning episode, the Club decided to support the idea of a plan, and at the end of the second, it agreed to support the plan itself. The educational campaign of the CPA was designed to win formal assent for the plan from the community and the city council. And, as the specialized agencies undertook their work, they knew that equally tangible results would be expected of them.

An Unanswered Question

The analyses of these cases demonstrate that the proposed program-design framework can be applied to a wide variety of educational situations. In making any such application, variant interpretations are quite possible, particularly since none of the accounts give exhaustive details about what actually occurred during the educational process. Thus the reader may prefer to assign any of the programs described to different situational categories than the ones here suggested and may consider certain procedures to illustrate other components than the ones to which they are ascribed.

But, quite aside from this possible variance in interpretation, an important question remains. Even within the framework, ignoring for the moment alternative systems of program design, have any basic situational categories or necessary components been omitted? Put another way, does the actual process of educational design and operation require any major factors not included in the model? The author, by presenting that model, has answered in the negative, but the reader should deal with the question himself to fully test the proposed way of analyzing or designing programs. If he does find another category or another component or prefers a different ordering of the present ones, he will have increased the utility of the framework for himself and may have helped in its eventual evolution toward a more precise and meaningful instrument of analysis and operation.

CHAPTER IV

Categories of Educational Situations

'Tis to create, and in creating live
A being more intense, that we endow
With form our fancy, gaining as we give
The life we image.

Lord Byron, *Childe Harold's Pilgrimage*

Much has been said, and rightly so, about the unity of man's experience and the impossibility of separating and defining all the attributes and actions of the seamless web of life. The eleven categories of educational situations suggested here do not come from an attempt to sort out all existing learning or teaching activities in terms of their form or sponsorship. Instead, the categories are dynamic. The educational planner or analyst examines the milieu in which he works, defines or chooses what appears to be the most logical or productive situation, identifies the category in which it falls, and shapes or guides his work in terms of the distinctive nature of that category.

At first sight, the eleven appear to reflect a shifting point of view. In C-1 there is at best only a fancied semblance of a leader and in C-11 the leader has no clear awareness of the nature of all the learners. C-1 through C-5 and C-11 are based on the act of education itself while C-6 through C-10 deal more broadly with the creation or operation of an administrative pattern. But beneath these surface differences lies a central unity—the categories describe the basic configurations of action used by an educator, a learner, or an analyst in pursuing a creative process, either alone or with other people.

C-1: Independent Study

Since independent study is, by definition, a wholly self-guided way of designing and controlling an educational activity, it can be examined in depth only by one who analyzes his own experience or that reported to him. As a result, knowledge about this category of situations is based largely on anecdotal accounts, most of them drawn from the biographies or autobiographies of distinguished men and women. Episodes in which learning plays a primary or significant part may occur in a life which is essentially private and contemplative (as was that of Montaigne or Spinoza), or in one which is fully rounded with activity but in which all actions aim at the fullest possible enlargement of the individual's potentialities (like that of the idealized "Renaissance man"). It has been taken for granted that any scholar at the forefront of his field must direct his own study, either alone or with the advice of colleagues. Such general patterns of independent study as these have long been cele-

brated as providing one of the wellsprings of major human achievement and as setting ideals for less supremely gifted men.

Little is known about the nature or frequency of independent
study in the lives of the undistinguished individuals who make up the
great majority of mankind. An investigation based on a national
sample estimated that in one year in the early 1960s, 8,960,000
American adults were engaged in episodes of this sort. It was discovered that "some subjects are almost always self-taught;" among
them are technical arts and hobbies, gardening, and home improvement skills.[1] The incidence of independent study is probably highest
among those who have had an extensive formal education. In a
Canadian study, Tough found that all but two of forty-four college
graduates he interviewed had recently engaged in self-directed
study.[2] But, as the examples of Walter Dan Griffith in Chapter
Three and many another workingman suggest, this kind of learning
can exist at any social level. Even in economically disadvantaged
societies, such as those of Africa, some individuals find ways to study,
often in situations in which their objectives are dictated by the fact
that they have access to only a single book or other learning resource.

The available evidence suggests that self-directed learning
takes place in a number of different ways. For some people, it is
an inherent part of the pattern of life itself. A scientist, for example,
may systematically keep up with the literature of his specialty, attend
conferences, and take part in continuous discussion with his colleagues. When he engages in research, he informs himself about
relevant theoretical work and previous studies and, by collecting
and interpreting data, acquires new understanding and insight. The
expression of the urge to know may be sufficiently paramount in the
lifestyle of such a man that learning and life merge together. He
has so completely mastered his own educational design that he
scarcely realizes that it exists.

Other equally self-reliant independent students are well
aware of the need to plan their learning. Their typical pattern is to

---

[1] W. C. Johnstone and R. J. Rivera, *Volunteers for Learning* (Chicago:
Aldine Publishing Company, 1965), pp. 38, 57–59.
[2] A. M. Tough, "The Teaching Tasks Performed by Adult Self-
Teachers" (unpublished Ph.D. dissertation, Department of Education, University of Chicago, September, 1965), p. 165.

accept some component of a learning design as central to what they wish to do and let everything else fall into place around it. One young librarian decided that she wanted to broaden her knowledge of the world and of her profession by spending about two years in each of five libraries in various parts of the United States. She carried out this plan, centered on her chosen method, altering it in one case to go outside the country to gain foreign experience. At the end, she felt that she had fully achieved her purposes, though she had never been certain precisely what they were.

Another example can be found in a prison experience of Malcolm X:

> I saw that the best thing I could do was get hold of a dictionary —to study, to learn some words. I was lucky enough to reason also that I should try to improve my penmanship. It was sad. I couldn't even write in a straight line. . . . I spent two days just riffling uncertainly through the dictionary's pages. I'd never realized so many words existed! I didn't know *which* words I needed to learn. Finally, just to start some kind of action, I began copying. In my slow, painstaking, ragged handwriting, I copied into my tablet everything printed on that first page, down to the punctuation marks. I believe it took me a day. Then, aloud, I read back, to myself, everything I'd written on the tablet. Over and over, aloud, to myself, I read my own handwriting.

He woke up the next morning, thinking about the words and proud of what he had done. So he went on, day after day, until finally he had copied the whole dictionary.[3]

Most learners who start such a program soon realize that their original plan lacks one or more important elements. Malcolm X found that he could read books with increasing understanding. "Anyone who has read a great deal can imagine the new world that opened" he said and embarked upon a broad venture in learning.[4] But many people find resources denied to them. Even so resolute a man as Winston Churchill had his difficulties. As a graduate of Harrow and Sandhurst, he had had an excellent early formal education, but when he undertook a program of independent reading of history and philosophy while stationed as a young officer in India,

---

[3] Malcolm X, *The Autobiography of Malcolm X* (New York: Grove Press, Inc., 1964), p. 172.
[4] Malcolm X, pp. 172–73.

he soon felt the need for guidance. "It was a curious education," he later wrote,

> First because I approached it with an empty, hungry mind, and with fairly strong jaws; and what I got I bit; secondly because I had no one to tell me: 'This is discredited'. 'You should read the answer to that by so and so; the two together will give you the gist of the argument'. 'There is a much better book on that subject', and so forth. I now began for the first time to envy those young cubs at the university who had fine scholars to tell them what was what; professors who had devoted their lives to mastering and focussing ideas in every branch of learning; who were eager to distribute the treasures they had gathered before they were overtaken by the night.[5]

Most people do not know of any systematic way to design their own learning activities. They choose independent study because they want the flexibility of approach it allows, because they are attracted by some new resource or method, or because they are unaware of any other way to learn what they want to know. Almost at once, most of them begin to feel inadequate. Tough's detailed record of forty learning episodes undertaken by college graduates in a metropolitan area shows that some learners felt they required assistance in every aspect of their programs and that the average learner turned to about ten other individuals for some kind of aid or support. In general, those who conducted the episodes felt inadequate about what they were doing, underestimated their accomplishments, and believed that their style of learning differed from that of everyone else.[6] Like Churchill, such people approach learning with an empty, hungry mind, and what they get, they bite. But when they encounter the confusion and difficulty usually posed by the reality of independent study, they grow insecure, stop far short of attainable goals, abandon their efforts, or try to find some other way of learning.

Why is this sense of stress and uncertainty so common? The answer may be that young people are seldom taught how to design and conduct their own education. A zest for knowledge may be fostered by a series of absorbing learning experiences in childhood

---

[5] W. Churchill, *My Early Life*, p. 127 (Thornton Butterworth, Ltd., London, 1930).

[6] Tough, pp. 160–61, 172.

and youth, but that zest does not automatically bring with it either awareness of the intricacies of a complex program or competence in designing one. What children and youth may learn by incessant practice is that education is a process guided by a teacher and conducted in a classroom. They may not be taught to separate the process from its embodiments, to understand its components, or to master their use.

It is interesting to speculate what would happen if such instruction were to become an established part of the schooling of the young, being taught by precept, demonstration, and practice, so that young people left school fully prepared to undertake independent study. The net result might be a vast increase in the number of people who initiate and carry out their own projects. It is less certain that such efforts would be more calmly and purposefully managed than is now the case. As a quotation in Chapter Two suggested, even researchers with extensive training and experience still proceed in a floundering and messy-looking way. Whenever man confronts the unknown with no sure guide, he is likely to be uneasy. But the researcher knows and accepts the canons of science which ideally should be embodied in his work and to which he can turn for guidance at times of doubt or stress. The independent student has a similar need to be aware of the fundamental design of learning.

In the system proposed here, the model used in self-directed study is the same as that in any other category, though a few of the elements or adjustments may be omitted or applied in special ways. An independent learner who works wholly alone may not need to think about leaders, social reinforcement, individualization, roles or relationships, or guidance. Alternatively he may want to test his plan with each such component in mind, particularly since he might wish occasionally to move into another situation, treating it as subordinate to his central endeavor. Thus a man who wants to learn statistics may seek guidance from someone about the best way to do so. If he decides to work his way through a textbook, he may find it useful to ask a friend to tutor him on the hard parts; in this way both leadership and roles and relationships would be involved. He may also find it pleasant to work in a library surrounded by other people, each of whom is studying independently but giving silent social reinforcement to one another.

As for individualization, the independent learner sees it in a special context. Unlike other situations where an educator must constantly consider how to reach each participant, the self-guided student has only himself to think about. But he should ponder how the process of his learning can best be adapted to his own nature and requirements. A C-1 situation is, in the deepest sense, a cooperative art in which learning must be guided at every point by the distinctive individualism of the learner. He must design and conduct his program with the realization that it is based on his own uniqueness, that it has meaning only as it changes him, and that at every point he must be its master.

C-2: Tutorial Teaching

Tutorial teaching exists in many forms and in some fashion or other it is universal to human experience. Most frequently it arises spontaneously as one person shows another how to do something, but it may be consciously fostered in institutions by the process which the English colloquially call "sitting next to Nellie." Such learning is an established aspect of some continuing relationships, such as that between a supervisor and a subordinate, and an occasional part of others, such as that between a physician and a patient. Tutorial instruction is also offered by private teachers who are usually paid for their work. The study by Johnstone and Rivera estimated that in a single year 1,670,000 American adults studied with such teachers.[7]

Patterns of tutorial teaching may also be institutionalized. In vocational rehabilitation and other ways of helping people reshape their lives, the counselor focuses directly on the specific needs of each client. The reader's advisor in a public library helps the patron choose the learning resources he needs. Much of Otis Griggs' time was given over to work with individuals. In many occupations, such as medicine, teaching, or industrial management, a master performer sometimes accepts an intern and gives him close and personalized instruction. In other situations, it may appear that instruction is occurring in a larger group (and, in some sense, it is) but the

---

[7] Johnstone and Rivera, pp. 53–57.

heart of the teaching lies in the relationship between the instructor and each student. The master painter or sculptor moves about the atelier helping his students one by one, and the same technique is used in teaching most of the other fine or practical arts and crafts.

The collaborative aspect of education as a cooperative art has its fullest expression in tutorial teaching, for the educator and the learner face one another directly. The starkness of this confrontation has led to deep analyses of the proper roles of the two members of the dyad. As Georg Simmel pointed out, it "contains the scheme, germ and material of innumerable more complex forms" but is itself completely unlike any other. "Each of the two feels himself confronted only by the other, not by a collectivity above him." If either party withdraws, the relationship ends, whereas if there are three or more people, the withdrawal of one person still leaves a collective social unit. The failure to have external social reinforcement gives the dyad its strength since it creates a "feeling of exclusive dependence upon one another and of hopelessness that cohesion might come from anywhere but immediate interaction." This bond is so great that larger groups often dissolve back again into smaller units. Thus the bonds and disunities, even in a triad, may "result in three parties of two persons each."[8]

In tutorial teaching, the dyadic relationship has been worked out in many different ways, some of which have taken established form. The Platonic dialogue was a method of eliciting truth by the process of directed questioning and the disputation of the middle ages demonstrated how subtly a line of investigation could be carried forward by the making of theoretical distinctions. In modern times, educational practice has relied heavily on work done in such allied fields as counseling, psychiatry, psychoanalysis, and industrial psychology, but many different ways of identifying the teacher-learner relationship have also arisen from practice or have been evolved from pedagogic theory. The following four patterns are among the most widely espoused.

The most common is straightforward exposition in which both parties expect the teacher to demonstrate or instruct and the

---

[8] K. H. Wolff, trans. and ed., *The Sociology of Georg Simmel* (Glencoe, Illinois: The Free Press, 1950), pp. 119–37.

learner to be a ready and willing recipient of his attentions. This pattern may be worked out in many ways but all of them assume that the two roles will be clearcut and well-established and that the members of the dyad will move through a series of formal steps. In a manual on industrial training, for example, the following procedure, paraphrased here and stripped of its reinforcing discussion, is recommended under the title *How to Instruct:*

> *Part I.* Prepare the Worker (Put him at ease. State the job. Find out what he knows about the job. Get him interested. Place the learner where he can see the operation clearly.)
> *Part II.* Present the Operation (Tell, show, and illustrate. Present one important step at a time. Stress key points. Instruct clearly, completely, and patiently. Teach no more than the learner can master. Summarize the operation in a second run-through.)
> *Part III.* Tryout Performance (Have learner do the job. Have learner explain key points as he does the job again. Make sure he understands. Continue until you know he knows.)
> *Part IV.* Followup (Put him on his own. Designate the person to whom he can turn for help on the job. Encourage questions. Taper off by returning to the learner at longer or longer intervals. Continue with normal supervision.)[9]

A second pattern (actually a special adaptation of the first but one which is now being heavily stressed as an independent system) is programed instruction, in which an educational task, usually the learning of a body of content or an established skill, is analyzed into a series of logical units, each of which is mastered by the student before he goes on to the next one. Cooley and Glaser suggest that this instruction follows a general sequence of operations:

(1) The goals of learning are specified in terms of observable student behavior and the conditions under which this behavior is to be manifested. (2) When the learner begins a particular course of instruction, his initial capabilities—those relevant to the forthcoming instruction—are assessed. (3) Educational alternatives suited to the student's initial capabilities are presented to him. The student selects

[9] S. B. Magill and J. E. Monaghan, "Job Instruction," *Training and Development Handbook,* R. L. Craig and L. R. Bittel, eds. (New York: McGraw-Hill Book Company, 1967), pp. 117–20.

or is assigned one of these alternatives. (4) The student's performance is monitored and continuously assessed as he learns. (5) Instruction proceeds as a function of the relationship between measures of student performance, available instructional alternatives, and criteria of competence. (6) As instruction proceeds, data are generated for monitoring and improving the instructional system.[10] A special feature of programed tutorial instruction is that the human teacher may be supplemented or sometimes replaced by an inanimate one such as a specially developed book, a teaching machine, or a computer, whose devisers have tried to take into account in advance all of the possible approaches of the students who will receive the instruction.

A third pattern is coaching, which is most commonly understood in its application to athletic accomplishment but is also widely adopted in the teaching of other complex skills, including those of management. Anselm Strauss defines this relationship as existing "if someone seeks to move someone else along a series of steps, when those steps are not entirely institutionalized and invariant, and when the learner is not entirely clear about their sequences." In each case the learner "has yielded himself (whether he knows it or not) to a teacher who guides him along at least partly obscure channels." The coach dominates the instruction by thrusting the student into unfamiliar situations, imposing demands, functioning "like a playwright, arranging episodes, setting scenes, getting supporting characters to act in a certain way", setting the timing, and devising such tactics in a delicately balanced process as "the prescription, the schedule, the challenge, the trial, and the accusation." From the beginning, however, the student imposes resistances and controls; eventually he achieves independence and usually he decides when the relationship will end. Strauss concludes, "The best pupils, like the best children, get out from under the control and the vision of the best teachers, and the best teachers are pleased that this is so. At the outer limits of learning, the stages can no longer be as standardized as at the beginning; and the pupil discovers his own style, whether we are talking of religious conversion, musical composition,

[10] W. W. Cooley and R. Glaser, "The Computer and Individualized Instruction," *Science*, 1969, 174, 574–75.

or anything else. For the coach, too, the process may be open-ended; he too may end with a different identity.[11]

A fourth pattern is nondirective instruction, often cast in the form of counseling or therapy. The learner asks for help but the person who guides him (counselor, therapist, teacher, or any other) knows that the seeker must find his answers within himself. He may do so by putting together previously unrelated elements of his knowledge, by searching beneath the surface level of his consciousness, or by discovering for himself the purpose and the motivation which will lead him to seek out independently the information, the skill, and the understanding he needs. In this permissive approach, the guide is far from being a vacuum; he is so strong and independent that he can turn his attention wholly to the needs of the person he is trying to help. Various specific methods have been proposed as appropriate to differing situations but Carl Rogers has suggested that in all cases the greatest help results from the ability of the therapist to communicate his own trustworthiness in an unambiguous fashion, recognize his essential separateness as a person from the individual he is trying to help, "experience positive attitudes toward this other person," respect his freedom "to develop a personality quite different from that of his therapist," "enter fully into the world of his feelings and personal meanings and see these as he does," act so sensitively in the dyadic relationship that the client "can begin to experience and to deal with the internal feelings and conflicts which he finds threatening within himself," free the client from any "threat of external evaluation," and accept him as a person who is in the process of becoming, of confirming or making real his own potentialities.[12]

As these four patterns suggest, tutorial instruction can be dominated from beginning to end by an established theory of the proper roles of the two members of the dyad, this theory being imposed on the relationship by the person who is cast as the educator. If such a theory is followed, its dictates influence all choices and actions taken during the designing and carrying out of the program. A coach and a nondirective leader will differ greatly from

---

[11] A. L. Strauss, *Mirrors and Masks* (Glencoe, Illinois: The Free Press, 1959), pp. 109–18.
[12] C. Rogers, *On Becoming a Person* (Boston: Houghton Mifflin Company, 1961), pp. 39–58.

one another in how they behave and how they require their learners to behave. However, some leaders are eclectic, choosing whatever pattern seems best to fit the situation or evolving a fresh approach out of the dictates of the moment. When such is the case, the relative importance of the definition of roles may diminish somewhat, but the very directness of confrontation of the two members of the dyad always causes such a definition to be an important element, even though it may be expressed in action, not words.

Leadership is sometimes provided by a group, not an individual. For example, a new public administrator may go through a formal indoctrination program provided by his future associates. If each person sees him separately with no collective planning in advance, he is subjected to a series of tutorial experiences. If the leaders work in terms of an overall plan, each experience will be limited and directed by that fact since each leader operates in terms of his assigned function. Occasionally, the leaders provide instruction simultaneously, so that the tutorial teaching ceases to be dyadic. In such cases, conflict sometimes arises among the leaders, particularly if they differ on their theory of approach; one person may feel he should be a coach and another that he should be nondirective. If this conflict cannot be resolved, the education of the learner will be impaired.

In the later stages of an episode, the nature of the C-2 situation often changes. The interaction gradually broadens and the role distinction between educator and learner disappears. In such a case, tutorial teaching is replaced by another situation, that in which a group of two or more people share in the learning.

C-3: Learning Group

A group is any collection of human beings which has a common purpose and among whom interaction occurs. Thus runs the austere sociological definition, but since some of the most crucial, creative, and inspiring elements of the human spirit result from the relationship of one person with another or others, there is great emotional power in the idea of the group, however small or large it may be. The goal to be collectively sought furnishes one source of inspiration but the very sense of interaction provides another. Thus Martin Buber, who applied Simmel's thought to his own career as an adult educator, identified the central importance of the group by distinguishing between collectivity and community:

> Collectivity is not a binding but a bundling together: individuals packed together, armed and equipped in common, with only as much life from man to man as will inflame the marching step. But community. . . . is the being no longer side by side but *with* one another of a multitude of persons. And this multitude, though it also moves toward one goal, yet experiences everywhere a turning to, a dynamic facing of, the other, a flowing from *I* to *Thou*. . . . Collectivity is based on an organized atrophy of personal existence, community on its increase and confirmation in life lived towards one another.[13]

All groups are learning groups in the sense that their members are constantly influenced by interaction with one another, but some groups have education as a primary or facilitative goal. Most of them are probably autonomous, arising from some spontaneously discovered sense of interest or need and continuing as long as they find their experience rewarding. Others are fostered and developed by an institution, such as a public library, a great books program, a sensitivity training center, or a health or welfare service.

Learning groups are so numerous and so variable in form that they can be neither counted nor catalogued. Some are brought into being by the common desire of several people to study a specific body of content. Others are created as literary clubs, scientific societies, or other associations designed to provide a generalized opportunity for learning; many clubs of this sort outlive their founders, occasionally by several generations. Others focus on the group process itself as a way to provide increased sensitivity to individual personality and human interaction. Others are designed to be vehicles of advanced study; most professions and scholarly disciplines have self-selected groups of leaders (known collectively as invisible colleges) who inform one another of outstanding new developments and research contributions.

Such learning groups as these are often highly significant both to the individuals who compose them and to the society of which they are a part. Few men in human history have had as

---

[13] M. Buber, *Between Man and Man*, R. G. Smith, trans., (London: Routledge and Kegan Paul Ltd., 1947), p. 31.

thorough a formal education in childhood as did John Stuart Mill; yet he said of a discussion group to which he belonged as a young man,

> I have always dated from these conversations my own real inauguration as an original and independent thinker. It was also through them that I acquired, or very much strengthened, a mental habit to which I attribute all that I have ever done, or ever shall do, in speculation; that of never accepting half-solutions of difficulties as complete; never abandoning a puzzle, but again and again returning to it until it was cleared up; never allowing obscure corners of a subject to remain unexplored, because they did not appear important; never thinking that I perfectly understood any part of a subject until I understood the whole.[14]

Illustrious learning groups may have a powerful impact on their societies, sometimes (like the Royal Society) continuing to influence it for centuries. Also the cumulative influence of many humble groups can sometimes be very great. In the twentieth century, Swedish study circles have done much to lay the foundation for the social advance of their country, and voluntary groups have had a powerful influence on the development of responsible electorates in Africa.

When a learning group is formed, its program may be created afresh, borrowed, or dictated by some aspect of the situation. In the first case, the members themselves decide how to deal with all components of the design. The success or failure of the group's endeavors reflects the extent to which an effective program was devised and followed. In the second case, the group which follows the example of another may find that the design it adopts fits its own need exactly or it may wish to consider how differences in the two situations require the original pattern to be altered. In the third case, the group accepts the fact that it cannot have full freedom to do as it wishes. Such a decision is necessary, for example, when a local chapter of a national association is formed, when a group decides to undertake a packaged instructional program, or when process is controlled by purpose, as in some forms of sensitivity training.

[14] *Autobiography* (Columbia University Press, 1944), p. 187.

Even when the situation requires that some of the components of the design be borrowed or accepted, a great deal of decision-making must usually be left to the group if it is to flourish or even survive. The quality of its life and experience depends on its capacity to be creative and to have the right to choose as freely as possible among alternatives. Thus a national association ordinarily allows its local chapters as great a freedom as is consistent with established overall policies.

The leadership of a learning group may take many different forms. The group may have no formal leader but let itself be guided only by the push and pull of the personalities in its membership; the individuals who exert more influence than others have a fluid kind of power which may shift at any time to other hands. In such cases, the role is not consciously accepted or ascribed by others, but it exists and, upon scrutiny, can be identified and defined. There may be both a titular and a real leader, and the two may or may not be in conflict. The group may be an amalgam of factions, each with its own leader. It may have a rotating leadership from among its members. It may recruit a leader from outside, or accept a leader at the time of its formation. He may or may not be trained for his job, and he may be completely pragmatic in his approach to his task or try to use some formal process. But essentially he is first among equals, and, though his role sometimes may come very close to that of a teacher, some distinction is ordinarily preserved so that the group retains the power of decision and action in collectively achieving its aims.

Of all the design components in a C-3 situation, social reinforcement tends to be most important, being at once a beginning point, a major determinant of continuity, and a basis of appraisal. It often transcends objectives in importance; the group remains in existence though its purposes change. As Hodgkin pointed out in his study of African groups, a truckdriver's "union may decide to run literacy classes; a football club may formulate proposals for constitutional reform."[15] But whatever it may do and however its purposes may change, Buber's observation states the central fact of its exist-

[15] T. Hodgkin, *Nationalism in Colonial Africa* (London: Frederick Muller, Ltd., 1956), p. 85.

ence. The group makes it possible for each of those who belong to it to experience "a turning to, a dynamic facing of, the other" members, and this relationship lies at the heart of the group's existence.

C-4: Teacher-directed Group Instruction

This category of situations is given its distinctive form by the combination of two attributes. First, the leader has a clearly defined role as a teacher which sets him apart from those whom he is to instruct and whose role is, in turn, defined by the fact that they are his students. He is aware of all that they are intended to learn, he has already mastered that knowledge himself, usually having gone well beyond it, and he operates in terms of some conception of educational method. Second, the instruction is provided to a group, and therefore a sense of community can exist among its members. By accepting the authority of the teacher, they relinquish—at least to some extent—their decision-making authority over the program design, but they can collectively provide a powerful aid to learning, both intellectually as a shared venture and emotionally as social reinforcement supports individual effort. The focused interaction between teacher and student which is possible in tutorial teaching is diffused when instruction is provided to a collection of individuals rather than to one, but skillful teachers and learners can overcome the apparent disadvantage by using the group itself as a means of achieving the rapport required when education is a fully cooperative art.

This category is widely used in adult education not merely in formal institutions which parallel those of youth, such as evening schools or colleges, but in many other situations as well. Among such activities are lecture series, training classes in industry or unions, educational tours, lifesaving and first-aid courses sponsored by the Red Cross, speeches delivered to meetings of voluntary and professional associations, and religious instruction carried out by churches.

Teacher-directed group instruction has always been a dominant form of education, not only numerically but also because it has been reinforced by the brilliant examples of masters with disciples, such as Jesus, Buddha, Confucius, and Socrates. The virtues of the teacher compared to those of other media of instruction have been stressed by such humanists as Bishop Grundtvig, who argued that by use of "the living word" abstract knowledge could be vitalized and brought directly to bear on the needs of adult students. The values of the group in fostering learning have been much celebrated by modern social psychologists. But the combination of the two elements has perhaps had its greatest reinforcement from the efficiency and economy with which it makes possible the spread of knowledge. In both ancient times and modern, the democratization of educational opportunity could best be achieved by teacher-directed group instruction.

The inherent values of the C-4 situation are reinforced by the fact that its use is so flexible in linking the periods of learning. One class session is an act and a coordinated series of them is an episode. An aggregate of episodes can be contrived to take place simultaneously in a school, community college, or other educational center, thereby establishing its basic pattern as an institution. The episodes can be put in series to make up a program leading to a certificate, diploma, or degree, and institutions can be placed in a graduated series such as that which leads from kindergarten through the graduate school.

The many values of teacher-directed group instruction have caused it to become so central to educational thought that, as was pointed out in Chapter Two, many people, both lay citizens and professionals, believe it is the only proper form in which learning can occur. The formal study of the nature and processes of education has matured around the teaching of children and young people in the classroom. Even when the content of pedagogical books and courses is professedly broader, purporting to deal with educational psychology, curriculum, administration, or the history of education, the customary central reference of the author is to the young person in the classroom in the school. Many of the findings and conceptions of this literature, if generalized sufficiently to remove it from the immediate situations from which it was derived, can have significance for the improvement of adult education. The principles used to state objectives, demonstrate a skill, determine readability, or construct achievement tests are as relevant to the learning of men and women as of boys and girls, particularly when the adults are engaged in teacher-directed group instruction.

Yet there are important characteristics of both the maturity and the life-style of adults which make the application of the C-4 category to them different from its use with young people and this difference is worth exploring at some length. The adult has had more experiences than a child, including some which boys and girls cannot have, such as marriage, getting and holding a job, and sensing the body's full maturity and subsequent decline. He may therefore bring to his learning a background of knowledge, skill, and judgment which can enrich his learning and that of his classmates. He may also grow rigid, opinionated, or forgetful, particularly if he does not keep his mind and body active with use, and thereby present special problems to anyone who tries to teach him. The instructor of adults does not have the same generalized power over the students as does the teacher in a school or college. He has a specialized authority unique to the situation which is based on his mastery of subject matter and teaching skill. When the class is ended, so is his power. But he can be challenged by the very maturity of his students to go far beyond the exposition of the familiar. The teacher of children almost never conveys a message of profound original truth to them. The teacher of adults, at least occasionally, does.

In the education of children, the teacher-directed group is a customary, familiar, and continuing experience which students take for granted. A high school boy, for example, spends most of his day attending classes which often have much overlapping of membership among them. More than that, he has moved through the previous school years with his same age cohort and expects to continue to do so. In adult education, the group is usually formed especially for each situation. The students may not know each other, for many of them the experience is a unique and unusual one, they are of varied ages and backgrounds, and, as a result, each class is a venture and often a challenge in building a new network of interpersonal associations.

In the lifestyle of the learner, there are significant differences between the child and the adult. The former conforms to some degree to the expectation of society that his main occupation should be learning, much of his time is spent within the environment provided by the school or university and under its administrative controls, and he expects to have a number of simultaneous classes. The

adult usually accepts noneducational tasks as primary to his way of
life; learning must be secondary to other major occupations. He
may have little contact with an educational institution except as it
provides the environment which he enters periodically for his class,
and his schedule may contain only that one experience of learning.
This limited effort may mean that education becomes so peripheral
to his experience that it has little impact on him. At the other extreme, it can mean that he continuously uses the knowledge gained
in his class to look with new insight at his own affairs and those of
society, thus enriching not only his learning but also his understanding of his whole pattern of life.

The normal child proceeds through the steps of an orderly
and successive educational progression. Society carries him along for
ten to sixteen years of schooling, sometimes longer. Ordained completion points exist, and while he may not achieve them the system
is set up to encourage him to do so. But when he ends his formal
instruction, age-grading ceases. In his adult years, any learning activity must usually be initiated by himself or by someone else, such
as his employer. The impetus to study comes not from the established expectations of society but from his interaction with the conditions of his life. He may elect to undertake a long-range series of
episodes, perhaps one leading to a certificate or a degree, but the
choice is his to make, not society's. If, by decision or default, he does
not continue to study, he will gradually lose his learning skills, a fact
which he may not recognize until, after a long hiatus, he undertakes
a new educational program.

Such distinctions as the foregoing make clear the fact that
adult C-4 situations, while similar in form to those encountered in
childhood, must be handled by both teacher and students with a
special awareness of the distinctive nature and lifestyles of the latter.
This necessity falls on both parties, but its burden lies heaviest on
the teacher since the designing of the activity is centrally in his
hands. He usually begins by accepting his own role as a leader, but
he then takes account of all the other components, either by himself
or with the collaboration of his students.

A C-4 situation is more likely to be repetitive than is one in
any of the other categories, since the teacher's usual pattern of em-

ployment requires recurring activity of the same sort. This repetitiveness can lead to staleness or rigidity. Early episodes may be planned creatively but with the passage of time routines are established and, in increasingly rigid fashion, applied to succeeding groups of students. This process can also occur in C-2 situations but there the directness of confrontation with a single student tends to reduce the danger. In a C-4 situation, the very generality of the group may blur the differences among individuals and lead the teacher to the comfortable belief that each succeeding class is made up of pretty much the same kinds of people. He begins to treat education as though it were an operative rather than a cooperative art. This danger can be resisted only if he sets himself the task of rethinking each act and episode in terms of its unique components.

C-5: Committee-Guided Group Learning

A C-5 situation is one in which the educational activity of a group is guided by a committee, usually composed of its own members. This guidance may be required because the group is too large to plan for itself, does not wish to do so, or does not have adequate time. Alternatively, committee planning may be required because the learning group has not yet been created, as when a council is appointed by a mayor to plan and undertake a conference on an important social problem. A C-5 situation is essentially a collective decision-making process which aims to make a proposed educational experience more truly cooperative than it would be if planned by a single person. But the committee must not allow itself to consider only its own concerns and thereby act as though it were in a C-3 situation. Throughout its deliberation it must think about what will be most educative for the learners for whom it is planning.

Program committees have highly variable tenures of existence. One may be called into being for only a single session. Another may have a life which begins with its first meeting and ends with the completion of the activity it has planned. Still another may have permanent status, though with rotation of membership; such might be the case in a continuing voluntary association. It sometimes happens during the course of an activity that one committee succeeds another. Thus a teacher-education workshop may be planned by one small group but, when the program begins, be replaced by another elected to represent the wishes of the participants in attendance.

The composition of a program committee also varies greatly among situations. It may be wholly derived from among the potential learners, as is the case with the education committee of a local union. Alternatively its membership may be drawn from many sources and be destined to play various roles in the activity itself. For example, the planners of a conference at a university center for continuing education may include faculty members from several disciplines, programming specialists from the center, delegates from institutional co-sponsors, experts in the topic to be considered, and representatives from funding agencies.

A C-5 situation may arise naturally and spontaneously. Often a learning group, perhaps because of growth in size or a sense of frustration, designates a few of its members to assume the planning function. Program committees have also become established parts of the work of many highly formalized institutions. Thus the Cooperative Extension Service has made great use of such committees in all aspects of its work, as the case of Otis Griggs in Chapter Three indicates, and experience in them is regarded as important in the continuing education of lay leaders. Some institutions or program formats are chiefly or entirely concerned with C-5 situations; such is the case, for example, with university conference and institute offices.

Planning groups ordinarily have a limited time in which to work and must often use much of that time to resolve individual or role differences in points of view. In order to compensate for the brevity of the planning period, specialists in program design have developed standard check sheets of decision points and components which are designed for use in industrial training centers and other settings where C-5 situations are common. Such a list presented to a committee makes it aware of the decisions which it must either make or delegate, and helps fix its attention on the total situation in which it finds itself. Even when such a check sheet does not exist, many institutionally based program planners have evolved a pattern of standardized decision making. As a result, systematic design may be more characteristic of institutionalized C-5 situations than of any other sector of adult education.

C-6: Collaborative Group Education

Every voluntary group is held together by the bonds of interest created by its purposes, activities, structure, and interpersonal associations. When a number of groups work together to enhance their combined programs, they are essentially trying to fuse these separate loyalties into some larger pattern of interconnected interest. Suppose, for example, that in a small city, the various voluntary associations (such as Rotary, Kiwanis, PTA, and the League of Women Voters) decide to sponsor an educational activity which none of them can undertake separately, such as a lecture-forum series of distinguished speakers. Every decision made in such a program-planning situation reflects not merely the capacity of the separate groups to accommodate one another but also their ability to transcend their separateness and join in a common effort.

While retaining this essential quality of supragroup cooperation, C-6 situations vary in many other ways. The planned educational activity may be designed for members of the constituent groups, for some other special audience (such as the functionally illiterate, the "downtowners," or the elderly) or the entire community. The collaboration may be undertaken solely for one activity or it may be continuing, as is the case with the countywide councils maintained in some Cooperative Extension Service programs. It may occur on a completely independent basis or it may be sponsored by an institution, as when the clubs in a settlement house plan for some general activity. The planning group may do all of its own work or it may have a full or parttime secretariat.

The formal structure for planning in a C-6 situation often looks very much like that in a C-5 situation, since both center on small groups working out the design for large group learning activities. There is an essential difference, however, since the C-6 planners are delegates assigned by groups to speak for them. Usually these delegates have only limited powers; they act under direct instruction or with clearly defined authority. Even when they are given unlimited freedom, they feel informal constraints and are careful not to go beyond the wishes of their constituencies or even of factions within them. These delegates must move collectively through the stages of program planning, making the decisions and acting upon them. Each such delegate is obliged to express the will of his own group as he understands it or, alternatively, be prepared to urge his group to adopt a new position. In the latter case, he knows that he has no power other than his personal stature or persuasive ability to win the support of his group for the educational program he has helped to design.

Institutions, Associations, and Organizations

Since the next four categories all deal with institutions, it is useful to begin by making several distinctions concerning their basic nature and their typical pattern of growth. The term *institution* itself is used as an overall designation to mean any comparatively stable, formally, and often intricately structured body of persons which carries out common purposes or advances common causes and whose members share a standardized and complex system of habits, attitudes, and material facilities. Institutions of adult education have countless structural patterns, but usually can be classified as either associations or organizations in terms of their allocation of function, the flow of power within them, and the intended beneficiaries of their services.

An association is a complexly structured body of members who join together, more or less freely, because of a shared interest, activity, or purpose, and who, by the act of joining, assume the same basic powers and responsibilities held by other members. This collective membership elects its officers, thereby giving them some degree of temporary authority. Sometimes this upward delegation is carried out at several political levels. Thus a large association may have local, county, district, state, regional, and national decision-making bodies. An association usually has its own members as its beneficiaries. It is distinguished from a group largely by its size and complexity and may be, in fact, a constellation of groups. It cannot maintain direct interaction among all its members, but must create an interlocking system of roles and relationships, often of a complex sort.

An organization is a body of people who work together to achieve a common purpose and whose internal structure is characterized by a hierarchical flow of authority and responsibility from the top downward, with relatively permanent (rather than periodically rotating) occupants of the seats of power who, when replaced, are ordinarily designated from above rather than from below. The basic authority of the organization may be derived from the general public, from stockholders or other owners, or from a self-perpetuating board, but its visible exercise is in the hands of a layered succession of policy makers and administrators. Organizations ordinarily exist to benefit their owners, a defined clientele outside their own membership, or the public at large.

An association or an organization is seldom found in a pure form, for each type tends to evolve toward the other. As an association grows in size, it creates a bureaucracy which may in time achieve dominance in both policy and its execution, though paying lip service to the all-encompassing power of the membership. On the other hand, an organization is often greatly influenced by the associations which enter intimately into the exercise of its power. A university has its academic senate and its student and alumni associations. Industry and government must deal directly with unions, professional societies, and employee groups. But though there are few pure examples of either an association or an organization, both are essentially different models for the exercise of power, so that in analyzing or dealing with any particular institution, it is important to know how the two different forms are mixed in its composition, which is dominant, and how each is tempered by the other.

Since many institutions, particularly public ones, are organized in a complex and interlocking fashion, it is often hard to define their boundaries. The term *institution* could be applied, for example, to any of the following entities of what is essentially an interwoven system: the government of a State, its legislative branch, the state university system, the land-grant university, the college of agriculture, the agriculture extension service, the statewide group of field agents, or the staff of a county extension program. In practice, those who design a program, operate it, or analyze it usually concentrate on whatever level of structure they believe to be most relevant to their actions, meanwhile taking account of the influence of the larger systems of which it is a part and the subsystems which make up its internal structure.

The founders and supporters of an association or organization usually believe it to be wholly unique. They are concerned chiefly with the immediate social and physical environment in which they work, and with their own personalities, interactions, and processes. But while every institution is in some respect like no other, students of organizational theory and practice have found a number of patterns and classifications that are useful in analyzing particular instances of institutional creation and growth.

In testing this point, William S. Griffith studied five dissimilar adult educational institutions: the Great Books Foundation, a suburban evening school, the educational activities of a central-city YMCA, the educational department of an international trade union, and the correspondence division of a university. Using a general growth model earlier proposed by Herbert Thelen, Griffith established the fact that these five institutions all passed through the same stages, though sometimes going back and forth among them and sometimes, with a new surge of life, repeating the sequence of steps.

This growth model has six stages, which can only be sketched here. (1) "A 'sense of issue' develops in a potential leader or leaders who feel that a strain in an existing system is not being reduced satisfactorily in the conventional, routine operating procedures." (2) The leaders are supplemented by the addition of other people and become a larger group which refines its objectives and develops a means of reducing the strain. "Decisions, both firm and tentative, are made concerning the structure, functions, and methods of the new institutions." (3) The institution comes into being and has its "first working interactions with the clientele and the environment . . . . As a result of the decisions made at this stage the institution may be said to acquire the beginnings of a 'personality' which includes . . . the generalized images held by those who work within it." (4) The institution expands at an accelerating rate and its program "is focused upon the successfully proven combination which produces a channeling of interest and resources and the productive utilization of resources that had been engaged in testing previously."

(5) For any one of a number of internal or external reasons, a strain sets in. Compensatory adjustments are made and some growth continues, "but when structural adjustments are no longer made and growth effectively ceases, the institution is mature." (6) The institution "comes into a fairly steady state in which a constant level of input and output is maintained. . . . The functioning is at that level which is adapted to the established structure, functions and methods of the institution in a particular environment. The personnel direct their efforts toward increasing the efficiency of each of the operating segments and may lose sight of the cosmic *raison d'etre*."[16]

At every stage of its development, those responsible for an institution must pay attention not merely to its program but also to its pattern of administration. The two constantly overlap, since the objectives, format, external relationships, and measurement of results of an educational activity are never separable from the staffing, budgeting, and reporting processes required to undertake it. Yet in practice a distinction is often made between a program staff and an administrative staff. In some cases a whole institution becomes bureaucratized into many interlocking units. Those who deal with various components, such as the provision of resources, the selection of leaders, interpretation, or finance, develop a sufficient tradition, size, or complexity of interacting operation so that each administrative unit develops a purpose and structure of its own distinct from that of the organization or association itself. The maintenance of one part of the system becomes the chief end of the people concerned with it, however much they may cloak that goal by using the rhetoric of service. As a result, the institution achieves a steady state from which it may be difficult to dislodge it.

The same result can be brought about when the program becomes unalterable. Even inspired administration can then do little to change the situation. One national association with adult education as a central purpose has maintained for years a membership of between 39,000 and 40,000, though its program invites the participation of all adult males. It is richly financed and has a large and skillful staff which has worked out refined administrative procedures and is innovative in trying new promotional practices. Yet

[16] W. S. Griffith, "Implications for Administrators in the Changing Adult Education Agency," *Adult Education*, 1965, 15, pp. 139–42.

unceasing effort can do no more than to keep the size of the membership stable, replacing those who drop out each year with an equal number of recruits. The reason for this failure to grow is clearly that the basic design of the program was "perfected" long ago and a conservative board refuses either to alter any element of it or to add new activities which might increase the membership.

The growth cycle of associations and organizations gives rise to many situations, but only the five most common categories will be considered. The four concerned with ongoing practice will be dealt with in this chapter. The complete redesigning of a mature steady-state program is the topic of Chapter Six.

C-7: Creating an Educational Institution

Adult educational institutions are constantly being created—by the government, by industrial and business corporations, by profit-minded proprietors, by people with a cause or those enamored of a solution to a social problem, and by countless others who seek to learn or to teach. Sometimes these institutions are wholly new in form; more often they are imitations or adaptations of existing structures. Their sponsors usually hope they will become enduring parts of the social fabric, and occasionally this hope is realized. For the most part, however, their life is relatively brief; they come into existence, survive as long as they are sustained by hope or need, and then disappear. The creation of institutions also occurs in elementary, secondary, and higher education but with nothing like the frequency that it does in adult education.

In a relatively few cases, the creators of an adult educational institution have complete freedom to design it in any way they choose. A sponsoring group may decide that its community needs a new cultural resource and make whatever plans for it they like, or a foundation may be created by an endowment of funds which imposes no limitations on those who administer them. In any such situation, the founders need only consult their own sense of what is appropriate and design whatever mix of components seems best to them.

Usually, however, the planning for a new institution is anchored by the acceptance of one or more components as being unalterable. The scarcity of money may impose limitations. The desire of the founders to remedy the wrongs or inadequacies of an existing social system may restrict them to the selection of certain goals. Personal capacities or resources may set limits to the format, as happens when the founders want to be the leaders themselves, to employ a method which they favor, or to spend funds for already defined purposes. When the controling desire is to replicate or adapt an existing institution, a fairly complete model of the proposed activity is already in existence. Thus a community group which decides to establish a public library has, by defining that goal, identified the major components of its program.

Freedom to choose may be further limited when new recruits to the cause are found, since they will have their own ideas about what is to be accomplished and by what means. The sponsors of the new public library may win support from the Chamber of Commerce by agreeing to stress industrial and technological books and from a local film society by promising to have an audio-visual service. While such alliances as these help make an institution possible, they influence the distinctive pattern which it evolves and which it may never subsequently be able to change.

Despite initial limitations, the range of choices open to the founders of an organization or association is usually greater than that available to their successors, who will always have to deal with both the tangible and the intangible legacies of its past. Therefore those founders should think through their program very carefully, considering each of its components and making choices which reflect the best available judgment as to what is required for initial success. The elements which must be accepted as unalterable can then be combined as effectively as possible with those in which freedom of choice is present.

It is also useful for the founders to retain an experimental approach, for the program will seldom work out exactly as planned. Early calculations, however expertly made, will be faulty in some respects. New staff members will want changes to be made, as will the people served. The social system which the institution enters will have aspects which were not taken adequately into account in advance calculations. Unexpected opportunities and resistances must both be coped with, and counterinfluences created by the program's presence must be met. One sector of the program may flourish and another wither, requiring a rebalancing of the total service. As time goes on, the social and physical environment will change, sometimes as a result of the program's success. These and other internal and external factors require that constant change in the design be contemplated. However steadfast of purpose the founders may be, they need to be as pragmatic as possible concerning the format of the services they provide and the way by which those services are fitted into the larger patterns of life of the society.

A growing modern sophistication about institutional growth models has led many founders of organizations and associations to be concerned with the rigidity of form and function which they often display. Occasionally programs are planned to have only a limited life because self-destruction is preferable to inevitable staleness. Alternatively, mechanisms or procedures are devised to aid creativity. Among them are the deliberate seeking out of innovative staff members, the provision for a periodical review of the program, the creation of a special staff freed of operational responsibility so that it can constantly plan for the future, and the engaging of consultants to provide independent critiques. These and other devices can be helpful, but only if they are consciously and continuously used by institutional managers. Innovativeness is the product of human thought and can never become automatic.

C-8: Designing a New Institutional Format

An institution's total program usually becomes established as a relatively limited number of accepted formats. For instance, a university extension division may maintain off-campus centers, a conference and institute staff, a correspondence division, and a lecture bureau; and its customary planning is entirely devoted to these four kinds of activity. Then the prospect may arise of a new kind of service, perhaps the creation of television programs, the development of a special baccalaureate degree sequence, or the local sponsorship of a national project. In any such case, the policymakers and administrators of the institution must ponder the new format, not merely thinking about it as a different kind of activity but also considering how it might be fitted into the aggregate of the present patterns of service.

An institution may add a new format for any of a number of

reasons, among which the most common are to respond to an expressed desire or demand, to meet a need perceived by the staff, to capitalize on past experience by using a new approach to a continuing goal, to provide itself with a broader base of service than before in order to spread opportunity or risk, or to take advantage of resources made available to it. Sometimes the decision to go into the new activity is swiftly made and executed. Sometimes it is reached only after long and agonizing consultation, which may involve a debate between those who want to remain true to the traditions of the past and those who insist that the demands of society or the needs of the institution require a broadening of scope. The strain is usually felt most keenly when an institution which has always specialized on one format adds a second one. A broadly generalized institution has less of a problem; if it already uses ten formats, it can fairly readily add an eleventh.

While a new pattern of service should always be examined on its own terms, it will be influenced at every point by the nature of the sponsoring institution and of the other educational activities it maintains. Sometimes the institution is not centrally concerned with education, as was the case with the 5th Army training activities described in Chapter Three, in which an academic program was strongly conditioned by the system of military control in which it was operated. In predominantly educational institutions, the staff draws on its past experience in designing the new format and usually tries to make it complement or supplement the existing pattern of services. In a sense, the distinctive difference between C-8 situations and those in other categories is the influence of the history of the sponsoring association or organization on the design of a new format.

The creation of a pattern of service can also cause profound changes within the institution itself. When it adds the new kind of activity, its administrators usually hope not merely to meet individual and social needs but also to reap such advantages as may come from greater financial and material resources, a larger staff, a better balance of program, and more adequate ways to take advantage of equipment, public relations, and other methods of facilitation and control. These gains may actually be achieved, but it is equally possible for losses to occur. Resources may not grow as expected so that the costs of the new format must be borne by the well-established programs. Long-time clients may be alienated, or, alternatively, their shift to the new activity may hurt the old ones, thereby providing no net gain in service. New staff members may be incompatible with existing ones. For these and other reasons, the institution may be weakened, not strengthened, by its larger responsibility.

A new format also alters the overall image of the institution held by those outside it, and that change may have either positive or negative consequences. When a community college which has offered only degree sequences begins to sponsor noncredit special interest courses, its image changes in the eyes of both the continuing clientele and the people it seeks to attract. Occasionally this change may pose such a threat that a manager goes to great lengths to avoid it. Thus the proprietor of a specialized correspondence school who adds a new program may pretend to the public that he is creating a separate institution when he is actually only broadening the base of the old one.

The risk of a C-8 situation can be minimized to some degree by developing and testing model programs, each with its own combination of design components. Only when an effective pattern is devised is it put into full-scale operation. Mr. Heylin used this procedure in the 5th Army program. While the preliminary testing of formats can also be employed in the other categories, it is particularly suited to those in C-8, which offers the opportunity for an institution to provide the shelter and support of its existing resources for the development of the new pattern of work.

C-9: Designing New Activities in Established Formats

Within the established formats of an institution, a constant inventiveness of new program ideas is usually required. For example, a local council on world affairs may have adequate staff and resources to administer about fifteen short courses, three weekend conferences, seven foreign tours, ten luncheon sessions, and fifty meetings with special groups. Some of these can be repeats of earlier offerings but most of them must be planned afresh each year if the council is to keep up to date with current developments. Other agencies, such as evening schools or community colleges, may be able to build up a large percentage of staples but each year some of them will lose their power to attract or to serve and must be replaced. The innovations constitute the essential growing edge of the institution's service.

The rapid national growth of adult education in recent years is attributable in large measure to the success of people in C-9 situations in identifying new needs and shaping programs to meet them. Usually the ideas come forward spontaneously and from many sources. The staff of the institution knows that its future depends in part on creativity and therefore keeps on the alert for potential programs. The members of an association put forward their ideas about what should be done. The students of an organization have proposals to make. And the outside community or constituency also presents its requests. Many come in fortuitously, or, as the phrase has it, over the transom. Others result from systematic outside contacts made by the staff. In fact, the administrators of a successful institution may need to do little creative thinking themselves but merely select the most promising activities which are brought to their attention.

In most cases, however, it is necessary to supplement chance and good fortune by a systematic effort to be creative, using as many approaches as possible to stimulate the ideas of the planners. Among the most frequently used such approaches are those in the four following groups, here cast in the form of questions which such planners might ask themselves. While these questions are most relevant to C-9 situations, many of them can be used (either as they are now phrased or as revised slightly) in each of the other ten program-development categories.

First, some leads to new programs come from within the institution itself. How can the principles which have made it successful in the past be applied in a new time or a new setting? What successful designs can be recast to meet different objectives? What are the logical points of extension of present programs? What institutional objectives are not now being adequately achieved? What topics of interest are being raised in association meetings that are not being adequately dealt with? What information can counselors provide about topics being raised in the interviews they conduct? What requests for service are unmet? What could be learned by questionnaires or systematic interviews of members or clients?

Second, some ideas for programs arise from the availability of a component or components on which a design can be built. What potential leaders, physical facilities, or resources are available but are not being used? Would some medium of public interpretation (such as a newspaper, a ministerial association, or a radio or television station) be interested in helping achieve a community-based goal?

Third, some programs can be borrowed or adapted from other institutions. Are institutions like ours doing interesting things elsewhere? Can we create our own version of a program which is successful in institutions unlike ours? Can we borrow program ideas from other cultures or subcultures? (American, British, and Scandinavian educators of adults have done a great deal such borrowing from one another.) Are schools, colleges, and universities maintaining programs for young people which should also be made available to adults? Are there associations of potential students which we should cultivate? Are there other adult educational institutions with which we might cosponsor programs?

Fourth, some sources of innovativeness are to be found within the community or constituency served. Are there special clienteles which we should reach and, if so, how? Are there social needs which should be met? Can we discover and get the advice of innovative men and women who generally tend to be ahead of other people in their interests? Are there topics which seem to be of increasing concern in the community? Are there widely discussed issues on which we can base programs before the present interest disappears? Could we learn anything from interviews with community leaders or other informants? Should we have continuing program-finding relationships with consultants, advisors, or advisory committees?

By asking such questions as these, administrators may be stimulated to have many ideas for programs which can be fitted into their service formats. These ideas can then be sifted to see which seem to be the most feasible. In doing so, it is useful to sketch out quickly in advance the way in which the various components might be handled in shaping each proposed design. Some institutions even use planning forms or checklists similar to those mentioned under C-5 above in which the pattern of a proposed activity may be quickly outlined. If there are then a number of alternatives from which a choice must be made, the decision can be made as to which

potential programs appear on balance to offer the greatest opportunities for fulfilling the institution's objectives.

In C-9 situations, the task of program planning is often
divided among the various levels of the administrative hierarchy.
Thus the director of an industrial training unit may identify a proposed activity, choose its instructor, and fit it into the scheduling,
guidance, financial, and interpretational framework of the institution. The instructor then does the rest of the planning, sometimes
alone and sometimes with the advice of the administrator or other
staff members. Complex institutions could not be operated without
such division of authority, which may be guided by conventional
practice or by agreements reached by the parties concerned. As with
all divisions of authority, conflicts and misunderstandings occasionally arise, a fact which often makes necessary some revision of
plans in the course of their execution.

C-10: Collaborative Institutional Planning

Adult education, unlike earlier schooling, cannot be viewed
in terms of the work of a few dominant institutions. Therefore one
important effort in creating the total service which should be provided by the field as a whole is the development of collaborative
institutional planning. If the argument of this book is correct, the
associations and organizations involved use the same fundamental
system of program creation and analysis and therefore have much to
learn from one another's experience. They all serve the same broad
clientele, the men and women of the community, and could provide
far better service than at present if they could devise ways of eliminating gaps and duplications of program, reinforcing one another's
endeavors, and seeking out and meeting jointly the needs which no
single institution can adequately handle.

The problem of coordination is essentially that of bringing
independent and often diverse institutions together so that they may
interrelate their activities in a harmonious fashion. This task is never
easy, as the work of the United Nations demonstrates, but it is
capable of being undertaken with some success by those who
genuinely seek to develop more comprehensive service than can ever
be achieved by piecemeal institutional planning. The social welfare
field with its councils of social agencies, its community funds, and its

extensive involvement of both professional and citizen leaders has gone further in this respect than other kinds of community-wide service (such a health, culture, recreation, and adult education), though it still has major problems to confront. All such endeavors have essentially the same need to find ways to broaden their scope and coverage of program. This need is particularly strong in adult education since it is so often a partial, peripheral, or supportive function of the institutions which maintain it. But it is equally true that the educators of adults have a special need to establish joint relationships outside their institutions in order to reinforce their work within them.

Collaboration can take countless forms but they can be analyzed in terms of a few basic dimensions. One of these has to do with the number of parties involved. In multilateral coordination, such as that undertaken by an adult education council, the institutions involved take a general and comprehensive approach, usually governed by an overall parliamentary body which follows the practices of representative democracy. In bilateral coordination, such as that undertaken by the extension divisions of two neighboring universities, there is direct confrontation by each organization of the other in an effort to bring their programs into harmony or to reinforce one another's efforts. In unilateral coordination, such as occurs when a public library undertakes to supply books and other resources for the educational activities of all community agencies, one institution sets itself the task of reinforcing the work of others.

Another dimension has to do with the contribution made by the parties involved. Sometimes institutions facilitate each other's work; they refer students, they promote programs, they support bills in the legislature or representations to government authorities, or they find other ways of offering assistance. Sometimes institutions complement the work of others by blending together dissimilar activities; a community college may provide physical facilities for other institutions and associations, an art museum may create a special display to illustrate the work in art history at a university, and a county agent may circulate books for the regional public library. Sometimes institutions undertake joint sponsorship of activities; several citizen associations may develop a state-wide study-action program, two universities may support a leader-training institute, or a number of institutions may support a television channel.

Still another dimension has to do with the complexity of the interaction. Here it is useful to think of a continuum ranging from simple to comprehensive interrelationships between two or more institutions. Thus the public school and public library systems in a city might agree only to hold a meeting at which key staff members of both might learn about each other's programs. At the other extreme, the two systems might work out a wholly coordinated effort from top to bottom, with both the central staffs and the neighborhood schools and libraries in close and continuing contact with one another, and with much use of contracts for service, joint appointments, problem-solving committees, liaison officers, or other collaborative mechanisms and practices.

Any form of coordination, no matter what its specific dimensions, may be initiated by the institutions themselves or result from the application of external pressure. Ideally there should be a desire to work together or, at least, a lack of antagonism toward the idea of cooperation. In some places, however, long-standing apathy, ancient quarrels, or a spirit of separatist empire building keep apart the people who could work together fruitfully. So long as such conditions prevail, no readily apparent way can be found to reduce indifference or antagonism so as to prepare the ground for positive cooperation. In such cases, the major hope for comprehensive service must rest on some outside development such as a pressing social need, the demand made by a governmental body, or the rapid rise of a new institution which compels existing ones to rally together for mutual defense.

In all C-10 situations, the individuals or groups involved in planning confront one another in new ways which require them to transcend accustomed habits of work and to rise above parochial loyalties. Each adult educational institution builds its own routines, special language, and procedural dogmas, and this superficial distinctiveness tends to make it feel wholly unique. The difficulties of collaboration can be lessened by the use of a generalized system of program planning. When people move through the decision points of a system such as the one presented in this book, they turn their attention away from themselves and their separateness toward the task they hope to accomplish and the community of interest which they all feel. This approach reinforces the desire to cooperate and thereby strengthens the program which is produced. The representatives of each institution are also provided with a new vantage point for examining and improving its individual efforts.

Administrative considerations influence both the planning and the execution of C-10 situations, particularly when the new interrelationship is a complex one, requiring the working out of many staffing, material, and financial arrangements at several levels of diverse hierarchies. The basic decison to consider collaboration must be made by the policyshapers of each institution and each one brings to the planning table its own structure and administrative code which set preconditioning frameworks for everything which follows subsequently. Thus questions of administration both precede and accompany program planning.

Each of the constituent agencies must usually invest resources in a coordinative program which it would otherwise have available for its own purposes. It is therefore essential that the planning process involve people with sufficient authority to commit their own organizations or associations to the decisions which must be made in sponsoring the new program. Failing such involvement, the planners must have immediate access to the people who can make the necessary decisions. Also, since the staff of each institution is oriented to its specific purposes, the planning group may include people who are not immediately involved with any of the collaborating parties, but can focus directly on the program itself as a new endeavor. Lay citizens, acting as spokesmen for the whole community, can often serve very effectively in this role.

C-11: Mass Education

The essential characteristic of any mass educational situation is that the individualities of the learners remain unknown to those who conduct the instruction. The sponsor of a mass program may design it to reach a generalized target audience, such as the members of an academic community, white suburban housewives, or people interested in modern art. The bull's-eye of any such target, broad though it may be, is surrounded by successively less well-defined penumbra, so that the persons actually reached may be markedly heterogeneous. An effort may be made to individualize mass teaching on a sampling basis, as when a lecturer watches the reaction of several people in his audience, but the number of learners is too great to allow awareness of each of the many men and women who participates.

The specifics of mass education are ordinarily defined by time, place, or method. When the learners are all participating at the same time, they may be physically present together as an audience, or they may be dispersed as small groups or individuals, as is the case with television viewing or radio listening. In some places (such as museums, fairs, or expositions) mass learners may present themselves one after another, either alone or in groups. Some methods (such as the lecture, the film, or the exhibit) foster group use, but others—most notably, reading—are essentially solitary and yet are mass educative, at least as viewed by the author of the material to be used.

Just as a C-1 situation can be planned and conducted only by a learner, so a C-11 situation can be planned and conducted only by an educator. He may seek to make his planning cooperative by working in terms of his conceptions of the nature of his learners or by doing some questioning of members of his target audience, but his capacity to have real involvement is limited sharply by his inability to do more than make a guess about who the learners will turn out to be. Once the activity has begun, its audience is likely to have only limited ways of interacting with the educator. Questions may be asked of a lecturer or telephoned in to a television panel show, and there may be some expression of the opinions of a few participants, but these devices can do no more than sample the full range of response.

So far as periods of learning are concerned, C-11 situations are more often acts than episodes, series, or aggregates. To be sure, the latter three are frequently designed. Radio and television courses or degree programs, integrated series of readings and lectures, related exhibits, and many other formats are undertaken with the aim of providing more learning than can be accomplished by a single act. Yet realists know that the continuity of contact with learners is almost always far less than the designer of the program hopes it will be. This is true because of the lack of group cohesiveness or discipline, the impersonal relationship between educator and learner, the distractions of the home or work settings in which much mass learning occurs, the tendency of many learners to sample a mass activity with no intention of remaining permanently, and the problems of adjustment required by fixed and demanding schedules. These difficulties are so great that mass educators often try to design each act to be as separately educative as possible while still linking it to the other acts in the episode or series of which it is a part.

While a C-11 activity is designed in the same way as those of any other category, many of the components must be treated in a special way. In order to overcome the impersonality of the approach and the lack of small-group facilitation, mass programs often mix noneducational with educational goals; efforts are made to amuse, to entertain, or to be topical as well as to teach. The role of the leader is stylized; even when he uses an intimate and informal approach, both he and his audience know that no actual intimacy of contact exists. The measurement of results is usually gauged by size of audience, warmth of applause, sampling studies of opinion, or ratings which estimate the number of participants. Social reinforcement can be created when people are physically present, but it is difficult or impossible to achieve in other situations. Guidance and the fitting of the activity into a total lifestyle must usually be left to the discretion of the learner, though attention to such matters as scheduling and finance may set an activity at a time when it is thought to be most convenient and least costly. Interpretation both within the activity itself and in its reinforcing public relations may help learners to decide whether or not they wish to take part.

In some of the other categories, thought about program components can become so generalized as to create a C-11 situation. A correspondence course (C-2) can be turned into a series of readings with no interaction between instructor and student, a teacher of a class (C-4) can lose sight of the individuals present and treat them as a group of types, not as real people, and institutional settings are often prone to impersonality of approach. In such cases, the full potentiality for learning inherent in the situation is not being realized, and the result is a loss of effectiveness.

Selection and Use of Categories

The eleven categories do not include all the situations in which education can be planned or analyzed, though they do identify those most commonly found in practice. Nor is the differentiation between categories always sharp and clear, for some situations lie in shadowy zones where one category merges into another and where arbitrary decision may be necessary for precise placement. But if the definition of the general outline and independent form of these clusters is accurate, they provide a basis for decision and action, thereby helping to make concrete the theory and practice of adult education.

It often happens that the designer of a program can work within only one category. Sometimes this limitation is imposed by the goal. The desire to have people learn how to participate in group decision making requires the use of C-3. In other cases, situational factors compel category selection. A learner may have to guide his own education because he can find no tutor, group, or teacher, and a television station is required by the dictates of its method to operate in the C-11 category.

Where the possibility of choice exists, the person making the selection must balance the situational factors to see which category is most suitable. The director of an evening college may wish to inform the people of his community about urban problems. Should he use the group discussion approach (C-3), formal classwork (C-4), a conference (C-5), an all-community effort (C-10), or a lecture series (C-11)? In making his choice, he must take into account how specific goals will be influenced by each of the available categories and also how well his resources permit him to undertake the possible designs.

Many tensions arise when those involved in a program disagree as to its basic category. If a small group plans a program paying chief attention to its own interests (C-3) when it should really be considering those of a larger group (C-5), the resulting activity is almost certain to reveal strains and disagreements. Similarly, if one staff member believes he is suggesting a new activity in an established format (C-9) but his colleagues believe he is proposing a wholly different kind of activity (C-8), conflict is likely to result. It sometimes happens that even when there is surface agreement as to the category being used, its actual practice is subverted by a covert use of another one. The members of a group may feel that its leader, whether he knows it or not, is using the force of his position or personality to manipulate the discussion to reach predetermined decisions, and therefore is acting not in a C-3 but a C-4 fashion. In any of these cases, difficulties can be remedied only by resolving the indecision over which category is dominant. Similarly, if there is a shift in category (such as when a group becomes a class or vice versa) that fact should be clear and acceptable to all concerned.

The use of the categories helps to solve one of the most critical conceptual difficulties of adult education. Even those people who have long believed that the field is crucially important to the realization of mankind's potential have realized that its breadth has led to diffuseness of approach. If men and women learn in countless situations in all aspects of their lives, either alone or with some kind of guidance, it becomes hard to grasp the scope of adult education and difficult to guide and direct it. But if the situations in which it occurs can be reduced to a manageable number of prototypes, vagueness and generality of approach can be replaced by a sophisticated conception of form and structure which gives some unity to the field despite its institutional divisons, makes possible distinctions which lead toward harmony and away from disagreement, and provides the basis for practical accomplishment. The educator who becomes aware of the variety of categories in which he can operate has taken a major step toward becoming the master of his field and the learner who understands the options open to him is helped to choose wisely among them.

CHAPTER V

Development of Program Design

The intellectual life of man consists almost wholly in his substitution of a conceptual order for the perceptual order in which his experience originally comes. . . . Had we no concepts we should live simply 'getting' each successive moment of experience, as the sessile sea-anemone on its rock receives whatever nourishment the wash of the waves may bring. With concepts we go in quest of the absent, meet the

131

remote, actively turn this way or that, bend our experience, and make it tell us whither it is bound. We change its order, run it backwards, bring far bits together and separate near bits, jump about over its surface instead of plowing through its continuity, string its items on as many ideal diagrams as our mind can frame. . . . We harness perceptual reality in concepts in order to drive it better to our ends.

William James, *Some Problems of Philosophy*

The themes explored in this chapter have long been central to the theory and practice of education. Most of the literature concerned with the science and art of pedagogy (and of andragogy, if it be accepted as a separate field of study) is made up of analyses of exquisitely refined topics, each of which is somewhere within the compass of an enormous and complex body of knowledge. This diversification both inhibits and makes necessary some integrating synthesis which can bring coherence to what would otherwise be a shapeless body of facts and principles. The emphasis here therefore is upon the establishment of a symmetry of thought and action, not upon a full treatment of each part of education.

It is assumed, as was pointed out in Chapter Two, that this symmetry is to be found in the interconnection of coexisting components, none of which is invariably more fundamental nor prior in time to the others. As in Chapter Two, the series of decision points is here put in the order which experience has shown to be most readily understood. But in either designing or analyzing an educational program, the mind does not proceed in any established sequence but plays back and forth over all aspects of the process. As Robert Oppenheimer has suggested, "The unity of knowledge, long thought of as corresponding to a structure in which the foundation stones imply the whole, has today a very different topology: very much more than a temple, it is a network, as William James foresaw, with no central chamber, no basic truths from which all else will follow, but with a wonderful mutual relevance between its many branches, and with beauty illuminating the growing tips of knowledge, even in the most recondite and unfamiliar branches."[1]

[1] "The Added Cubit," *Encounter*, 1963, 12, 45.

Identifying Possible Educational Activity

The awareness that a learning activity might occur can arise from many sources and in many ways. It may be an extension of a previous action of the same kind. An experienced tutor talks with a potential client (C-2), a teacher contemplates the resumption of her work during a new term (C-4), or the staff of an institution considers new activities in an established format (C-9). The situation is often such that awareness of a possibility is followed almost automatically by a decision to take action. But, particularly in the education of adults, such an awareness may also arise in a context which makes a negative determination at least as likely and as wise as a positive one.

A potential activity may enter the consciousness of an individual as a result of either internal reflection or response to external events. As people think about themselves, they develop desires, grow dissatisfied with their lives, realize their lacks of ability, see disparities between present and desired accomplishments, sense their needs to grow in capacity or usefulness, and distinguish in many other ways between what might be and what is. This self-knowledge may either precede the awareness of a possible learning program or be precipitated by it. Thus a poster describing a music appreciation course may create in its viewer a recognition of his ignorance of that subject. External events can create needs, present challenges, or offer opportunities. A man has an accident and finds that a rehabilitation program would help him recover. A marriage fails, and both parties seek to find out why. A woman has an increase in salary which permits her to fulfil a long-standing interest. Almost any event of life, whether it enlarges or limits the range of potential action, can give rise to a recognition of the possibility of learning.

As with individuals, so it is with groups. During a social conversation, in a meeting of a club, at a conference between a worker and his supervisor, or in any other form of direct human association, the potentiality of a learning activity may arise from a consideration of the interests and needs of the participants themselves, of some body of potential learners, or of society as a whole. This possibility may grow from an initial suggestion made by one of the persons concerned, or emerge from the interaction and stimulation of a discussion, as several approaches and notions are considered.

People vary greatly in their receptiveness to the idea of education. The threshold of awareness of the value of learning differs from one individual to another. One woman may be so conditioned by past experience that study is an ever ready option in her mind, while another woman may never consider it for herself nor even be aware that it is a possible way of meeting the challenges which confront her. The threshold also varies from one situation to another; thus a businessman or a farmer may frequently consider education as a way of refining his capacity to carry out his work while never thinking of it as a way toward a better family, community, or recreational life.

The idea of learning or of teaching may be born with or without marked emotional overtones. Some theories of adult education have been based on a conception of needs or interests which implies the existence of either tension or pleasure. It is true that the facing of a need (if that term is understood as a lack of some necessary or desirable good) may have an aura of grim necessity and therefore be unpleasant, while the opportunity to engage in an interesting activity may be accompanied by a feeling of keen enjoyment. In either case, emotion can lead to fruitful action. It can also prevent it. Too negative a feeling creates immobility or an inability to learn, even as too positive a feeling prevents the establishment of the discipline usually required by any worthwhile educational activity. But experienced observation suggests that strong emotions are not essential to the undertaking of learning. It is possible to decide coolly and rationally about participation in an educational activity.

Deciding to Proceed

The decision about proceeding with an educational activity may flow directly from the awareness of its existence. A group is formed, a man is asked to join it, and he says "yes" or "no" at once. But in other cases, an element of judgment enters in. A choice among alternative programs may require that their relative merits must be weighed. Even when a decision is focused on the acceptance or rejection of a single opportunity, some consideration may need to be given to it if the persons concerned are to avoid either an unrewarding venture or a missed opportunity.

In most of the cases in which a decision is called for, it is negative. Certainly this fact is true if awareness means simply a casual consideration of a wide range of possible actions, such as occurs when someone leafs through a catalog, looks at mailed brochures, or scans announcements or advertisements in the mass media. Similarly a tutor may reject a client, a cluster of people may choose not to form a learning group, and a teacher may decide not to offer a course. Momentary regret may be felt at the negativeness of the decision, but it is usually tempered by the belief that the regret would be greater if the activity were undertaken.

Even when the decision is positive, later experience may show that it was unwise. A learner embarks impulsively on a program of self-guided instruction, a student is registered in a course with no counseling as to its relevance for him, or a new institutional program is launched with an inadequate understanding of its potential audience. Rapidity of decision leads to many of the failures of adult education—the insecure, self-guided learners, the low retention rate of students, the waning enthusiasm of groups, the canceled courses and conferences, and the death of institutions. In some such cases, a negative initial decision would have been wise; in others, further thought about possibilities might have created rewarding designs for learning.

The depth of analysis involved in making a decision varies greatly from one situation to another. An opportunity presented to an individual may require him only to accept or reject an established program. A man receives an invitation to a conference and, looking it over, sees that all the design components have already been arranged. In such a case, he needs only to consider whether he can accept the announced aims and fit the program into the pattern of his life. But the original decision to sponsor the conference may have required its planners to consider at length whether or not to proceed with it in terms of their knowledge of all the many components which would need to be blended in its design.

It is often necessary to review several alternative programs before a wise choice can be made. Thus when a new educational institution is to be created (C-7), several designs may be constructed so that a determination can be made as to which is best in the situation. Sometimes everything, including the goal itself, may be uncertain. A man may have only a generalized desire to learn and no clear purpose or pattern in his mind. Alone or with such counsel as he can secure, he must map out several possible courses of action and either choose the one which appears to be most appealing or discard the idea of study. Otherwise he will make a blind plunge into some activity and will be fortunate if the results happen to prove rewarding.

The decision about proceeding is essentially a matter of subjective judgment, for it is impossible to demonstrate in advance that either a positive or a negative choice will be wise, considered either in its own terms or as the best of alternatives. Those who make the choice must try to consider all aspects of the situation and then, on balance, decide what to do. Both facts and feelings must usually be considered. Thus in a C-8 situation, the proponents of a new program may present data and arguments in support of their position, but its acceptance or rejection finally reflects the existence of many nuances of interpretation and emotional response which are apparent only to those aware of the intricacies of the situation.

In the application of judgment, particularly in institutional settings, it may be useful to have policies or principles to use as standards or guidelines. The staff of an agricultural extension service may wish to concentrate on serving commercial farmers, the staff of a general extension division may believe it should offer only work of university-level complexity and rigor, and the staff of a settlement house may choose to work with those people who have the fewest opportunities for progress open to them. Such principles as these may be carried by tradition and precedent or they may be worked out into a set of codified policies. Their use can never be automatic, however, for discrimination is required in making the judgment as to whether or how a general rule applies in each new case.

Identifying and Refining Objectives

The identification of the objectives to be sought in the learning experience is usually a major step in designing or analyzing it. They have been inherent since it was first contemplated and have usually been somewhat clarified during the process of decision. Indeed, the very act of making a choice may establish the initial goals; for example, a group which decides to study a packaged course has, by that decision, indicated both broad and specific purposes. Usually, however, the planners of an activity must think carefully about what it is designed to achieve.

The shaping or analysis of objectives is never an easy task, since they are always at the heart of an activity, not on its surface. Whether or not they are stated explicitly, they always give both focus and direction to the program. When put into words, they usually express a desire to achieve some such rational end as to teach illiterates to read and write, to help practicing surgeons acquire a new operating technique, to study modern poetry, or to confer on ways to reduce air pollution. Any learning activity is, however, a force field in which many other purposes than the professed goals are in operation, some leading to harmony, others to conflict.

The classroom, for example, is a simple form of teaching and learning, but several discernible spheres of influence intersect within it. The teacher has ideals about the mastery of content which may not be achievable with the present class but still serve as guiding stars. He also has a point of view toward teaching which is consciously or unconsciously expressed in his performance of his art and he has personal purposes and motivations which influence his work. Each student accepts to some extent the aspiration, the instructional style, and the personal needs of the teacher, but he also has his own requirements and ambitions. He may come to the classroom because of his ideals or because he wants to learn whatever the teacher has to teach, but also he may be present for reasons which may seem extraneous to the formal purposes of instruction but which make his participation meaningful for him. The course is also influenced by external forces. It may need to fit within the broader aims of a series of which it is a part and it may be sponsored by an institution which has an overall purpose. Beyond such formal boundaries are the larger controls and expectations imposed by the sectors of influence in the encompassing society. As all these hopes and intentions blend in the classroom, the group generates and fulfills its pressures toward achievement.

This complexity of goals is present in all educational settings, but it is particularly evident in those designed for adults. The child or youth goes to school essentially because it is his expected way of life. His own feelings and intentions are often not focused on a particular activity but generalized to cover the whole curriculum. Even his nonschool education may be compulsory, as every piano teacher knows. Some of his learning is specific and voluntary; his clubs, projects, and independent reading programs reflect his own concerns and interests. In society's view, however, such learning is peripheral to the main business of education which is carried on by schools and colleges. The adult however ordinarily embarks on a learning program because it has an immediate and direct meaning for him. Education is usually not his expected way of life; indeed he may be hard pressed to find time for it. While compulsory or generalized adult educational programs exist (such as those in the armed services, industry, or formal evening schools or colleges) society's root conception of adult education is of specific learning freely undertaken with the intention of achieving clear-cut and definite objectives.

Three terms. In such learning, no matter in what situational category it occurs, three terms should be distinguished from one another. They are *motive, aspiration,* and *objective.* The three are not sharply different; they are sometimes identical, sometimes merged in practice, and always related, but they are analytically separate.

A motive is an inciting cause which helps to determine an individual's choice of an objective and his behavior in seeking it. In any learning episode it is possible to discern many motives, some more strongly held than others. The difference between announced objectives and motives can be demonstrated by asking adults why they take part in various kinds of courses. It would be generally assumed perhaps that enrollment in such groups of subjects as vocational education, religion, English, and practical nursing indicates that the aim in each case is to learn the indicated content. A national sampling survey shows, however, that 13 per cent of the people who enroll in vocational courses do so in order to meet new people and 9 per cent do so as a means of enjoying their spare time. Of those who take courses in religion, 19 per cent do so in order to gain help in their everyday tasks and 17 per cent to escape the daily routines of life. English is a highly utilitarian subject; 23 per cent of those who enroll do so to prepare for a job and 45 per cent do so to help them with their present jobs. Practical nursing, on the other hand, has a broad appeal. Exactly the same number of people (21 per cent) take it because they want to meet new people as take it in order to get help on a present job.[2] No similar studies have been made of the motives of educators, but observation suggests that they are not wholly motivated by a desire to convey a defined content. In the light of this distinction between announced objectives and motives, a great deal of the content-based discussion of educational aims seems narrow and limited.

An aspiration is a desired perfection or excellence based on an ideal. It exists only as a conception in the mind of either learner or educator. It may arise from such sources as carefully thought out philosophic positions, the expression of basic human needs, internalized cultural patterns of belief, or simple surface values derived from reflection or from interaction with other people.

An objective is an intended result of an educational activity. It does not exist until the decision is made to take action, and it is then the effect sought by that action. It is essentially different from an aspiration. The latter is a theoretical statement of what might or should be, the former is a practical end toward which actions are aimed. An aspiration is, in fact, two steps away from an objective. An individual, a group or an institution may have an aspiration but contemplate no action. It may contemplate action but never take it. Or it may take it. Only in the third case does an objective come into being. A hunter sees a whole landscape full of possible targets, and he may consider shooting at several of them, but not until he points his rifle intending to fire does he have an aim. Similarly, there are countless things which it might be good to understand, to appreciate, or to do; and one might contemplate learning many of them; but not until the process of learning is set in motion is an educational objective created.

Some attributes of objectives. The determination of objectives before, during, or after the learning process is a complex operation, particularly when an objective is defined in its fullest sense as being the actual intended result of learning, not merely the formal expression of that intention. The task may become more manage-

---

[2] J. W. C. Johnston and R. J. Rivera, *Volunteers for Learning* (Chicago: Aldine Publishing Company, 1965), pp. 146–50.

able if several interrelated attributes of objectives, which follow from
the above definitions, are made clear.

An objective is essentially rational, being an attempt to impose a logical pattern on some of the activities of life. Only a zealot
believes that all life can be reduced to a wholly charted existence. As
Pascal said long ago, "the heart has its reasons which reason does
not know;" men can never be certain about the wellsprings of their
own behavior. Moreover, though planning may be exquisitely
refined, it is impossible to devise a set of goals which will take care
of all contingencies. Anybody who sets out on a voyage by land, sea,
air, or in space identifies his ultimate destination and the waystations
which lead to it, but he expects that events will arise which call for
change in his plans. Finally, no statement of aims can be completely
comprehensive. Usually the planner or analyst of an activity can do
no more than identify its major rational guides to action, leaving
accepted but unstated the vast sea of motives, aspirations, and specific goals in the lives of those who undertake the educative process.

An objective is practical. It is neither an attempt to describe
things as they should be nor an effort to probe to the underlying
nature of reality. Such concerns as these are theoretical. In preparing
for action, it may be useful to construct ethical, esthetic, or scientific
systems, to define the nature of broad concepts, or to describe ideal
patterns. An objective comes into being, however, only when a plan
of action is devised to achieve some concretely defined change in a
specific person or persons. The ultimate test of an objective is not
validity but achievability.

Objectives lie at the end of actions designed to lead to them.
Many good things in life are achieved by serendipity, but an objective is not merely the attainment of a fortunate outcome. It is the
result of effort designed to bring it about and is always inextricably
related to such effort in both theory and practice.

Objectives are usually pluralistic and require the use of judgment to provide a proper balance in their accomplishment. To learn
a foreign language, for example, it is necessary to build vocabulary,
to perfect prounuciation, and to understand and use grammatical
construction. The teacher employs the limited time available to seek
to achieve all three goals, allocating to each its proper share of
emphasis. Sometimes objectives impose limits on one another. Thus

a major American industrial firm has defined the goals of its training department as "the improvement of our business and the personal development of our people." The great majority of the company's educational activities can lead toward both ends but in some cases, they may run counter to one another in their application. In any such case, the acceptance or rejection of a specific course of action can only be determined by the use of judgment.

Objectives are hierarchical. A broad educational purpose is made concrete by the provision of subordinate purposes which in turn are made even more definite by specific goals. It is possible to build an ordered statement of aims which runs from the broadest relevant purpose of an educational series to the specific and detailed identification of what is to be achieved in each minute of each act. The folklore of curriculum analysis contains accounts of such earnest young teachers as the one who prepared an outline of 2,728 objectives for the first semester of seventh grade English. Ordinarily the identification of goals in this detail is not only wearisome but also uses up time better spent in learning or teaching. In practice, it is customary to identify the major purposes of an activity at two or three levels of analysis, leaving to the good sense of the participants the continuing determination of more specific goals.

Objectives are discriminative. By indicating one course of action, they rule out others. A public library staff which says that its function is to help people improve themselves can make such a statement meaningful only by making some further decisions. For example, it can have a "comprehensive" book-purchasing policy with the result that its coverage is so thin that nobody is served with any depth; or it can emphasize some areas of knowledge, thereby scanting others. Since means are almost always limited, the selection of one choice inhibits or denies the selection of others. In determining objectives, therefore, it is necessary to go beyond an identification of all the possible aspirations which might apply in the situation. The next and crucial step is to decide which ones will be operative in guiding further action. If selection is not made at the start it will have to be done later by choice or default.

Objectives change during the learning process. In all situational categories, the beginning of action makes concrete what was formerly only potential. A young man deciding to learn to play the violin begins with a romanticized view of his eventual level of accomplishment; his experienced tutor will have a different conception of what can be achieved. The hopes of both may change at the very first lesson and continue to do so as time goes on. The teacher in a classroom often has a carefully worked out set of objectives whose accomplishment can be measured by observable behavior and may hold fast to them to the very end of the course, but they are only a skeletal framework of what is to be achieved, representing neither the full range of possible goals nor the varied measure of achievement of the students. Practically speaking, therefore, the educator or learner needs to make an initial judgment about what the objectives should be, but then be prepared to abandon some, add others, and change the emphasis of those retained.

Refinement of objectives. Now that objectives have been defined and described in general, it is time to inquire how they may be chosen or identified in specific situations. In introducing this topic, it is useful to begin with some examples.

(1) The dean of a university evening college decides that his institution should try to improve directly the conditions of life in his city. Where is he to start? The topic of urban development broadens out to include the major elements of modern culture and narrows down to involve such persistent problems as the billowing smoke from factory chimneys, the crying child in the jungle of the slum, and the sharp conflict at the frontier of racial expansion. In this milieu, many individuals and groups need education but the dean's attention finally focuses on one target audience—the members of the various boards and commissions which control and manage the public and private health, welfare, recreational, and cultural agencies of the city. Such people learn whatever they know about discharging their functions only by the slow process of trial and error. But the dean knows that there are books on board structure and function, and that a professor of social welfare at the university has specialized in this content. Both dean and professor believe deeply in the need for responsible citizenship and this view is shared to varying degrees by the board members. So a new program of service is developed in which lectures, reading, and discussion are intermingled. Before very long, the professor discovers something he might well have known before but did not. Many of his students are

present for other reasons than because they want to be of greater service to the city or to gain mastery of the content. They hope, among other things, to take part in a highly publicized community activity, to learn skills which will win the respect of others, to identify promising new members for boards which need them, or to become known to leaders who might choose them for such boards. Without ever identifying these motives openly, the professor shifts his procedures to allow them to be more fully achieved by the activities of the course. Some of the learners, meanwhile, note that the professor seems deferential to his more prominent students and make some judgments of their own about his motives.

The objectives of the course are therefore defined by the simultaneous interaction of six factors. The beginning point was the *milieu,* the city itself in its full social and physical context. The nature of the specific *learners* was identified next. The *content* existed; a body of developed knowledge was available and could be taught, and a *design* for teaching it could be devised. The *aspiration* was the achievement of responsible participation of citizen leaders, and the *motives* were the personal desires and hopes which led both learners and educators to take part. A change in any one of these key ingredients would have altered the goals of the program as well as its format.

These same factors determine the objectives of every adult educational program. The planner or the analyst may begin with any of them but he employs each of the others in refining his eventual goals. It may be useful to see how this process works by taking one of the five latter factors as a beginning point for each of the following examples.

2. The president of a club speaks, "When I retired I went through the usual period of disorientation but it ended when I found some other fellows—professional men and managers—like myself who didn't know what to do with themselves. Some of us got together and set up this little club. We're all reasonably well fixed and we live in the same part of town; we all belong to the country club. We decided that we didn't want to be a Golden Age Club or a Senior Citizens' Group or engage in artsy-craftsy kinds of things. We wanted challenge—to our minds and to our sense of independence. So we have a weekly lunch and afternoon at the club. Sure, we have

fun and games in the late afternoon but earlier there's always a serious part. Our program committee brings in a speaker who talks on something really serious and then we go after him and each other in a hammer and tongs discussion. It has worked out rather well. We have to make allowances for some of our members who aren't as serious as the rest of us, and some fellows are more interested than others in a given subject or lecturer, but, taken by and large, we get along very well."

3. At a sensitivity workshop, the director of a local adult educational council becomes convinced that the use of a new theory of interpersonal relationship would vitalize the overly formal programs of his member agencies. With a grant from a local foundation, he sets up a series of residential weekends at a vacation retreat with good food and recreational facilities, and engages a trainer from a nearby university. The staff members of the agencies are invited to apply, but a final selection is made on the basis of who seems to have the most influence in the various programs. After the first weekend, the director has to suggest to the trainer that he play down his apparent desire to become a paid consultant to the agencies represented. As the series proceeds, some of the more "practical" members of the group have difficulty in understanding that the content of the course lies in the acquisition of interpersonal skills rather than of a body of knowledge. But each successive conference is better accepted by its participants than the one before.

4. A wealthy man dies, leaving his country estate and funds to maintain it to a private university, with the sole stipulation that it be turned into a residential conference center. The university board accepts the bequest, and the president appoints a committee of faculty members and administrators which he asks to deal with the following questions: What would it cost to put the mansion in proper condition to serve as an educational center? How many conferences could be held there each year? What purposes should they serve? Why should people want to come to them rather than taking regular courses in the evening? What faculty members and other resource people would be available and interested in taking part in the center's program? What conference topics would interest the faculty? What kinds of people would attend? What could the university hope to achieve by operating such a center?

5. "The ultimate best hope of mankind lies in building a better understanding among the peoples of the world," concluded the speaker at the annual Chamber of Commerce luncheon in a flourish of rhetoric. The unspoken response of most of his hearers was that he had not uttered a highly original thought, but one listener, the new President of the Chamber, took the idea seriously. The city had an increasing number of companies engaged in foreign trade, most of which was with the Common Market countries. What about setting up a study group led by several industrial, commercial, and financial experts which could go to Europe and observe matters at first hand, each company paying the cost for its own representatives? The members selected for the tour should be men and women who had an enduring stake in the city's economic life and who would accept the responsibility to study and learn, though naturally a trip to Europe would lend spice to the idea for everyone. Would such a tour work out well? Why not try it to see?

6. The West End Settlement House, located in a markedly deprived neighborhood, had had some success in reaching children and older adults, but almost nobody between the ages of twenty-two and forty ever entered its doors. What are such people interested in? the director asked himself, and his answer was jobs, making a home, raising children, and getting established in the community. What could he do to help these young people become more fully participating citizens? Well, perhaps he could begin by persuading other community agencies to use the settlement's facilities. Would the Board of Education provide a literacy teacher? Would the Department of Health offer a well-baby clinic? Could a vocational counselor be found to teach young men and women how to present themselves more effectively to prospective employers? Should there be a family-planning center? Some of the activities suggested by these questions are inherently educative; others are facilitative services which might lead to education. Several approaches would need to be made simultaneously; the kinds of people to be reached are highly resistant to influence and nobody knows what will appeal to them. So the Director scheduled a series of exploratory meetings with the heads of other agencies.

In each of these six cases, the beginning point was different. In succession, it was: a milieu, a group of learners, a body of content, a resource which required a certain kind of educational design, an aspiration, and a cluster of motives. But in each case the initial factor was insufficient to establish the objectives; for that purpose, the other five were needed. In practice, it often happens that a statement of objectives is the expression of only one factor, most often an aspiration ("to achieve better interracial understanding"), a body of content ("to convey an appreciation of modern poetry"), or some component of an educational design ("to use the expertise of the university's faculty to help solve urban problems.") The maker of such a statement assumes that others will know what he is trying to achieve, but in the absence of further information, they cannot know—and it sometimes turns out that he does not know himself. Before objectives can fully emerge as guides to action, it is necessary to consider how the six factors mesh together.

The process by which this result is brought about can, to some extent, be observed and, to a lesser extent, be made systematic. Essentially, however, the meshing is a creative process, having to do with the capacity of individuals and groups to weigh and evaluate available information and to establish priorities based on the assessment of present and future conditions. The beginning educator or learner must ordinarily think his way laboriously through the process of identifying and stating objectives but gradually, as a result of experience, his capacity to make decisions in particular cases is improved, so that he can simultaneously take account of all the factors and make them mesh together smoothly.

Statement of objectives. Objectives may be implicit and undefined, but often they are stated in oral or written form for any of a number of reasons, among them: to help shape a format, to restrict the sphere of action, to provide a brief description of the activity, to clarify the thought of planners or analysts, to create a sense of unity, or to serve as a basis for public relations. The actual form of the statement varies; it may be conveyed in oral discourse, in a syllabus, in a promotional brochure, in an annual report or catalog, in a law, or in other ways.

The educative process is usually facilitated by the clear expression of purpose. Even in very simple situations, as when a man maps out a course of reading for himself or a tutor guides a learner, the statement of aims may help to raise the eventual level of accomplishment. Such statements are even more necessary in formal and complex situations in which individuals play differing roles or when many people are involved. An institution achieves unity through its sense of purpose and therefore tends to suffer if that purpose is not clear.

Any effort to state objectives must begin with the realization that they are the actual guides to action embodied in the learning program and express the hopes of those who take part in it. A first essential therefore is to make written or orally expressed objectives conform as closely as possible to reality, taking account of the factors in the situation, making judgments about them, and fitting the results together to shape those specific and tangible goals at which the learning process may most profitably aim. Otherwise the statement may be essentially a relic of the past, an embodiment of fantasy, or an effort to attract attention and support.

However refined a statement of objectives may be, it can never be more than a notation in abstract terms of the goals which are actually sought. "To gain an understanding and appreciation of Shakespeare's plays" is an announced aim which shows a clear direction and can be the apex of an extensively outlined hierarchy of statements of skills, knowledge, and attitudes, worked out with elegant precision according to the best canons of curriculum making. Yet a sensitive understanding of Shakespeare's plays as it is realized fully in the minds of learners has a richness, depth, variety, and scope which is related to the formal definition of the various levels of goals as a mountain is related to the cross-hatched lines on a map which symbolize it. Some writers on education have failed to make this distinction and have treated the statement of a goal as though it were the goal itself; they study the map, not the terrain. A cartographer uses an essential and highly developed art and so does a writer of formal statements of objectives, but both work with abstractions, not with the realities which they describe.

Educational objectives may be stated in terms of the desired accomplishments of the learner. He is to become a different person because he has gained the knowledge, ability, or sensitiveness the experience is designed to provide. The measurement of change requires observation of his behavior. Does he, for example, voluntarily read and reread the works of Shakespeare, bring them into his conversation, get a high score on written examinations concerning them, and, in other ways, demonstrate both mastery and enjoyment of them? To help answer such questions, goals are sometimes stated in terms of the actions which would demonstrate their accomplishment. But unless care is taken to distinguish between the developed power of a human being and its exercise in specified ways, the latter itself becomes the goal, not merely the means of measuring achievement. The path of a subatomic particle is traced by the chain of droplets its passage leaves in a cloud chamber, but the particle and the evidence of its behavior are clearly different from one another. Similarly, growth in the ability of a man may be measured by evidence of his actions, but the measurement is not the ability.

Educational objectives may also be stated in terms of the principles of action that are likely to achieve the desired changes in the learner. A teacher planning a class in human relationships may wish to proceed through a process of individual and group self-discovery; he might say, as one educator did, "I aim to (1) excite the student's curiosity about aspects of behavior which he has hitherto overlooked, taken for granted, or considered insignificant, (2) motivate him to discover his own insights, and (3) help him to absorb these insights in a personal-emotional way rather than merely to accumulate them as so many psychological facts."[3] Such a teacher is aware of the depth of insight of master psychologists and of the existence of established concepts, but he is skeptical that the accumulation of psychological facts will be significant for most learners. He believes that they will be profoundly changed only if they are stirred by the process of self-analysis and the excitment of self-discovery. He therefore states his goals in terms of principles, not accomplishments.

The understanding and acceptance of educational objectives will usually be advanced if they are developed cooperatively. He who has had a share in deciding what is to be done will understand it better and be more interested in doing it than he who must accept a goal developed by someone else. This principle can be applied in only an analogical fashion in C-1 and C-11 situations—the independent student may hypothesize an educator and the mass educator

[3] D. I. Malamud, *Teaching a Human Relations Workshop* (Chicago: Center for the Study of Liberal Education for Adults, 1955), p. 1.

may hypothesize the nature of his students. In the other categories, it can be made to work in varying ways through the mutual effort and thought of the individuals and groups concerned. Thus the teacher (C-4) plans with certain kinds of potential students in mind, then adjusts those plans with the help of the actual students when they appear. In a C-5 situation, representatives of the potential learning group may, from the beginning, be members of the planning committee.

An objective should be stated clearly enough to indicate to all rational minds exactly what is intended. Otherwise it will give rise to countless interpretations, many of which contradict each other, thereby fostering confusion rather than comprehension. Goals are sometimes stated in single words or brief phrases ("brotherhood" or "a higher standard of living") which do not provide an adequate understanding of what is being aimed at. It may be argued that ambiguity of this sort is desirable since it allows the maximum subsequent freedom, but since an objective exists to provide shape and focus for action, obscurity in its wording leads to formlessness. After the activity begins, changes will occur in its goals, but revisions can be made most intelligently only if the original statement is clear enough so that any change in purpose can be understood.

In many teaching and learning situations, but particularly in those sponsored by institutions, objectives can be stated not only in terms of the outcomes of education but also in terms of changes in the design components which will presumably make those outcomes better. These facilitative objectives have to do with such matters as the acquisition of learning resources, the improved training of leaders, the establishment of more efficient counseling procedures, and the discovery of new sources of revenue. Thus the board of a cooperative grocery store may wish to strengthen its work in consumer education and therefore set as an objective the hiring of a full-time specialist in that field (an accomplishment goal) or the provision of more product information by all staff members (a principle goal). Either is a facilitative rather than an educational purpose, and yet here as elsewhere the two kinds of objectives are intimately interrelated and sometimes hard to distinguish from one another.

A threat to learning arises when facilitative objectives crowd out educational objectives. It is relatively easy to identify the former and to measure their accomplishment. An administrator expresses the need for more money, better methods, increased resources, and more effective public relations and as a result of his efforts, the budget is increased, the techniques used are diversified, more books and visuals aids become available, and additional students are enrolled. The facilitative goals have been achieved, but what of the educational ones? Are desired changes being brought about in the learners served? As long as an answer to that question seems important, educational objectives remain, but to the extent that it ceases to be significant or even relevant, the program becomes bureaucratized as the improvement of process proceeds without proper attention to the results which it is intended to achieve.

As the designer or the analyst of an educational program refines both educational and facilitative objectives, he must engage in creative thought as he makes judgments about how the six factors are meshed together in the situation with which he is concerned. It is true that many prefabricated adult educational programs already exist or can be quickly devised. In a rough and ready sort of way, they are applicable to a variety of situations and thereby give some aid to learners, just as a pair of eyeglasses bought in a variety store can sometimes provide help to those who need to correct their visual deficiencies. But most discerning people would prefer to have an ophthalmologist use his advanced skills of diagnosis and prescription in analyzing their individual needs rather than to rely on the untrained assistance of a clerk to choose the right pair of lenses from his limited supply. A really good educational program requires careful attention to the unique nature of the situation and skill in identifying the objectives which are uniquely appropriate to it.

Developing Format

During the time that a decision to proceed with a program is being made and later when objectives are refined, the mind of the planner is constantly darting ahead to consider the components of the proposed design. As noted above, objectives are determined at least in part by a foreknowledge of the availability of certain elements in the format, but at some point it is usually necessary to consider whether all of them are adequately cared for. Otherwise important deficiencies may subsequently appear. Some elements (such as the method of measuring progress or of making the program pattern clear) may be overlooked entirely. Others may be only narrowly applied. For example, the dictates of program scheduling and of budget may require a television station to offer twenty-six week courses and to use the lecture and demonstration method, but within that apparently rigid framework, creative thought about leadership, resources, and sequencing may greatly enhance the effect of the activity. Moreover, while the selection of objectives limits the range of choice as far as various elements are concerned, some freedom to decide among alternatives remains. One who wishes to learn to swim can make relatively little use of either the lecture or the discussion method, but he may still choose to hire a tutor, join a class, or try to teach himself by using a manual.

A format blends together the various elements, each interacting with the others. For example, decisions about roles and relationships influence decisions about leadership or social reinforcement and vice versa. There is no invariable order in the determination of the elements. Often several of them are inherent in the situation; then others are decided; and, at the end of the format-designing process, the whole pattern is reviewed and adjusted until the necessary harmony is achieved. After the episode begins, adjustments are usually required. If it is repeated, still further alterations may be made. In the 5th Army case reported in Chapter Three, the best overall pattern of instruction did not emerge until the fifth episode in the series.

The acceptance of education as a cooperative art is particularly important in designing the format. In such cases as C-2, C-3, and C-5 situations, decisions about the various elements can be made collaboratively. In others, such as C-4 situations, the probable needs and desires of the learners can be estimated in advance and taken more fully into account after the episode begins. In every category, the elements of a format are evident and important to all who share in the educational process. They may have difficulty grappling with the intangibles of objectives, which, in many cases, are not completely clear to learners until the entire educational process has been completed, but everybody has an immediate reaction to such matters as the books, visual aids, leadership, and social reinforcement which are used in the format. All participants usually want, in one way or another, to help make decisions about the elements and fit them together into an acceptable pattern.

In analyzing an educational activity, either during its progress or after its completion, judgments about its relative success often center on one or more of the format elements, such as scheduling, individualization, or sequence. By reflecting over his experiences, the planner comes to realize that he must be aware of all the elements of his format if he is to have the greatest possible measure of success. Eventually he may become so accomplished in designing a harmonious pattern that he scarcely needs to think about each of the elements in turn, but when he has a failure, as even the most experienced planners sometimes do, he usually realizes that he has either overlooked one of them or handled it badly.

Selecting learning resources. A resource is here defined broadly as any object, person, or other aspect of the environment which can be used for support or help in an educational activity. Resources may be categorized in any number of ways as materials, instruments, media, facilities, and so on. While a resource exists independently of any usage, it gains its educational meaning from its application to learning in a particular situation. Thus the shell of a chambered nautilus may be handled and admired as an object, but it may also be used as an instructional resource in marine biology, art, architecture, cultural history, American literature, the study of submarine design, psychology, and as an illustration of the diversity of educational uses to which a single object may be put.

Ordinarily the resources used in a program, taken collectively, make up one of the two chief means by which content is conveyed, the other being leadership. (As already noted in Chapter Two, a leader can be viewed as a resource but ordinarily his active role in guiding instruction makes such a classification of him inappropriate.) In some cases, other elements become important in conveying content, as method does in any program in which a heightened awareness of interpersonal relationships is a goal. Even then, resources usually play an important though secondary part. Thus in sensitivity training the physical setting may greatly facilitate or hinder the interactive process whose understanding provides the content.

While resources and methods are always interrelated, they can usually be distinguished from one another for planning or analytical purposes. In some cases, the existence of a resource implies the method by which it is used—the book and reading, the film and its showing, or the art museum and the tour of its paintings. In other cases, as noted in the preceding paragraph, the resource supports the method. But the proper design of an educative experience requires that the two be thought of separately, for the selection of resources and the choice of methods are essentially independent processes. Thus the question "what books will be used?" is different from the question "how will the books be used?"

Because resources are so important in conveying content, they have often been considered the heart of the educational format. Some institutions, such as libraries, audio-visual centers, and industrial displays, are based on the collection and use of resources. For centuries, the college curriculum was defined as the mastery of certain books and in adult education the coordinated course, the farmers' bulletin, or the display of a museum's treasures has sometimes provided the focus of instruction. But resources cannot be educative unless they are used and the manner of that use does much to determine their effect. Thus if a film is well-introduced before it is shown and is then discussed afterward, it has a greater impact on its viewers than if it is merely screened. Maximum learning occurs only when resources are effectively combined not merely with method but also with all the other elements in the format.

Resources vary greatly in availability. Some are absolutely nonexistent; no book or other piece of material exists which can teach mankind how to cure cancer, control genetic coding, create life in the laboratory, or travel to the distant reaches of space. Most resources are limited in their distribution. Primitive parts of the world have a great scarcity of instructional materials (most people now alive cannot use a book and may never have even seen one) while complex, urban, industrial societies have them in profusion. But even where either scarcity or glut generally prevails, variation still exists. An underdeveloped country may have a university as a sanctuary for learning, and an advanced society may have places of cultural impoverishment.

The greatest variance in adequacy or resources, however, has been over time. In earlier eras learning materials were so limited in quantity that they could be used by only a very few people, usually those in a monastery or a royal court. To the man who chiseled out inscriptions in stone or who laboriously copied a manuscript, the printing press came as a new instrument full of promise as it offered enlightenment to more people or full of danger as it threatened to open the sacred mysteries of learning to vulgar eyes. The spread of print has had both effects, and so have the other media of communication which followed it. A transformation has also occurred in the availability and attractiveness of physical facilities. The first history of adult education, published in 1851, says of the mechanics' institutes of that day that "their Parnassus is reached from a back street by a narrow intricate stair, dimly lighted on winter evenings."[4] In the modern city, facilities for learning, such as universities, evening schools, proprietary institutions, libraries, museums, and residential centers, abound and are located on main thoroughfares.

The growth of such resources has brought about both quantitative and qualitative differences in education. A lecturer's ideas used to be available only to those within sound of his voice at the time he expressed them; now they can be sent throughout the world by satellite and captured for posterity by book, record, and videotape. The development of high-fidelity auditory systems enables countless people to study music who would earlier have been denied that opportunity. The growth of new communications materials has expanded not only the reach but also the scope of learning. As Andre Malraux pointed out, the reproduction of pictures makes possible new dimensions in the understanding of art since it enables the student to place side by side the representations of works which are actually far away from one another and thereby to make detailed comparisons and contrasts hitherto denied even the greatest authorities. The same kinds of results have flowed from the computer and from other new media and instruments, and are likely to continue to do so from communications inventions not yet perfected or even contemplated.

Thus it has come about that while the scarcity of learning

[4] J. W. Hudson, *The History of Adult Education* (London: Longman, Brown, Green, and Longmans, 1851), p. 44.

resources is still the major problem for most people in the world, for others the central difficulty is one of choice. Decisions must be made not merely about which materials are best to achieve a given goal, but also about which goal is best among the many made possible by the existence of profuse resources. In making either kind of choice, the central point of reference is the situation itself. At a specific time and place and with a known audience, which of the available resources will be most useful as it is combined with the other elements of the format to achieve the desired goal? Or, if many resources are at hand, which of them should be chosen and combined with other factors to determine the goal? In answering such questions, the designer must rely on his experience and his intuitive grasp of what is immediately important. He also has available an impressive and growing body of knowledge about the assessment of learning resources. Much is known about such matters as readability, the display of exhibited material, the way to arrange items of content so that they are maximally educative, and the best use of such resource categories as sound motion pictures, filmstrips, teaching machines, and computer-based courses. Here, as with the other components, both the practical wisdom which comes from experience and the principles derived by research can be used to enhance the outcomes of learning activity.

Choosing leaders. As already noted in Chapter Two, those who take part in any educational activity tend to occupy one of two major roles—the educator or the learner. The first role is a broad one and includes professional program planners, curriculum specialists, administrators, and supervisors, as well as those who are here called *leaders,* the people who directly assist learners to achieve their objectives. A leader works in various ways and in all categories from C-2 through C-11. Even in self-guided learning, the person concerned may consciously separate two ways of behavior, sometimes planning as a leader might do and sometimes carrying out the plans he has made.

The source of a leader's influence is often crucial in determining the nature or the results of an educational activity. If a leader is presumed to be a master of content or process, he must demonstrate his capacity clearly to his students. If he has been chosen only because some aspect of the situation confers status or responsibility upon him, he must be careful not to claim any special knowledge of the educational content or process. Sometimes a mixture of two or more kinds of influence is required. It may inhere in a single leader, as when a supervisor uses both his special knowledge and his institutional authority to guide a worker, or it may require the complementary service of several people, as when a conference has speakers, discussion leaders, and chairmen. Also a group may rotate leadership or a conference may follow a procedure in which participants serve as leaders on some occasions and as learners on others; at any given moment, it is usually apparent who is occupying each of the two roles and the authority of the leader is accepted as long as he exercises it well.

Leadership in adult education is far more fluid and fluctuating than it is in the schooling of children and young people. With adults, the authority of the leader is usually restricted to the situation itself and does not broaden out to create a caste system as it tends to do in schools and colleges. Furthermore, while some people devote their careers to adult education, far larger numbers undertake it as a part-time or occasional activity. This fluidity has saved the field from the sterility of a rigid professionalism, but it has occasionally diminished the caliber of leadership and thereby made the outcomes of learning less significant than they might have been.

Insofar as a profession of adult education exists, its structure does not resemble that of any of the other educational professions. They tend to be oriented to institutions and are designated as school teachers, school administrators, college professors, university administrators, or librarians. The highly trained adult educator, like the physician, lawyer, architect, social worker, or nurse has an expertise which is applied in any of a number of settings, each of which may be central to his own work but not to that of the whole profession. Moreover, the full-time career adult educator sees himself as part of a network of other people whose service he may guide or direct but from whom he does not separate his own work sharply since he regards them as colleagues essential to his own endeavors. For example, a university extension division may have only fifty full-time staff members but plan for and direct the activities of two hundred faculty members who teach adults on a part-time basis, three hundred nonfaculty members who are engaged occasionally to teach, and a hundred lay citizens who serve as volunteers in various capacities. This broadly based pattern of leadership is likely to continue and to set limits to any tendency to establish a separate adult educational caste.

The selection and use of leaders in an adult educational program is usually not a task of filling well-defined slots in a table of organization with people already trained for their work, but of considering and acting upon a conception of format in which the relevant elements (including leadership) are meshed together to achieve a defined goal in a specific setting. It often happens that the planner of a program intends to become its leader, as when a teacher organizes a class. In such a case, this element becomes the starting point in constructing the format, influencing from the beginning all other aspects of the design including the objectives. In other cases, the designer must take account of the requirements of the intended activity to determine what functions its leaders should perform. He must then find the people with the desired qualities of personality and the specific competence required and reinforce the efforts of such people in any way necessary.

Such reinforcement is often essential because most adult educational activities cannot be based on a teaching profession whose members have been trained for their work and whose competence is certified by some authority. Even when the members of an educational profession can be used, they often need special training for their work with adults. Thus an elementary school teacher accustomed to working with preadolescent children may require help in adjusting her outlook and procedures when she undertakes a literacy class for adults.

Leadership training directly geared to the situation is often essential, particularly when new institutions or institutional activities are created. If Congress establishes a program to train the unemployed, its staff must be recruited from available manpower but then it must be prepared for its work. When a settlement house launches a nutrition program for welfare mothers using other women on welfare as aides, the latter group requires preparatory education in both content and method. This preservice preparation must usually be supplemented by in-service training by means of supervision, manuals, stimulation of reading and attendance at conferences, staff seminars, and the fostering of advanced study. The leaders of adult education promote the continued learning of others and therefore believe in it for themselves.

Selecting and using methods. A method is an established and systematic way of work used to achieve an educational objective. In traditional schooling, it is exemplified by lecturing, discussion, recitation, laboratory work, and coaching. In recent years, many methods have been created or expanded in usage, such as the case method, programed instruction, role playing, psychodrama, and simulation games. In the situations in which adults learn, the range of methods broadens out from these well-established procedures to include other aspects of life deliberately manipulated to increase their educative effect. A self-directed learner may choose certain experiences because he knows they will help him, a tutor may try to become a role model for his student, and a group may diversify its membership to achieve a broader viewpoint. Activities which are not centrally educative may also use instructional methods; a television program designed for entertainment may introduce serious content, a manager may handle problem-solving processes so that they yield maximum learning for his staff, and recreational activities may be conducted to build character and interpersonal skills.

Throughout the twentieth century, American educators have been preoccupied with method, and, as a result, the term itself has acquired countless shades of meaning. It has been narrowed to signify a specific way of conducting an act of learning, such as the use of mnemonics or drills. In a broader view, it includes all of the aspects of learning or teaching which are here identified collectively as elements in a format. In the most sweeping sense, as in the work of Dewey and his followers, it encompasses the entire educative process, erasing customary distinctions between ends and means. The term and its synonym *technique* are used, as noted above, in a pragmatic sense to mean an identifiable and generally recognized procedure, sometimes overlapping others but distinguishable from them, which is used by a learner or educator to achieve his objectives.

Every method has its own rules of excellence which must be learned if it is to be performed well. To give a lecture, lead a discussion, or conduct a panel is an art which can be greatly improved by experience, study, and the conscious effort to excel. Some people have natural talent and learn to use a method more swiftly and effectively than do others, but it may be doubted whether any natural-born teachers exist. Any individual so designated has usually put himself through a process of self-guided instruction to gain his mastery, and the height of his art lies in its concealment. For when a method has been truly learned, it is so absorbed into the personality of its user that other people may not be aware that he is employing a technique. The twin enemies of method are self-consciousness and obviousness of use.

In designing a program, therefore, a major consideration in choosing methods is the capacity of leaders to use them. Other considerations also come into play. The method may itself be the beginning point in the design of a format, as is the case with a television program or a correspondence course. Other aspects of the situation which influence the selection of method are the amount of time available, the number of people involved, the resources at hand, the level of sophistication of the learners, their personal preferences, the cost, the sequence, and the schedule.

The definition of objectives limits the range of alternative techniques. If the goal of a program is to teach a physical skill, appropriate methods might be drill, coaching, demonstration, and guided experience; other techniques such as role playing, panel discussion, field trips, debates, and buzz groups would be less useful. The relationship also works in reverse, for goals are usually implied by method. For instance, anyone who admires T-group training usually indicates by that fact that he has a high regard for the improvement of understanding of human relationships.

Most activities need to use several methods. For example, the teaching of a complex skill ordinarily requires several complementary approaches—presentation of theory by reading, lecture, and other means, demonstration by a master performer, practice by the learner, and continued coaching by the instructor. The use of several methods instead of a reliance on one has other values as well; it broadens the range of achievable objectives, stimulates the interest of both leaders and learners, encourages participation, and takes account of the differential response of individuals to various approaches.

It follows from these comments that no method is inherently and universally superior to all others. Again and again during the last half-century some technique or cluster of techniques has been advanced as having such supremacy. The case for discussion, for example, has been advanced on the lines that adults have had more experience than children and therefore the essential element of adult education is the sharing of experience, that the best way for minds to interact is by discussion, and therefore that discussion is the best method to use in all circumstances. New methods sometimes seem to have such limitless horizons that their advocates believe they will replace all other techniques. Claims of this sort have been made for the use of audio-visual materials, group dynamics, nondirective leadership, programed learning, and computer-based instruction; other such claims will doubtless be made for techniques not yet invented. But experience demonstrates that a method has limitations as well as advantages, and eventually it takes its proper place in the inventory of techniques available for choice and use.

Making a time schedule. A schedule is the timetable of an educational activity. It may be simple, as when a group decides to meet on ten successive Wednesday afternoons from 3:00 to 5:00. It may be complex, as when a five-day conference of four thousand people has plenary sessions, simultaneous sectional meetings, group discussions, dinner and luncheon programs, and opportunities for counseling. It may be rigid, as when an activity must be fitted into a college semester or a television season. It may be flexible, as when a correspondence course student proceeds at his own pace. Scheduling has several aspects which must be considered simultaneously: the total elapsed time, the various kinds of sessions required, their frequency, their duration, and their placement in the day, the week, the month, the year, or other period of time. Proper choice among these aspects becomes harder as the time frame grows more complex. It is more difficult to determine the timing of an episode than of an act and scheduling a series or an aggregate is even harder.

Scheduling has been less extensively studied than other format elements, perhaps because schools and colleges (the chief foci of educational research) have well-established patterns governing the timing of their activities. In recent years, many ideas about the diversification and rearrangement of schedules have been tried, but objective studies of the value of such innovations are scarce and the conventional system resists change. Research on such generalized topics as the relative value of spaced or massed practice has chiefly been done under laboratory conditions and its results have more relevance to educational acts than to episodes or series of episodes.

Despite the scarcity of studies on adult educational scheduling, the topic has great practical importance. For adults lead complex and varied lives and are widely distributed in space. Finding the timing for an educational activity which will best fit into the life patterns of participants is often crucial to its success. More general problems also arise. What are the values of concentrated learning, as in a conference, contrasted with spaced learning, as in a course? In the worlds of business and government, when should a course be offered on company time and when on personal time? How long can a session last or a series of sessions be maintained without encountering diminishing returns? How can a complex activity be designed to provide sustained variety and interest? How can the adult educational use of an essential resource, such as a computer or a laboratory, be best accommodated to its other uses? Such questions constantly accompany the designing of new educational activities and the operation of ongoing ones.

Most present decisions about scheduling are determined by tradition, necessity, the best available judgment, or an arbitrary choice among alternatives. Many institutions have a standard format or policy. The courses in an evening school may run for a set number of weeks on a fixed pattern of hours, or an industry may follow the principle that all its education must be on company time. In any such case, the schedule becomes a beginning point for planning. Where greater freedom to develop a schedule is possible, choice must be made in terms of the objectives, the other elements in the format, or the adjustment of the activity to the participants' lifestyles. Judgment about scheduling tends to be improved by experience as planners learn how to take these diverse influences into account. Learners too become habituated to established schedules. For example, they have grown used to having school and college begin in the autumn and it seems appropriate to them for adult educational activities to do so as well.

Devising a sequence. Sequence has to do with the order in

which content is learned. It may itself have an inherent structure (geometry moves from axioms to postulates to an ordered series of theorems; history is chronological) which establishes a pattern of progression. But in education the requirements of the content and the needs of the learner must be kept in balance. One must start with people where they are, as the old saying has it, and where they are at any given time determines the next step they must take to get where they want to be. It is equally wrong for a teacher to be so true to content that he ignores the abilities and desires of his students and for him to be so concerned with their wishes and feelings that he forgets or denies content.

In the last quarter-century, perhaps no other aspect of education has had more lay or professional attention than sequencing. Debate has been continuous about the proper way to teach reading. New national curricula in mathematics and science have radically revised the ordering of topics. Programed instruction which seeks to elevate sequencing to a science has become a permanent part of education, and its earlier application in teaching machines and self-instruction manuals is being supplemented by the use of computers which take account of the varied approaches of different individuals to the learning task.

This variance among learners is particularly important in adult education. Men have had more experience than children, have had kinds of experience that no children can have, and the pathways of maturity are much more diverse than those of childhood. These facts have many implications for the selection and presentation of content. Since the time of the ancient Greeks, it has been recognized that some bodies of knowledge cannot be fully understood until adulthood. As Aristotle observed, "One may enquire why a boy, though he may be a mathematician, cannot be a philosopher. Perhaps the answer is that mathematics deals with abstractions whereas the first principles of philosophy are derived from experience: the young can only repeat them without conviction of their truth, whereas the definitions of mathematics are easily understood."[5] When an adult learns an exact science, therefore, the sequence he follows may be very like that used by a child, but when

---

[5] *Nichomachean Ethics,* Book VI, Chapter 8.

he wishes to gain broader, less precise kinds of knowledge, his starting point and his continuing pathway are influenced by the depth and breadth of his own experience and that of his fellow learners.

Sequence is also influenced by the fact that adult learning ventures usually arise from specific needs or desires. The generalized social reinforcement of education characteristic of childhood does not apply. Adults must have a continuing sense of tangible accomplishment or they will abandon their efforts to learn. The designing of instruction must incorporate rewards or interest-maintaining features to ensure continuity of effort. Thus a literacy teacher may establish certain accomplishments such as writing one's name or a simple letter which his students can use in daily life, even though these evidences of progress are not inherently necessary in achieving the ability to write.

A desirable sequence is most readily accomplished in C-2 or C-4 situations where the teacher has a grasp of content and an opportunity to interpret it to a specific group of students with known capacities and concerns. The task of sequencing is particularly difficult in programs which have no content leader, particularly in self-directed study where the learner may never know where next to turn. In each of the other categories, the arrangement of the subject matter has special aspects and problems. In C-11 situations, for example, where the nature of the students can only be guessed, the sequence is determined by the planner's estimate of what is appropriate for his hypothesized audience.

Providing social reinforcement of learning. Learning almost always occurs in a social context. Even the self-guided student usually reaches out to other people for help in informing or reinforcing his efforts. In each of the other categories, individuals are brought together into some established or improvised form of intercommunication. One motive for doing so is economy; a teacher can handle thirty students in a classroom much more quickly and inexpensively than if he served as a tutor to each of them separately. But in modern educational theory, the resulting loss of individualized attention is usually thought to be balanced or outweighed by the gain in social reinforcement in which each learner is helped by his interaction with the others. This fact is particularly true in a mass society in which learning activities have become the surrogates for waning forms of collective action such as those provided by religion, farm, and village life, and of the extended and inter-dependent family. As a result, the socializing possibilities of organized education have become more and more important to both learners and educators.

When people work together to achieve a purpose, an ethos is created by the interactions of individuals with one another, but it is far more than a blending of personalities. Before long, idiosyncrasies are savored, group-originated anecdotes are enjoyed, special terms and shadings of meaning are established, differentiated roles are developed and performed, and subgroups with congenial interests appear. Incorporating but transcending these behavioral patterns is a community spirit and a desire for its preservation. This ethos can be planned, fostered, or analyzed to discover its subtle blend of awareness, acceptance, cooperation, and challenge.

A special question must be asked, however, about the collective spirit of an educational entity: how can it reinforce the desired changes in the nature of its members? Put another way, how can the behavior of everyone stimulate the learning of each one? The easy answer is that the higher the morale, the greater the amount of learning which will occur. In a sense, this answer is usually true. A warm, positive, and inviting social climate within the activity helps to offset the ill at ease feeling of many adults when they enter a new learning experience, particularly when they have little support from their customary associates for doing so. Yet too great an attention to building a social spirit may eventually lead to a reversal of ends and means. Learning objectives can be lost because the members of the social entity become so concerned with its preservation that they forget the task it was intended to accomplish.

The proper balance is most likely to be struck if the cooperative nature of education is manifest at every stage in the planning and execution of a learning design. In the short run, warmth of personal relationships is rewarding and valuable but, in the long run, the chief cause of high morale is a sense of social reinforcement which is directed not merely to the maintenance of the group or institution but to the accomplishment of its goals. If the members share in refining objectives and choosing the means of their accomplishment, they are likely to remain task oriented, not letting the creation of a positive social climate outweigh the other elements of the format.

The designers of programs have many ways to foster social reinforcement. Physical arrangements have an influence; when a group can sit around a table, each member having direct eye contact with the others and sharing the physical and psychological support provided by the table itself, the sense of community is likely to be stronger than when the group sits in rows of chairs facing the same way. There should not be so many people as to create facelessness, nor so few as to lead to tedium. The people concerned should be neither too similar nor too heterogeneous. Leaders can display attitudes of acceptance and support and use techniques which create good rapport, such as the careful introduction of each participant to the others, the fostering of discussion, and the use of wit and vivid illustration. The experiences of the individual members can illuminate and enlarge the comprehension of the content. An activity should last long enough so that the people involved come to know one another but not so long that they grow bored with each other. And wise planners realize that some of the most rewarding learning occurs between sessions, not during them. For example, experienced conference planners insert what they call *white space* between their work sessions to give time for reflection, the reassertion of individuality, and the recreation of a zest for assembly.

Each of the categories imposes its own requirements. The foregoing comments have been most relevant to C-2 through C-6. As suggested, independent learners may seek support from other people. In a C-11 situation, a speaker to a large audience can use the arts of the lecturer to build a powerful social reinforcement, but the author of a book can do relatively little in this respect. Institutionalized programs have many ways of providing social reinforcement. Some are obvious though often ignored. A public library can appear to be warm and inviting or it can seem to be a fortress protecting its riches. An evening college can make its physical plant attractive and conducive to informal gatherings, build student councils and advisory panels, schedule all-college social activities, and select administrators, counselors, secretaries, and other staff members who are open and friendly. Other institutional supports are less obvious. With the best intentions in the world, a director of a center may streamline registration, abolish attendance records, and discontinue the awarding of grades and certificates, only to discover that his adult students like to talk over their programs with counselors, want to establish their presence at class, and feel a need for evaluation and a record of accomplishment. Such feelings are not merely a holdover from outmoded patterns of schooling. Learning, particularly in adulthood, is enhanced by social reinforcement, and anything which provides it and does not negate some other element is worth introducing into the educational format.

Adjusting to the nature of each learner. The central concern of all education is the learner and the effect of the educational process can be most directly measured by its changes in him. The planner of a program must try to design and conduct it so that the growth of each participant is fostered. Occasionally it is enough to consider how learners vary idiographically in terms of some trait which is crucial to the instruction. Thus the teacher of a simple motor skill may give selective assistance to his students only as it is required by their varying physiological aptitude. Since most education is complex, however, each learner should usually be considered nomothetically in terms of his whole personality, not some defined dimension of it.

The effort to keep the path of progress open for each individual is never easy. The wide range among adults of ability, experience, interest, sense of need, previous education, and other personality dimensions means that any effort to take account of all such factors in providing individual attention is costly in terms of time and resources. Sometimes the brevity of the activity, the size of the group, the desire of the learners for privacy, or other reasons prevents any substantial effort to incorporate this element into the design. But, as far as possible, the effort should be made.

In every form of education, the learner considers his own desires and needs, particularly when, as an adult, he is required to accept personal responsibility for each act of learning. This fact is the essence of the C-1 situation. In other cases, the responsibility is shared as in C-2, by the tutor, in C-3, by the other members of the group, in C-4, by the teacher, in C-5, by the planning committee and the leaders they choose, and so on. In institutional situations, individualization may occur not only in the learning itself but also by such administrative reinforcements as testing and personal counseling. Even in C-11 situations, efforts may be made to individualize by paying attention to a few selected learners, though this practice sometimes hampers the leader's capacity to influence his entire audience.

Clarifying roles and relationships. A role may be defined as the characteristic behavior expected of an individual in a situation as perceived by either himself or others. Though he is a unique human being, his attitudes and actions are influenced by what he thinks it right to do or what he believes is expected of him. This role expectation helps to define his relationships to other people. A woman can be a teacher of one group, a presiding officer in another, and a student in a third. Each role differs from the others and so does the way by which she relates herself to the members of the group. In educational settings, roles and relationships may never be stated but they are usually deeply felt, and the planner or analyst of a program needs to take account of them. As already noted, the primary role distinction is that between the educator and the learner, but there are countless other complexities of formalized relationships in educational settings, particularly those in which many people are involved.

Even the minimum social relationship, the dyad, is remarkably complex. For example, county agricultural extension agents are usually responsible to district supervisors, each of whom oversees a geographic area within a State. The county agent is an officer of local government, a representative of the State land-grant university, and a part of a nation-wide Federally-supported endeavor. The district supervisor represents only one of these sources of power and influence, the university, and therefore is not the boss of the county agent in any simple sense. In a study of this relationship, Durfee[6] identified three kinds of role performance. The supervisor is simultaneously a superior officer with authority to require certain actions, a stimulator who takes the initiative to influence the county agent, and a consultant who stands ready to furnish help and advice on demand. Durfee identified ninety-six topics with which the dyad

[6] A. A. Durfee, "Expectations Held Toward the Extension Supervisor's Role," (Unpublished doctoral dissertation, The University of Chicago, August, 1956).

might concern itself, including items in such areas as budgeting, building morale, maintaining relationships with other people in the county, inservice training, and evaluation. He then asked a large number of county agents and their supervisors to identify which of the three roles the supervisor should play with respect to each topic and was able, as a result, to draw up a detailed analysis of both roles and relationships. He also demonstrated that the most satisfactory dyads were those which had the greatest similarity between the expectations of the county agent and those of his supervisor.

A research investigation of this sort is too complex to serve in most program building but it does suggest the importance of defining the roles and relationships of any situation as far as is practically possible. This fact is particularly true in C-7, C-8, and C-9 situations, where it is often necessary to consider very carefully how a new institution is to be organized, how a new program is to be added to an existing framework of service, or how new activities can be provided in an existing format. The need for adequate definition is even more crucial in C-6 and C-10 situations where no overarching structure of authority exists and the activity can be maintained only if roles and relationships are clearly understood and agreed upon.

Complete freedom of choice seldom exists in any of the eleven situations. Tradition is usually important, since people tend to behave in accepted though often unexamined ways. In large institutions, the need for hierarchy and structure may create a complex bureaucracy which establishes firmly set roles and relationships among its members. When well-established professions are involved, they impose standardized patterns of behavior; the doctor, the nurse, the lawyer, or the clergyman expect (and are expected) to behave in ways appropriate to their callings. And always personality breaks through, giving uniqueness to the performance of even the most well-established role.

Sometimes the potential service of an institution of adult education is limited because no satisfactory way can be found for establishing a new educative role. In public libraries an effort was made in the 1920s and 1930s to create the position of reader's advisor, a person who could help patrons learn by using books and other resources. This attempt proved to be unsuccessful and no other helping relationship of an adult educational sort has been defined and widely adopted. As a result, the public library remains an invaluable educational resource but has only limited significance as far as the guidance of adult learners is concerned.

Other institutions perform several functions and must define adult educational roles in the light of that fact. In a university, a community college, or a public school system, young people (often significantly called regular students) occupy the center of attention. In museums, industrial concerns, labor unions, and voluntary associations, education is paralleled by such other functions as research, economic production, and the fostering of fraternal feeling. In all such cases, those who are concerned with the education of adults may have a feeling of marginality which pervades their performance and the continuing relationships they have with other people both inside and outside the institution. This feeling can be either inhibiting or challenging. In the latter case, it may give rise to determined efforts to make the roles more significant in the prestige system of the institution or to redraw the lines on the organizational chart so that adult education has a more exalted place in the hierarchy than before. In the long run, neither effort is likely to succeed unless it is accompanied by a greater capacity to design and execute programs and by the demonstration of that capacity in the performance of the role.

Identifying criteria for evaluation. From the start of an educational activity, it should be clear what standards, rules, or tests will be used to judge relative success or failure. Criteria of evaluation are suggested by the objectives; some people would argue that the two are interchangeable. But "to learn the basic principles of economics" is related to but different from "to learn the content of a specified textbook on economics." The second establishes a criterion for the decision as to how well the first has been accomplished since it sets the framework for the construction of tests of the learners' knowledge.

Many kinds of criteria are available to the designer of an educational format. Some measure the accomplishment of defined skills, content, or appreciation. Others have to do with the principles of action by which desired changes may be brought about, measuring, for example, group interaction and cohesiveness, the satisfaction of the learner with the process of learning, the growth of problem-solving ability, or the heightened self-awareness of an individual. Some criteria are easy to apply and understand, while others are difficult to use, requiring elaborate interpretation and inference.

An awareness of the criteria to be applied in measuring the extent of learning gives concreteness and definition to an educational activity. A goal may be clear ("to learn to play the organ," "to understand statistics," or "to be sensitive to group processes") and yet lead the learner on forever, since he would never achieve full mastery. When precise levels of accomplishment or exact principles of action are defined, they structure the whole endeavor. Both educator and learner know what is expected by the end of the activity and can have the gratification of assessing concrete accomplishment. It is the lack of clear criteria which gives to many adult educational activities (particularly those in the C-1, C-3, C-6, C-10, and C-11 categories) a sense of vagueness and lack of significance.

The criteria used in adult education are broader in scope and less sharply defined and developed than those of childhood and youth education. In the latter, heavy reliance is placed on formal achievement tests, many of which have been standardized and have well-established norms. Sometimes these tests can be adapted for use by adults and, in even fewer instances, tests specifically devised for them have been developed. For the most part, however, pencil and paper tests for adults are teacher prepared or are used as inherent parts of the instructional rather than the evaluative process. Adults enjoy taking self-evaluative tests, as both magazine editors and the arrangers of museum displays have discovered, and this fact has been extensively used in the construction of self-directed instructional materials.

Most of the criteria now used in adult education are inferential, such as those based on the belief that the higher the participants rate their enjoyment of a program, the more they are learning from it. Some of the most frequently used inferential measures are those of enrollment, attendance, number of meetings held, number of registrants, extent of circulation of books or other materials, and cost indices. Alternatively, a learner or an educator may feel that if he uses an established process, the proper results are bound to occur; he judges his success by the rigor with which he follows procedures. (One is reminded of the oriental hunter who, while returning from a fruitless day in the field, asked his gunbearer what had gone wrong, to which the quick-witted servant responded: "Master, you shot divinely, but Allah was merciful to the birds.") While inferential criteria have some values (measures of volume of service seem to have a particular appeal to financing authorities) they do not directly measure growth in terms of the accomplishment of objectives and therefore cannot meet the basic test of evaluation.

In many cases, however, that test can better be met by adult educational activities than by those provided for children and youth. The success of the latter may not be measurable until many years after the learners have left school but much of the education undertaken by men and women is designed to make an immediate change in their life patterns. They want a promotion or a better job, an increased or improved productivity in a vocation or avocation, a capacity to handle a family problem, or the ability to adjust to a physiological handicap such as a stroke or diabetes. Alternatively, an educator may have social goals, such as the reduction of disease or illiteracy, the improvement of economic life, or the acceptance of a new governmental policy, whose accomplishment can be measured by community statistics or other tangible evidences of success.

As an activity proceeds, original criteria may change, some being altered or abandoned and others added. Thus an association formed to study a social problem may initially measure its success in terms of growth of resources and membership and maintenance of a high morale. As time goes on, its leaders may realize that its actions are having an effect on society and that the measurement of that effect constitutes evidence of the educative impact of the association. But while criteria are often altered in this way so that eventual judgments are different from those forecast at the start, the original design will lack both definition and the capacity to measure movement if it does not include a statement of the criteria which from the beginning seem to offer the best available indications of success.

Explaining the design. When any program is initiated, those who take part in it should understand, so far as possible, both its objectives and its format. As learning proceeds, any change in goals or processes should also be made clear. These observations are truisms but they are frequently violated in practice. It is often said of an educational activity that its purposes or design are not clear to its participants. The planner may know so exactly what is to be undertaken that he assumes that other people share his awareness; he does not take the apparently minor but actually crucial step of informing them. They know neither what they are supposed to accomplish nor the principles they are being asked to follow and, as a result, they wander through the dark, sometimes developing such a sense of frustration that they abandon the program or even the quest for knowledge.

The need for providing as much clarity as possible (particularly for the learners) is made all the more important because the nature of education as a change-inducing process makes a complete awareness of either goals or format impossible until the changes have actually been brought about and the activity completed. The ability to operate a lathe, the knowledge of the essentials of cultural anthropology, or the possession of insight into the wellsprings of behavior be stated as abstractions but are never fully grasped until they have been mastered by the learner. Similarly one may understand the general format of a program's activities but fail to grasp the actual nature of the experiences to be undertaken. A mariner's chart suggests what a traveller may encounter but only he who has actually lived through the voyage knows what it is really like. But while the learner can never understand everything at the start, he should be as aware as possible of the goal toward which he is moving and of the paths he will take to get there. Otherwise he is likely to feel he is wandering through a trackless territory toward an unknown destination.

Fitting Program into Life Patterns

In a strictly logical sequence of program planning, a format might first be devised and then fitted into larger patterns of individual, group, or institutional life. This rational order is seldom followed in practice. Even while the elements of a format are being considered and decisions made concerning them, attention is being given to the ways by which the proposed activity is to be incorporated into the lives of the persons concerned. Awareness of the need for financing, for example, runs constantly through all planning for learning. The consideration of a possible activity may even begin with one of what are here called *adjustments*. A man may change his career or inherit money and thereby be required or enabled to undertake a new educational venture.

The establishment of the proper relationship of learning to the rest of life requires a planner or an analyst to take innumerable details into account. Most arise from the situation itself, though some are generally characteristic of one or more situational categories. The four adjustments considered here are required in some fashion or another in every category. Guidance, financing, the alteration of lifestyles, and interpretation may be so intimately interwoven with the creation of the format that they cannot be distinguished from it, but analytically a differentiation of function can be discerned, particularly when adjustments are determined by influences outside the program itself.

There are at least three prime foci of attention in making decisions about how educational activities should be fitted into larger patterns of life. In all situations except those in C-1, the learner confronts an activity which he may have helped to plan but which is essentially external to him. He must therefore consider how he is to accommodate himself to the new venture. The educator who plans a program must think of its influence on his own life and on that of the learners, making a proper allocation of time and resources in both respects. And an institution which sponsors a program must provide reinforcing supports for it. Specialized personnel, such as administrators, supervisors, counselors, financial officers, public relations specialists, and clerks, may be required to bring harmony to the design of the whole institution and to reinforce each of its separate programs.

An illustration may help to make clear the need to consider the situation from these three focal points—the learner, educator, and institution. The principal of a suburban evening school may invite a teacher to offer a course on the culture of the new African nations. The format itself may be left completely in the hands of the teacher with such guides and restrictions as general institutional policy requires. He must also give some thought to how he will fit this new activity into his present work pattern, what kinds of students will most profit from the course, how he can keep the cost reasonable, and how he can help to interpret its objectives to the community. Every potential student will consider such matters as the influence of the course on his customary pattern of life, whether he has the financial resources to undertake it, whether he understands what it will require of him, and whether he prefers it to some other course he might take. But the heaviest responsibility for accommodating the activity to the lives of the people of the suburbs will fall on the staff of the evening school, which must underwrite the program's financing, interpret it to the public, fit it into the overall schedule of courses, and counsel students into it or out of it. The course merges into the aggregate of activities undertaken by the institution and benefits or suffers by the competence with which such matters are handled.

Guiding learners into or out of the program. A question often asked about an educational program is: who should be included, who excluded? It sometimes happens that this query arises at the time a decision is made about proceeding with the activity, when the matching of suitably qualified and interested learners with appropriate formats may be an important factor in the decision. (In C-1 or C-2 situations, the decision is crucial; the activity cannot be undertaken if the judgment is negative.) The same issue continues to arise even after the activity has begun. A learner may ask himself from time to time whether it is appropriate for him, and the educator may often consider whether or not a specific learner should be encouraged to drop out.

In many cases, guidance poses no severe problems. A group chooses and retains the people its members regard as congenial. A teacher identifies the nature and level of competence required in a course and excludes overqualified, underqualified, or aberrant applicants. In institutional settings, formal or informal methods help potential learners decide whether they wish to take part; it often happens that such efforts, even simple ones, work well enough in selecting and retaining participants that the activity survives. Even those learners who might have been excluded if there had been rigorous admission procedures may finally profit from their study, particularly if the leader can individualize his instruction.

But it would be wrong to take for granted, as many educators do, either that adults know what they want or that they would resent any effort to guide them into or out of learning activities.

While both assumptions are sometimes valid, it often happens that men and women have only vague and ill-defined feelings about how to improve themselves. They come to an educational activity because they feel need or deprivation, their memories of the repressiveness of early schooling haunts them, they encounter resistance to study at home or work, they feel inadequate about their ability to learn, and they are unfamiliar with the program patterns of adult education. This last problem is particularly prevalent in institutions, where the array of courses or other learning opportunities, the interlocking requirements, and the complexities of scheduling seem formidable to those unfamiliar with them.

The initial need for guidance continues throughout the learning process. Within a program, effective individualization helps achieve objectives, but the learner may require help in fitting one activity to another or in adjusting to his general pattern of education. It is not easy for adults to become so fully oriented to the organized learning process that they can pursue it in a normal, natural fashion, without occasional self-consciousness, frustration, or depression. In every situation, therefore, attention should be given to providing the appropriate kind and amount of guidance. Realistic assessment may indicate that no help can be given. Even in such cases, some explanatory material about an activity may be offered to help people who want guidance—a summary of a library's services and service points, a map of a museum which indicates the location of its chief collections, or a description of a lecture or television program which identifies its central theme, its level, and its target audience. Though only a few people are reached by these or other devices, they help establish the fact that the institution cares about the people it serves.

The failure to provide guidance for adults has important consequences, the most obvious one being a low retention rate. Many men and women enter activities in which they are not fundamentally interested, which require more work than they originally contemplated, or which are not designed to achieve the purposes they want to accomplish. As a result, such people drop out. A chain reaction may then set in. Those who remain begin to wonder whether the decline in attendance is an indication that the program is faulty; perhaps they should leave, too. Some of them do. The leader grows uneasy and shows it. More people leave. The program limps along or is abandoned. A second consequence of failure to provide guidance is the loss of one of the most fruitful ways of improving programs, since unmet needs or desires of individuals are often discovered in counseling interviews. A third consequence is a failure of recruitment, for the guidance process draws people's attention to programs they might otherwise overlook or misunderstand.

One major difficulty with providing guidance for adults, particularly in institutions which require special staffs to perform the function, is the establishment of an appropriate interpersonal relationship between counselor and client. The counselor must go beyond the provision of information about requirements, fees, and schedules to take a sincere interest in the individual or group he is helping. Many men and women turn to education out of a sense of need and frustration and with the belief that they are inadequate to life's tasks; they need sympathetic reinforcement. Yet the counselor is not a psychotherapist and should not allow himself to adopt that role. Other adults turn to education with an almost religious spirit; they want to undergo a spiritual or humanistic rebirth or to have their values reordered by someone or something beyond themselves. Some educators, both religious and secular, are ready to try to provide that service. Others have different aims which their counselors must explain to those who would otherwise expect something more exalted than they will actually find.

Various approaches are used to establish the right framework for guiding adults into or out of educational programs. The most customary way of handling the matter is simply to provide necessary information with a warm and accepting manner. A second way is to adapt some psychotherapeutic or psychometric approach, such as nondirective counseling, the interpretation of tests, or group encounter. A third way is to use a pragmatic, common-sense approach, giving information but also trying to discover a client's deeper, rather than more apparent, needs and desires, quickly terminating any interview which seems likely to lead to problems with which the counselor feels he should not try to cope. This last approach may be the most useful one at the present time, since no systematic and sophisticated theory of adult educational counseling has yet won widespread acceptance.

Modifying lifestyles. An adult educational program must

always be fitted into the life pattern of those who undertake it. In childhood and youth, schooling takes precedence over most other affairs, but, in adulthood, the individual must find the time and place for study, he must spend money for this purpose rather than another, he must alter his associations with his family, fellow workers, and friends, and he must give education a high enough priority so that he will not neglect it. Education is never simply added to the actions of a life; it replaces something else; and that replacement must be carefully considered both when an activity is planned and throughout its duration.

In a C-1 situation, this reorientation must be enforced by the individual himself. He can be as flexible in fitting study into his life as he likes, but he must also be ready to make changes later on and to be resolute in carrying out his plans. In other categories, educators must adjust activities to help learners fit the into their patterns of life. Some attention is usually given this matter at the start, particularly in terms of scheduling, but a format may need to be reexamined periodically to be sure that it conforms to the life patterns and resources of the learners.

Most activities also require alteration in the previously established patterns or routines of the educator. The tutor, the leader, or the teacher must fit the student, the group, or the class into his schedule, and the institution must reshape its ways of work since its aggregate of activities is changed. This adjustment is particularly essential in C-6 and C-10 situations, where groups or institutions must be prepared to alter their existing programs to conform to the requirements of the collaborative venture.

Arranging financing. To a learner, the question of finance varies greatly in terms of his situation. He may be paid to go to school, his required outlay may be nonexistent or negligible, or his cost may be high and include tuition charges, incidental expenses (such as payment for transportation, lodging, meals, and child care), and the sacrifice of income which he would otherwise earn during the time he spends on education. Thus he must accommodate his learning pattern to the resources available to him.

Adult education is usually financed by: taxation; student fees; grants from government, foundations, or other sources; income from endowment; or allocations from the general funds of such sponsoring institutions as universities, voluntary associations, or industrial corporations. Much of the real cost, however, is indirect and comes from contributed service, physical facilities, or other resources. Adult education, like other community functions, makes extensive use of volunteers, and other workers receive compensation substantially below their customary levels. For example, a college professor who teaches an overload class of adults usually gets only a fraction of what he is paid for a similar class of regular students. The task of financing an activity requires the use of all of the available resources in the best fashion possible to achieve the desired results.

The field of adult education has traditionally had three major fiscal problems. The most familiar is inadequacy of funds which prevents an activity from coming into being, restricts its effectiveness, and limits participation to those who can afford it. An equally serious, though less frequent, problem occurs when too much money must be spent too rapidly. It sometimes happens that a government bureau or a philanthropist cannot or will not allow time to shape and perfect a new pattern of service but requires that it be created at once and spread immediately to large numbers of people. In such cases, early optimism is usually followed by disillusionment. A third problem arises when an institution or activity has unstable resources; feast and famine alternate, no capital accumulation is built up to assure a steady flow of income, and the program leads a precarious life.

One question perennially considered in one form or another by program planners is whether people appreciate education more if they have to pay for it. Folk wisdom and "common sense" suggest that the answer is yes, and that view is often supported by anecdotal evidence offering examples of how high-priced activities succeed while low-priced activities do not. However, at least as many examples can be given to support a negative answer. Free public libraries have not been driven out of existence by rental libraries, the imposition of a fee by an evening school or a museum often limits attendance, and American agriculture has been revolutionized by the essentially free assistance provided to farmers by the Cooperative Extension Service. Moreover, it is seldom suggested that a high fee can by itself save an activity whose other aspects are poor. The issue must be regarded as unresolved. No objective studies have isolated fee payment as one component of design and assessed its relative influence on various kinds of adult education. Whether or not this form of financing is used depends on the judgment of the planner and the necessities which his situation impose upon him.

Interpreting the activity. Those who plan an adult educational activity must usually try to win support, approval, or acceptance for it from outside persons or publics. A wife wants her husband to agree to her absence from home for several weekend conferences. A high school teacher of literature feels she should explain to other teachers why she offers a class at night. An administrator hopes in increase enrollment in the activities of his institution. The need for interpretation arises out of such simple and direct desires as these.

The learner may encounter no such need if he lives within an enclave of associates who accept the value of education, or, alternatively, if his temperament is so autonomous that he feels no need for social reinforcement. Many individuals believe their families and other intimates oppose their desire to learn. A study of young mothers in homemaking clubs showed that only 55 per cent of them thought their husbands approved of their participation, only 63 per cent thought their mothers approved, and only 60 per cent thought that their best friends approved.[7] Such figures as these, even for a simple, practically rewarding, and easily interpreted activity, suggest why so many adult learners feel they must either hide their participation or find ways of "explaining" it if they can.

The educator who designs a program usually tries to present it in a way that will win public support. In a tribal, peasant, or small-town culture, education may threaten powerful mores and folkways. It must be introduced with great care or it will be summarily rejected. Even in more sophisticated societies, attention must be paid to accepted values. Occupational advancement, getting to know the "right" people in town, or the achievement of a college degree may be socially accepted; a course of study which may not be centrally concerned with any of these objectives may need to be presented in terms of its possible contribution to one of them. In

[7] E. L. Goble, "Participation of the Young Homemaker in Group Learning Activities." (Unpublished doctoral dissertation, The University of Chicago, 1964), p. 72.

complex societies, competition for attention is so great that the designer of a program must often find some special way of heightening or expressing its appeal if it is to attract learners away from other forms of activity, including other adult education programs.

The desire for effective public relations must not endanger the integrity of the program itself. Most adults have been subjected to a lifelong barrage of promotional efforts and easily recognize overselling or deceitful promotion. Even if initially deceived, they do not remain so very long. A celebrity may be chosen as a leader because his name will attract enrollments, but the novelty of his presence will quickly wear off and if he does not perform effectively, the participants will soon grow disillusioned. An advertising campaign may create widespread attention, but if the activity itself is not a good one, word of mouth soon negates the paid promotion. When people are asked why they enrolled in a program, the most common answer is because it was recommended to them by some person who had already taken it or who knew of its reputation. The frequency of this response suggests that, at least in the long run, the most effective way to interpret a program is to have a good one.

General institutional interpretation can provide powerful support for the specific activities which an association or organization sponsors. As soon as it establishes itself in the public consciousness, it commands a ready-made audience for its entire offering. Thus an institution must define the image which it wishes to create and then establish and reinforce it by interpretational strategies and techniques, symbols, and the use of other means available to it. It will then have greater power to recruit students, increase its resources, win community support, and demonstrate its accountability to society.

As a program or institution continues, its interpretive needs are likely to change. A place may have been won in the community's consciousness, but the resulting conception may be so constricting that it limits any growth which is not in accordance with the accepted pattern. This problem was touched on in Chapter Four in the description of the C-8 category. When an institution tries to introduce a wholly new format, it may have great difficulty in interpreting its wish not merely to its desired new public but also to the established clienteles who may feel betrayed by the change.

As the foregoing paragraphs suggest, no widespread generalized climate of opinion now supports and reinforces all adult educational efforts and minimizes the need for constant interpretation and reinterpretation of them. Despite the enormous recent growth of the field, those who engage in it use a fragmented approach in which the several parts do not add up to a coherent whole. In such comparable areas of concern as welfare, health, conservation, or recreation, it is generally accepted that a broad social function can be performed in many ways and by many institutions, each playing its distinctive role but all orchestrating their efforts to reinforce one another. No comparable recognition of adult education exists, a fact which greatly impedes the growth of the field. The most immediate consequence is that every new learning activity must be separately interpreted to the publics influenced by it with little reinforcement from a general social understanding of the human need to continue education to the end of life.

Effecting Program

In a customary time sequence, such as that followed by most forms of schooling, a learning design is first devised and then carried out. It is usually expected that however well-laid the original plans may be, they will almost at once require changes, since even the most experienced educator or learner working within a well-established framework can never foresee all of the contingencies which must be cared for. He may have ignored crucial elements, made wrong decisions concerning others, or find that the situation he actually encounters is different in some way from the contemplated one. In every such case, the abstractness of his plan must be altered in terms of the concreteness of reality as he confronts it.

In other cases, a complete design is not possible until after the activity begins. A residential conference may be sketched out only in broad outlines, so that the participants can help determine its pattern. In other forms of learning, particularly those which have to do with problem solving, original inquiry, or sensitivity training, only a few general guidelines can be set at the start; everything else must be developed after the program is under way. A community development worker may plan to help citizens learn how to work collectively but he does so by using the difficulties they identify. The elements in the evolving educational design will emerge only during the activity itself and may not be fully identifiable until it has been completed.

The time period of an educational activity helps determine how faithfully it adheres to original plans. In an act, changes must be accomplished quickly or not at all, and if reality differs significantly from the plan, the activity may have to be abandoned, as when an announced lecturer fails to appear. In an episode, greater latitude for variation is possible. In a series of episodes, planning and action alternate and may even overlap one another, so that gradual improvement in execution is possible. The accounts of the 5th Army program and that of the 528 Club in Chapter Three suggest how this process occurs. In an aggregate of simultaneous episodes, each may reinforce the others, as a teacher or a learner discovers how to improve one episode by the experience of what is occurring in another.

In sum, the execution of a program is never merely the working out of a design already made in preparation for an evaluation which will come later. It is a time of both the accomplishment of plans and their constant readjustment.

Measuring and Appraising Results

While a program is under way, its quality is constantly being appraised by its participants. After it has been completed, they all make a summative judgment of how good it has been. When the members of a group, class or conference disperse, never to be reassembled, when the spirit and harmony of their community of interest disappears, when the final speeches have been made and the good-byes said, what values remain? Has it all been worth while?

The answer to this question is provided by the use of a dual process. The first is measurement, the determination by objective means of the extent to which learners have achieved the criteria of evaluation. The second part is appraisal, a subjective judgment of how well educational objectives have been achieved. Appraisal may incorporate the data provided by measurement but it goes beyond them to sum them up, to reflect about their meaning, and to make a final culminating assessment of the value of the activity. A simple illustration of the interworking of these two processes is given in this project report prepared by a county home adviser:

> The standard set for completion of our project on the reduction of obesity (which we called *Lines and Figures*) was that each of the 100 rural women included should attend at least half the lessons and actually reduce her weight. By the first standard, there was a 60 per cent finish. In terms of the second, the women averaged losing one pound per week. When final classes were held, a total of 601 pounds had come off. The most anyone lost was twenty-four pounds. I believe that this project has resulted in more changed habits and practices than any other project attempted in the last two or three years. The changes recommended were very basic and self-discipline not easy. The success of the sixty finishing members was gratifying but 60 per cent is not enough to satisfy me.

As noted earlier, the establishment of criteria for evaluation is one element of a format. Wherever possible, data relevant to them should be collected from the beginning of the educational activity, and information on progress should be reported and interpreted. While it is useful to have many kinds of evidence to provide the basis for a balanced appraisal, only as much measurement should be undertaken as the situation allows. Otherwise evaluation becomes an end in itself, which may be appropriate in research investigations but which distorts its proper purpose in most educational activities. Sometimes, too, the concept of an exquisitely refined assessment of achievement is so daunting that it keeps educators from doing any evaluation at all.

The science of measurement has grown apace in recent years, but relatively little is known about how its results can be harmoniously combined into a balanced appraisal. Education has to do with the human mind, body, and spirit, all highly resistant to mechanistic formulations. The precise refinement either of objectives or of measurement instruments is itself a sustained exercise in the making of choices. The effort to be completely objective can lead to a tendency to seek only those goals whose accomplishments are readily measurable and to forget the rest. It may be easy, for example, to test the skill of a worker but hard to assess his sense of craftsmanship; the first may therefore be stressed at the expense of the second. Even making a distinction between physical skills and values calls for the exercise of judgment; putting together the lines of evidence which harmonize them requires an even greater subjectivity of approach.

The learner or the educator must therefore examine all available evidence and make his appraisal of how much the educational program has accomplished in terms of his sense of the realities of the situation. The basic questions he must ask himself are simple and direct. How well was each objective achieved? If I did better than expected, why? Was the goal too high or was the design poorly planned and executed? If the latter, what specifics were wrong? If the objective was reached would I have done better if I had set higher levels of accomplishment? If goals changed during the course of learning, should they have? What additional criteria of evaluation should have been used? Can I make an estimate of how well I would have done on them? Such questions call for judgmental answers, but are the only kinds on which appraisal can be made and the process of evaluation completed.

Repeating the Educational Cycle

Even as appraisal looks backward to judge the past, it should also look ahead to help shape the future. The questions asked in an appraisal can be recast to give this foreward orientation. In a C-4 situation, for example, a teacher can consider such matters as these as he thinks about repeating a course for a new group of students: Should the original goals be used? Should there be additional ones, or should any of the previous ones be deleted? Should new criteria be used? Should standards on the criteria be the same or made higher or lower? What elements in the format or in its accommodation to lifestyles should be changed? Such questions can only be guides to subjective thought but it is only by trying to answer them fully and honestly that improvement is likely to occur.

For if learning is to be lifelong, new acts and episodes will constantly occur, and both learners and educators should gain through contemplative practice an increasing understanding and mastery of educational design. In Figure 1 of Chapter Two a line connects the final step of measurement and appraisal in one activity with the first step of the next one. The learner or the educator has completed one cycle and is now in a new phase in which he is ready to identify a possible new activity, to decide whether to proceed, and, if the decision is affirmative, to embark upon a new process of educational development using the same steps as before.

Conclusion

The length of this chapter may serve to defeat its purpose, if it has caused the central unity of good educational design to be obscured by the consideration of each of its components. Some people may treat the system mechanically at first, as a series of formal steps, but, even as they use it in this fashion, they will come to see that its parts have interconnections not solely determined by time. Whatever they may learn about each component can be incorporated into the overall system without destroying its unity. With increased practice they can move forward more and more confidently because they will need to think less and less about the several decision points. Finally, as in the mastery of any other complex process, they will achieve that highest form of art in which they seem not to be using any art at all.

CHAPTER VI

Major Program Reconstruction

The art of progress is to pre-serve order amid change, and to preserve change amid order.
Alfred North Whitehead,
Process and Reality

186

Sometimes the normal revision of an educational activity as it moves through its cycles is not adequate to bring about a needed or desired level of performance. A concert violinist grows dissatisfied with the results of his customary learning and practice schedule and retires for a year to restudy his basic technique. A teacher realizes that a course she is teaching should be completely revised. The staff of an institution comes to believe that it is not serving modern social purposes. In these and other situations, the need for reconstruction may arise from many causes: measurement and appraisal may be neglected, insufficient, or incorrect; a major new event or trend, either internal or external to the program, may alter conditions drastically; performance may reach a plateau from which not even the most strenuous efforts can start an upward thrust; or old ways of work may grow monotonous and unchallenging. Whatever the cause, someone raises the question whether fundamental redesigning of the activity would be desirable. This chapter deals with the way by which this question may be answered and, if the decision is made to proceed with the reconstruction, how it may best be brought about.

Redesigning Institutional Activities

While reconstruction can occur by the same basic process as does the creation or the cyclical revision of a program, the planning and analysis needed in the basic redesigning of an activity require a depth and comprehensiveness of approach to each of the decision points which cannot be quickly sketched or illustrated. Therefore the effort to include individual, group, institutional, and mass learning which characterized the approach in Chapters Three, Four, and Five must now be abandoned. To illustrate and deal with the distinctive aspects of each category would be tediously lengthy. Only the reconstruction of an institution will be considered and, since the four cases used in Chapter Three do not describe this process, it will be illustrated by events which once took place in the public library of Centerville, a not wholly fictitious Midwestern community.

One reason for concentrating on institutions is that their reconstruction has greater difficulties than does that of individual, group, or mass activities. In an organization or an association, the task of galvanizing and refocussing the efforts of many people, who often represent a wide spectrum of opinions and whose creativeness is highly variable, presents major challenges. The problem of change is usually accentuated by the fact that a new order must be conceived and carried out while the old order is still in full operation. Therefore most of the planners' time must be devoted to the maintenance of established routines and only a small amount of it can be spent on creative development. Desired changes may be incorporated gradually as they seem desirable, a series of phases may be planned leading from the old to the new, or the existing pattern may be continued intact until a wholly new design can be adopted. Such circumstances influence the pace and sequence of reconstruction, but they do not alter the fact that the complex interactional patterns and habits of the people involved must be permanently changed.

For purposes of analysis and illustration, it is assumed that the institution is a relatively small one with from five to thirty staff members who are close enough together geographically to have fairly ready access to one another or can be assembled as a group whenever necessary. This range and compass would include most institutional forms of adult education—extension services; training departments of business, government, labor unions, or hospitals; professional continuing education units; libraries; evening schools; museums; foundations; the staffs of voluntary associations; and other programs. The special problems faced in the reconstruction of large, complex, or widely dispersed associations and organizations will be considered at the end of the chapter.

Need for Reconstruction

The public library is one of the oldest institutions of Centerville and for many years was deeply cherished by the people of its community. Late in the nineteenth century, the city fathers shrewdly took advantage of Andrew Carnegie's offer to construct a library building, and he, equally shrewdly, required them to maintain its service at a prescribed level. For many years, the library fulfilled the original hopes of both parties, growing with the times and the town, adding services, remodeling the late Victorian building to take as great an advantage as possible of its limited flexibility, and offering recreation, information, education, and culture to literate people of all ages.

As the years wore on, however, a decay set in which was so gradual as hardly to be noticed. The staff was made up almost entirely of women who had grown up in Centerville and considered it to be a unique place and the very fulcrum of the earth. There were few retirements and few recruits, personal conflicts were resolved or endured, ways of work were stabilized, and occasional proposals for change were defeated by appeals to the virtue of accepted and tested practices. Circulation figures and other measures of service remained constant, thereby providing a sense of established accomplishment; scarcely anybody noted that while the number of people served remained about the same, they made up a declining percentage of the city's population. Centerville was growing, industries were coming to town, and in a long-sustained period of prosperity new institutions were being created, among them an art center, a community college, a museum, an extension office of the state university, and an evening school. Meanwhile the library continued on its placid course.

It was suddenly brought from obscurity to an unpleasant prominence by several events which occurred almost simultaneously. A modern group of city fathers, less sage than their predecessors, made a series of bad decisions which were culminated when two major highways were allowed to intersect near the heart of town. When completed, they effectively divided it into quadrants. The library found itself cut off from almost three-quarters of the population by swift-flowing rivers of traffic and at once the circulation plummeted. A new mayor was elected to office on a reform ticket. It happened that his elder sister was on the staff of the library, a fact which may or may not have been significant for its future. He soon appointed to its board two vigorous young community leaders who made clear their intention to challenge the elderly oligarchy of trustees who had guided the institution's policies for many years. The chief librarian, astutely reading the handwriting on the wall, announced her retirement, pointing out as though it were news that she was nearing seventy.

The time for reconstruction had come. The library's tradition of community support ran so deep that the proposal of one city council member that it be closed was quickly squelched. But certainly it could not continue in its accustomed ways. The two new board members were determined to appoint a chief librarian from outside, a decision which the continuing trustees did not care to oppose, particularly since no outstanding candidate for the position was already on the staff. After a widespread search, the choice was finally made of a woman who had already demonstrated her creative capacities in a smaller city in another state. She came to her new post with every intention to reform the library's program but with a shrewd awareness of the problems she confronted.

Thus is was that in Centerville the effective impulse toward reconstruction of the library came from outside the institution, though nobody could accurately assess the influence of the mayor's sister. In other situations where change is undertaken, it may be initiated by a maverick trustee, a chief administrator determined to make his mark, a single staff member or an informal group of them, or a staff association. Sometimes the source of an effective desire for change is less tangible. A sense that things are not going well grows up without any notable cause. An accepting and complacent climate of opinion is somehow replaced by a general belief that things cannot continue as they have been and that the time for drastic change has arrived.

Such an awareness can arise from a sense of success as well as from a feeling of failure. A vigorous and progressive institution may reach the limits of its capacity for growth under existing conditions. A hard choice must be made to either stabilize the program at its present level, taking the risk that decay and decline can be avoided, or maintain the momentum of growth or improvement by some profound alteration of ends or means. For instance, a university conference and institute staff may, through able and creative programming, use all the space available to it. If new conference facilities cannot be found, service must level off, with the possible risk that key staff members will seek greener pastures and be replaced by mediocrities. Alternatively, challenging new programs may be developed and old ones abandoned, or a new center for continuing education may be built.

The awareness of a need for program reconstruction must reach a certain level of pervasiveness or intensity before it can lead to a formal decision to take action. The mere expression of discontent is not enough, for a dynamic institution always exhibits tensions which are reflected in disagreements among the staff members or other persons involved with its future. These differing viewpoints may not be keenly felt or, if they are, may cancel one another out or be accommodated by alterations in practice brought about by normal processes of cyclical revision. A sufficiently powerful momentum to lead to drastic change is reached only when a widespread body of opinion agrees on the need for reconstruction or when that view is held by some person in a position of key authority. During the old regime of the Centerville library, such a threshold might have been reached by the board, the chief librarian, or the staff. Nothing happened. Then, in the new order of events, the necessary level of concern was reached, though it would be hard to say precisely when or by whom. Whatever the effective cause, it is clear that for a long time the threshold had not been reached and that at some later moment it was.

This result may be brought about by the actions of either or both of the two major institutional systems of power—the administrative and the collective. The first is exercised through the formal hierarchical structure depicted by an organization chart. The second may be formalized as an academic senate, a staff association, or a union, but often operates informally by some never wholly clear process of social climate formation in which personal influence, timing, and negotiation play a part. Each system of power can operate separately from the other and the two are occasionally at loggerheads, but ordinality a successful reconstruction of a program cannot be achieved without some harmony between them. The new chief librarian at Centerville knew that she had the administrative power to force through changes, but, being experienced, she also knew that to be truly successful she had to win not merely the assent but the cooperation of her staff.

Deciding to Proceed

How could she do so? More broadly, looking across a full panorama of situations, how can anyone who thinks program reconstruction necessary achieve his end? Such a person may belong to either system of power and even be dominant in one of them, but he also knows that he must influence others to accept his point of view. The arts of persuasion and political trading are sometimes brought into play and occasionally coercion is used. If matters have gone so far that the institution is in jeopardy, drastic and ruthless action may even be required. But within the normal dictates of program development, several strategies of varying depth and subtlety may be used, each of them designed to lead to a decision to proceed with major alterations of the program but none of them sure of success in achieving that aim.

Five strategies. The simplest and boldest strategy is for an administrator or some member or group of the collective power structure to assume that a decision to reconstruct the program has been made and to move at once to the identification and implementation of new objectives. This step may result from impatience, the pressure of time, or skepticism about the value of any study of the present situation. It may also result from the belief that the crucial element in direction finding springs from the application of judgment by those who have the power to decide, and that they already possess within themselves all the knowledge required to set the main lines of direction for the future. They need only find some way of freeing themselves from surface distractions, difficulties, and tensions so that they can chart out a course of action for the future. One problem often encountered when using this strategy is that the present ways of doing things usually have an inherent consistency so that changing any one practice jeopardizes the proper performance of many others. The awareness of this difficulty often leads to a feeling of frustration which finally results in either inaction or an acceptance of some superficial change as a way of retreating from the issues raised. Another problem is that sometimes the bold assumption by an individual or group that change is essential leads to the crystallization of contrary opinion. Polarization occurs between the "conservatives" and the "progressives," with the result that either stalemate or a reaffirmation of the status quo occurs.

Other strategies are based on the belief that some preliminary process of inquiry or investigation is essential before a decision can be made to proceed. Since the future must grow out of the past and present, it is argued that any rational effort to create a new design should follow or accompany a survey of the current situation. Even an administrator who believes that circumstances compel him to be bold and ruthless wants to be sure that he has made enough of a study to justify his actions. A more gradual initiator of major change, whatever his point of vantage, believes that an assessment of current status is essential to the making of wise decisions for the future and usually wants to involve other people in the process of reassessment.

A second strategy, therefore, for those who wish to change the direction of an activity is to propose a full-scale survey and reconstruction effort, spelling out with some clarity the course of action which such an effort would probably follow. While this strategy is straightforward and honest, it may have the disadvantage of seeming too bold. The people who need to be persuaded to engage in the effort may shrink back from the time and expense involved or be filled with dread about what might happen to them or to their established ways of work.

A third strategy is merely to recommend a survey. The rhetoric used may take the following line: let's have a good hard look at what we're doing; perhaps we'll find that we have excellences of which we are as yet unaware; perhaps we'll find growing points or ways we can improve; perhaps we won't want to do anything at all and certainly we ought not to decide until we have the facts; but if we don't get those facts, how can we ever know what we ought to do? Those who use such rhetoric believe that a survey will highlight the need for change, and that getting people involved in collecting or studying facts is likely to have the effect of getting them to want to do something about their implications. While this strategy often works, it can run into serious difficulties. It does not usually deceive anybody, least of all the people with a vested interest in the status quo who want no close examination of it. And a survey is likely to seem too large and unknown a task, one which intimidates the shy and threatens the lazy.

A fourth strategy is to apply some available criteria of excellence of performance. The public library standards of the American Library Association and the evaluative procedures of college and university accrediting associations illustrate two kinds of full-scale effort to assess a current level of performance. More specific measures are the various indices used by health and welfare institutions. When the staff of an agency realizes, for example, that the illiteracy rate or the incidence of a disease is twice as high in its service area as in other similar communities, the effect of that awareness is likely to be profound. Unfortunately, criteria and indices are often not available and, even when they are, those who oppose change are likely to find many reasons why their own agency or community presents a special case to which general standards do not apply. Also, while such criteria can be used to suggest that a poor institution should be better than it is, they are less useful in helping to make a good institution excellent.

A fifth strategy is to ask probing questions or make detailed suggestions concerning any of the components of an educational model which seem most vulnerable to attack. Since all components are interwoven, the change of one of them will lead to change in the others. While any component will serve for this purpose, the one most likely to have an effect is evaluation. Anyone who asks and, if necessary, keeps on asking, "How well are we doing?" (in all the variant forms which that question can take) is likely to arouse an uneasiness among his colleagues which leads eventually to a broader awareness of the need for considering fundamental changes in the program. In a sense, he is asking for a total survey while not seeming to be doing so. He merely inquires how much learning is occurring, whether it is the right kind, and if it is as much as it should be. But before such apparently artless questions can be dealt with, the whole issue of institutional excellence has been raised.

In the first strategy, a movement is made at once toward objective setting. The fourth and fifth strategies require subtle processes of intervention and negotiation which are so influenced by situational factors that they cannot well be abstracted for consideration. But the second and third strategies require the making of a survey, and the generalized technique for doing so is worth consideration.

The survey. In Centerville, the second strategy was used. The chief librarian knew that nothing less than a major alteration of service would suffice for the regeneration of the public library, and she felt that that fact might as well be clear from the start. She also believed that the whole program should be studied, not merely some aspect of it. She therefore proposed a plan which won the assent of her board and staff members, though with varying degrees of support. She suggested that the basic work of making a survey and identifying new goals should be carried out by the staff itself. A surveyor from outside the system might work rapidly and efficiently and would almost certainly write a clear and comprehensive report, but he would always remain external to the situation. While he would grasp the main outlines of the problem and bring a practiced expertise to bear on its solution, he might be insensitive to the nuances perceived only by those who had lived with the situation and expected to continue doing so. More than that, work by the staff would encourage its support of change later. Finally, the local board and staff were not so divided into armed camps that only an external mediator would be able to operate efficiently.

But the board and staff did not know how to go about the task of reconstruction; nor did she. A point of view from outside the system was needed. The board therefore provided enough money to engage a consultant who agreed to serve one day a month for a year. To assist his efforts, the staff was divided into two committees, one to make the survey, the other to formulate new objectives. The chief librarian held herself free, so that she would be able to supervise, assist, and coordinate the work. It was also decided that the survey would be as open as possible, its results being made available to everyone interested in them.

By these actions, the first stage necessary in any survey was accomplished—its basic framework was established. The scope was defined, responsibilities were assigned, the time and effort required were identified, a way of work was established, and a policy of disseminating findings was adopted. Other situations require other frameworks, depending on such factors as the amount of money available, the need for outside authority to resolve internal differences, and the nature and wishes of external decisionmakers. In many cases, for example, a survey is involuntary; it occurs because an outside authority sends in an examiner. But while various alternative arrangements may be devised to suit the distinctive requirements of situations, some framework needs to be established at the start. Otherwise, surveys are likely to continue indefinitely or peter out leaving no residue other than piles of paper, outmoded charts, and long-lingering distrust.

The definition of scope often presents special problems. In Centerville, the whole library was made the subject of study, not merely some aspect of it such as cataloging or reference service. In other cases, decisions about the extent of the survey are often complicated. As noted in Chapter Three, the choice of what shall be accepted as the institution to be considered often requires a selection of some central focal point within a complex fabric. For example, a trade association will have to decide whether the whole institution itself should be studied or only its educational department. When that determination is made, is all the activity of the unit to be studied or merely some part of its work, such as the conferences it provides? On such choices rest some of the important aspects of a survey, not the least of them being the decision as to what is internal to the program itself and what is peripheral to it but important for it. The proper conclusions about such matters grow out of an analysis of the situation and result from the use of judgment, not from the application of unalterable general rules.

A second stage of a survey, the definition of its central emphases, overlaps or closely follows the first. While the general objective is always to learn the truth about a program, the whole truth is impossible to achieve and the mere amassing of facts is tedious and self-defeating since perspective is lost in the accumulation of detail. Some focus must be set. It may be changed later, in the light of deeper understanding, but that change will be a further clarification of matters which have already been firmly outlined. One good way to begin is to identify the central or outstanding problems which have led to the survey. Once they have been properly defined, a long step will have been taken toward finding their solutions.

In Centerville, the survey committee began its work by setting down a list of questions. Included were these: What forms of outreach (branches, bookmobiles, deposit stations, or others) should be used to bring service to the whole city? What should be the chief functions of the central building and how should it be related to the outreach services? How can the library serve its customary patrons more effectively? How can it reach new clienteles, including those who belong to sectors of the population that have seldom used library services in Centerville or elsewhere? How can the library win greater public support? Should it collaborate with other agencies and, if so, how and with which ones? How can the members of the staff work together more efficiently? How good is the present collection? What policies should be followed in book selection?

Such questions might be answered merely by introspection without the use of any data on actual performance. But the survey committee believed it needed to look objectively at both past and present practices. Some forms of outreach had already been tried and their success could be appraised. The present functions of the central building could be analyzed. The opinions of current patrons could be discovered by questionnaires or interviews. Unserved clienteles could be identified. The public relations program could be examined and past patterns of collaboration with other agencies could be reviewed. The staff members could be asked to give their suggestions for more desirable ways of work. The book collection could be checked against established standards and the literature of librarianship could be studied to discover alternative book-selection policies. Thus the survey committee, by asking questions, made tangible the ways by which it could begin its work, realizing always that deeper and more fundamental questions might well emerge as it moved beyond preliminary stages.

The initial identification of problems introduces into the survey from the start an element which might otherwise be ignored —how do people feel? Any surveyer wants to get the facts about a program and they often present themselves in a temptingly objective fashion in terms of available statistics of size, nature, and use. But the way the people concerned with an institution feel is also a fact to be considered. What are their attitudes and opinions? What are they ready for? What obstacles do they see or sense? Unless the surveyor takes account of such matters either formally or informally, his report is likely to be merely a compendium of data, and the chances of any appropriate ensuing action are minimized. The danger of misperceiving points of view can never be avoided even under the best of circumstances but it is reduced when it is recognized from the beginning that the problems with which the survey deals must be solved not by machines but by people and that therefore the survey must take full account of their beliefs and attitudes.

The next stage is the collection of data. Here several overlapping frames of reference must be considered simultaneously, though they can be loosely divided into two groups, those "outside" and those "inside." Every institution (however it is defined for the purposes of the survey) is given its distinctive form as a result of the influences brought to bear upon it by its physical and social environment and by decisions and capacities of its staff and of other people concerned with its operation. There are many kinds of external and internal forces. Thus the Centerville Public Library was influenced by a macroenvironment which included the state of the economy, national and state laws and regulations, and the policies of the profession of librarianship. It was also influenced by the microenvironment of its own community—the nature of the population in terms of age, educational attainment, race, geographic dispersion, and other factors; the social structures which had been created to deal with economic, social, political, cultural, welfare, and other functions; the core value systems which the people of the community possessed or believed themselves to possess; the subtle influences of social class, the exercise of power, and the pattern of informal social relationship; and the existence of other educational institutions which could provide reinforcement, cooperation, or competition.

Many kinds of internal data are usually also available; in fact, the observation of the program itself ordinarily makes up the heart of the survey. The historical development of the institution may be examined, with some accounting for reasons why central program emphases have been developed and also some suggestion of the probable course of future development if present trends continue. The formal objectives need to be considered and their accomplishment assessed, as does the impact of policy or budgetary controls imposed by external authorities. Attention must also be given to many or all of the components of effective design identified in Chapter 5.

Countless techniques may be used to collect both external and internal data. One common means of securing relatively objective facts is by documentary research which examines such sources as census reports, other general complications of data, and formal descriptions of the institution and its community. New data may be collected by administering tests, using questionnaires, and conducting interviews. The surveyor can also use methods which offer insights, unifying principles, or evidences of value and belief, though such subjective findings must be interpreted with caution. Among these methods are observation, nondirective interviews, the analysis of relevant problems by groups familiar with them, and introspection by the surveyor or people associated with him.

Gradually the fourth stage of the survey emerges when the data are ordered and examined to determine their significance. The present can most profitably lead into the future when a thoughtful mind sifts and ponders relevant data and draws interpretations from them. This process starts early; it is implied in the definition of scope of the study, the asking of the crucial questions, and the selection of the data to be collected. But as the survey progresses, the emphasis on interpretation grows stronger. Tentative answers to the initial questions are suggested. New problems are uncovered and considered. Some effort is made to distinguish between surface facts and their deeper significance. The chief obstacles to change are identified, and the most promising growing-points are suggested. Finally, recommendations emerge which may turn into objectives if they are accepted and acted upon.

Some action always flows from any survey even though major change does not occur. Untidy places are cleaned up and inappropriate relationships or inefficient ways of work are altered either before the surveyor can notice them or after he has done so. Obvious inequities are remedied, shifts in function or authority are made, delayed decisions are taken, and postponed actions are put into effect. Such changes are normal, but the survey merely quickens the pace at which they are made. Even as the survey proceeds, events occur which alter the situation. In Centerville, for example, two additional members were appointed to the seven-member library board, thus changing the formal balance of power between the old and the new trustees. As a result, a major deterrent to innovation was removed. But reconstruction is usually delayed until after the survey is completed and studied. At that point, the decision is made whether or not to undertake substantial changes and, if so, which ones. This decision may be consciously taken by formal action or may evolve as a result of later events. The survey may live on in the minds of the staff members and subtly guide their future actions though they are scarcely aware that it is doing so. But it may be ignored and forgotten. Throughout the world, countless surveys molder on shelves or in filecases, their results unread, their recommendations unaccepted.

Identifying and Refining Objectives

Whatever the eventual effect of a survey may be, its completion is the most appropriate moment to consider which of its recommendations should be accepted and therefore give rise to objectives. The same point is reached in various ways when any of the three nonsurvey strategies is used. In the first, action is taken at once. In the fourth or fifth, a climate of opinion leading to change is achieved as a result of introspection or discussion; in some sense a survey has been made, though it is far from being comprehensive. In any of the five cases the time comes to plan for the future.

Whatever the circumstances or the theory in terms of which objective setting occurs, it sometimes proceeds with no clear sense of method, and, as a result, either trails off inconclusively or ends with sudden and arbitrary decisions. A weekend retreat is held in the belief that it will lead to completely changed directions but Sunday evening finds the participants still exploring their differences. A series of weekly staff meetings is scheduled to run "until we have a clear idea about future policy" but that clarity is not achieved and the sessions are finally abandoned. An administrator picks and chooses among the recommendations of a survey, counting on his authority to put his program into effect. A board or other policy-making body uses customary political processes to accommodate the wishes of its members, thereby evolving a compromise plan for the future. However common these procedures may be in the work of the world, none of them operates in terms of any general method of selecting objectives.

Such a method is outlined in the following paragraphs. It is by no means novel, for in some fashion or other it is used in the decision-making processes of government, industry, and other enterprises. But, so far as is known, it has never been conceptualized in its present form nor has it been applied widely in adult educational institutions. It rests on familiar principles: the fixing of central responsibility for a task; the involvement of every individual concerned; the need for collective discussion and decision; the use of objective data; the establishment of a clear-cut time dimension; and the need to carry on present assignments while new ones are being identified.

The first step in the process is to select the individual or group which is to guide the formulation of objectives. (For convenience, it will be referred to as the committee, but the task is not always a collective one and, even when it is, the chairman has a special responsibility.) Work assignments should be shifted to allow time for this new duty.

Second, all of the persons involved in improving the program meet together for a general discussion of the nature of objectives and the process for choosing them. (The analysis of objectives presented in Chapter 5 may be useful in dealing with the first of these two matters.) The purpose here is to acquaint everyone with the broad design of what is to be accomplished and how, to set the timing for the various stages, to allay doubts and worries, and to provide an opportunity for questions to be answered.

In Centerville, this meeting was attended by both board and staff members. The chief librarian presided and gave the full weight of her authority to the plan. The consultant then talked about the nature of objectives and their major attributes. He also indicated how he felt that the staff should proceed. Since these were practical people, they were not interested in going deeply into the theory of objective setting and the proposed sequence of activities apparently seemed reasonable to them. A number of questions were asked, however, for purposes of clarification or to establish particular viewpoints that librarians or board members wanted to be sure were not overlooked. Subsequently it was agreed that after this first meeting the board members would not participate actively until they were provided with a set of objectives upon which the staff had agreed. It was felt that in this way the appropriate distinction between board and staff responsibilities might best be carried out. The consultant made the following note about this first session:

> Given the Centerville situation, the meeting went as well as could be expected. The staff clearly represents several different points of view ranging from enthusiasm to indifference to, in one case, mild hostility. It seems clear that the chief librarian is the strongest personality in the entire group. She leads both the staff and the board and her decisions are unlikely to be opposed by either

group. In general the group seemed to understand the plan of procedure and to be willing to cooperate. Mrs. A had already done good work on the survey and seemed anxious to do more and to get new ideas. There was a tendency on the part of both staff and board members to be carried away by certain individual enthusiasms and to become excited over the possibility of some single solution to problems which presented themselves at the moment. It was necessary to underscore the importance of considering all possibilities and weighing the comparative values of various alternatives, rather than following through hurriedly on whatever seemed to be a good idea at the time.

Third, every person in the group writes down his own statement of objectives in any form which he wishes using any opinions or information he may have. These statements are turned over to the committee. This step is perhaps the most crucial in the entire process since it is the one in which the deepest and most substantial involvement is secured. Staff members ordinarily seek guidance in knowing just how they should set down their objectives but care should be taken to avoid too much direction lest it destroy the creativeness in which individuals are encouraged to say whatever they have in mind in whatever form they think is appropriate. If they ask whether they should be thinking about the total institution or about their own specific work, the answer is that they should be thinking about both. The main effort is to have everyone record his own ideas about policies, procedures, aims, and anything else which seems appropriate to him. Ordinarily this process is helped if there has been a survey because it will have aroused many individuals to a keener sense of the needs which should be met than would be the case if purely subjective judgments were given.

The practice of having individuals independently record their ideas about objectives has several values. It encourages creativity as it fixes responsibility. It requires everyone to participate. It reduces worries about having ideas overlooked; everyone knows that he will have the chance to present his views in the way he chooses. Clarity is encouraged by the need to express ideas exactly. Most important perhaps is that the time of the entire group can be used constructively to discuss major issues and policies and to resolve ambiguities of meaning and interpretation, not to work through all of the irritations, frustrations, partial conceptions, and personal conflicts which so often bog down discussions of objectives making meetings fruitless. While some people find it hard to write down their ideas and a few may never do so, the requirement of written, reasoned thought seems inherently appropriate for the staff of an educational institution.

Fourth, each member of the committee makes his own list of objectives, paying particular attention to the results of the survey and to the whole program of the institution. The committee members will have another opportunity later to incorporate their viewpoints into the evolving framework of the statement of objectives. At this point, however, each member should record his initial ideas and impressions about probable goals so that his special viewpoint is expressed.

Fifth, the committee examines the statements submitted to it as well as those its members have produced to make a broad distinction between those objectives which are stated as achievable accomplishments and those which suggest principles or ways of work. The distinction between these two forms of objectives is made in Chapter Five. A proposed accomplishment in Centerville was "to establish three branches in parts of the city now remote from library service." A proposed principle was that all major matters of library policy should be discussed by the staff as a whole before being recommended to the board." In practice, the distinction between accomplishments and principles is often not easy to make and may depend on the intentions of those who propose them. Thus the objective "to promote the use of books dealing with current community problems" may be treated as an achievable accomplishment if specific problems are identified and used as guides for the purchase and display of specific books. However, the statement may also be treated as a principle which suggests a desirable characteristic of practice (as differentiated, say, from the maintenance of a "well rounded" collection) but which is not used operationally in any specific fashion.

The committee will find that some of the statements which come to it are mixtures of accomplishments and principles, and rational analysis is difficult until the two are distinguished and defined. People may have strong feelings about the present state of affairs in the program. They may believe, for example, that staff members should cooperate, not compete, with one another and insist that a statement to that effect be written down as a desirable aim. Once it is accepted as a principle, the task of defining accomplishments can go forward; otherwise, the task may prove to be impossible because people cannot think constructively about them until the issue of principle is settled. From this point forward, the committee may consider itself to be working with two formulations, not merely with one. Usually the principles are stated as a simple list but sometimes they may be divided in terms of their relative importance or may be placed in some hierarchical order.

Sixth, the committee combines all of the statements of achievable accomplishments into a hierarchical form. Ordinarily, one member of the committee accepts this responsibility and the others check his work. In making this first rough formulation of the comprehensive statement which will eventually result, no idea should be omitted; if it is, its formulator is certain to take offense later. If the committee has difficulty in understanding precisely what was intended by any statement, its original framer can be asked for clarification. The same objective may have been suggested by several people; if so, the committee can combine the various statements into the most appropriate form.

At this stage, the hierarchical document, as it ranges ideas in terms of some conception of genera and species, will be loose-textured, fragmentary, and possibly filled with contradictions. Occasionally the framework accords with the organizational structure of the institution so that each major cluster of objectives is undertaken by a specific group of people. On other occasions, objectives are stated so broadly that they cut across the hierarchy of the employees.

In establishing this first formulation, the committee uses its judgment to group and rank objectives. Sometimes it works from the top down, beginning with the broadest statements and fitting the others somewhere beneath them. Sometimes it works from the bottom up, clustering specifics and moving toward generality. Often it works in both directions at once, identifying broad statements and specific ones and then juggling their relationships to one another until as good a fit as possible is found. The identification of the intermediate goals is often the hardest task of all. It is easy to have great aspirations and equally easy to identify needs for immediate action, but it is hard to relate dreams to impulses. Tocqueville suggested that this problem is characteristic of Americans. "They are haunted by visions of what will be; in this direction their unbounded imagination grows and dilates beyond all measure."[1] But the aim of imagination "is not habitually lofty; and life is generally spent in eagerly coveting small objects that are within reach."[2] Perhaps Americans still have this characteristic and perhaps other people also possess it.

Seventh, the committee scrutinizes the whole document to locate and remedy logical gaps and deficiencies. When many statements have been put together into a single formulation, new ideas will emerge, and the committee may add them at this point so that they can come under the scrutiny of the whole group when it is reconvened. For example, the Centerville staff members had suggested that the library should issue pamphlets, films, filmstrips, and pictures. The committee had grouped these under the broad goal "to extend the range of communication materials circulated by the library." It then seemed clear that another specific goal should be subsumed—the issuance of recordings and tapes.

Eighth, the committee checks the statements formally against any external controling provisions and notes restrictions that may be imposed thereby. All institutions operate within the laws and in terms of past agreements. Staff members sometimes know nothing of such matters and propose objectives which are either illegal or violate current interinstitutional arrangements. In Centerville, one staff member felt that library services should be provided to the people who live in the surrounding country. The committee knew, however, that this policy was expressly forbidden by the city council. The purpose of noting this fact on the committee's initial report was not to delete the objective but to indicate that its acceptance would require a request to the city council for a change in its regulations.

Ninth, the committee reports back to the entire group for a broad discussion of what has been done so far and for such guides to action as it may wish to give. The group now has before it the com-

---

[1] A. de Tocqueville, *Democracy in America*, 2 (New York: Alfred A. Knopf, 1945), 73–74.

[2] de Tocqueville, p. 245.

bined list of proposed accomplishments and the separate list of
principles. Each staff member ordinarily looks first to see how his
own ideas have been incorporated in the total statement. If he finds
that his wishes have been faithfully presented, he ordinarily feels
that the committee has taken him seriously. At the same time, the
whole group now sees its ideas presented in a larger framework than
had previously been possible. Some very specific proposals ("keep
the library open until ten o'clock one night a week") or highly
general statements ("we should try to achieve maximum efficiency
in every department") are readily seen to be too narrow and procedural or too vague to serve as useful objectives. The staff will often
suggest that such items be eliminated. On the other hand, the discussion may reveal an unexpected enthusiasm for some principles
and support will grow for some proposed accomplishments. The
committee must note both omissions and emphases and get as much
guidance and direction from the total group as it can, but several
steps remain to be taken and therefore nothing can be accepted as
final or conclusive.

At this stage in Centerville, the consultant made the following notes:

> The chief librarian suggested that following a revision of the out-
> line and its presentation to the board, she would soon like to
> bring in some lay people to discuss it. She felt that certain inter-
> ested laymen would be helpful in working with the staff. A local
> priest, for example, has already expressed an interest in some of
> the objectives. The chief librarian would like to call in the mayor,
> some newspaper reporters, people working on surveys in the com-
> munity and other service people for their assistance and to gain
> their interest. I suggested that some of the school authorities
> might also be consulted because of the value of gaining their co-
> operation if certain of the objectives for the children's department
> are to be gained. I warned, however, against the inclusion of
> carping critics or outright enemies of the plan until it was more
> firmly established. Staff reaction to the work so far is excellent.
> Miss B mentioned that it had been difficult at times to put into
> writing what she wanted to say but agreed that it was worth the
> effort to have these objectives stated. The chief librarian felt that
> one of the greatest benefits of the work so far has been the im-
> provement in interstaff communication and understanding. I felt
> that a very definite improvement in the attitude of the staff to-
> wards the entire project was discernible. It was clear that all

persons involved in drawing up the objectives now felt themselves part of the plan and that those who had at first been indifferent or even hostile now seemed friendly and willing to make suggestions of their own. On the whole, progress seems satisfactory; whatever weaknesses there are in the outline can be rectified by following the next steps in the agenda.

Tenth, the committee reexamines and revises the statements of accomplishments and principles in the light of the discussion by the group as a whole. At this point, the role of the committee changes. It ceases to be essentially a synthesizing and editorial body and begins to take a more decisive and positive stand than before— adding, refining, combining, and, in some cases, eliminating ideas and statements. Much, and perhaps all, of the committee's work at this point is centered on considerations which are internal to the document and to the agency. But external sources of information may come to light which the committee will wish to take into account. Among the internal or external matters are these:

(1) The general philosophy or set of conceptions held to be valid in the kind of work in which the institution is engaged is considered. While norms or standards of this sort are usually carried within the lore of professional or organizational practice, the committee may wish to consult the basic texts and pronouncements which attempt to define its field of work.

(2) The prevailing criteria of excellence governing the accomplishment of specific objectives is reviewed. If such standards are available, the committee can use them to test the feasibility of proposed goals. In Centerville, the committee thought it ought to consider what might be required if the library were to develop collections of films, tapes, and recordings which would meet generally accepted standards. The probable cost in time and money appeared to be greater than anyone had thought it would be, a fact which was noted for later consideration by the staff.

(3) Significant evidence concerning the nature of the community and its readiness for change is weighed. The committee needs to reflect about what has been learned in the survey and also what additional ideas and facts have come to the attention of the committee members. At this point it may want to consult new sources of data or to interview additional informants.

(4) Evidence concerning the nature of the present persons served and their readiness for any change in the program is interpreted. Every institution builds its own clientele and any proposed change in the program should be considered in terms of its influence on the people now served. In considering this point the committee might reflect on the results of the survey as well as on any other general facts which have become known.

(5) Evidence concerning programs elsewhere is considered. It is always useful to know what similar institutions are doing so that present practices and possible objectives can be checked against any relevant experience in other situations. If an idea which seems good in theory has generally failed in practice, the committee should realize that it must find a distinctive new approach if it hopes to succeed. If institutions elsewhere seem able to achieve an objective satisfactorily, the committee can have some confidence in proposing it.

(6) The advice of experts is solicited. The committee may wish to consult specialists, who can often enlarge its understanding or save its time because they can help it analyze knotty or complex problems or understand the best ways of proceeding in the future.

In refining the document by consulting such sources of information as these, the committee must not use up too much time. The fascinating process of self-education which is possible at this point may be disastrous to forward motion. Throughout this phase, the committee should constantly be moving toward its final statement of a hierarchy of proposed accomplishments and a list of principles. It must decide what should be included or excluded and how priorities should be ordered. It must be both firm and venturesome. It cannot assume that it will please all the members of the larger group, though it must remain constantly aware of the collective will of the staff and of the strongly held beliefs of the leaders. It also has the responsibility to assert its own views forcefully. The ultimate lists of accomplishments and principles must be ones which the committee is prepared to support and defend at least until better alternatives are presented to it.

Eleventh, the entire group discusses the statements of goals and principles at whatever length is necessary to reach substantial agreement. The discussion at this stage is usually lively and thought-provoking. The group has a document which it has helped to develop but which it now sees with a sharpness and clarity not previously possible. In the process of deliberation, modifications, and revisions of the original statements are likely to occur, for people will always have different points of view about what future directions should be. Yet consensus must somehow be achieved, though the process of reaching agreement should not so blunt the statement that it is no longer discriminative.

In Centerville, the earlier decision to distinguish between the role of the staff and that of the board meant that three separate discussions had to be held before full agreement could be reached. The staff adopted a set of proposed accomplishments and a list of principles which were then carried to the board by the chief librarian with her own endorsement. But the board was still divided between the long-time and the new members. The principles were accepted but two of the proposed accomplishments raised issues of policy which needed resolution. The upshot was that the board agreed upon changes in wording and emphasis, saying that if they were adopted, it would approve the statement. The matter then went back to the staff which was not entirely happy with the suggestions but which eventually agreed to accept them. With that action, the new objectives were declared in effect.

Twelfth, the committee derives from the master statement the objectives which are to be sought first. While it must use its own judgment in identifying immediate goals, it can often usefully ask itself certain questions as it does so. These overlap one another but each provides a way of focusing on the task at hand.

(1) What is most important? This question implies that some aspects of the program are more significant than others for any number of reasons and that primary attention should be given to them. Important goals are usually long-range in character, so that in an initial period some preliminary or exploratory work needs to be done. In Centerville, the library staff felt that its most crucial task was to extend its service to the three quadrants of the city from which it was separated by the intersecting highways. It was thought that this problem should be met in phases. In the first year, a bookmobile should give citywide service. In the following years, as rapidly as funds permitted, storefront branches should be opened,

the schedule of the bookmobile being altered to adjust to these new forms of outreach.

(2) What is most urgent? Some problems require immediate attention. They may not be important in the long run but in the short run they certainly are. The Centerville library had had no program of positive public interpretation for a long time. The committee concluded therefore that during the first year a campaign should be mounted to use the press, radio, television, and appearances at voluntary groups to describe the resources of the library and explain what it was trying to do in the community.

(3) What logically comes first in providing a groundwork for later development? In Centerville, the chief nonusers of the library were the families of the bluecollar skilled and unskilled workers and those who were perennially unemployed or underemployed. The committee decided that the staff did not know very much about these people and that during the first year it would study them to see whether new services or approaches would make the library more useful to them.

(4) What will be most readily accepted? It had become apparent in Centerville that the library had an unusually forbidding appearance both inside and out, that there were unnecessary rigidities in the issuance of library cards and books, and that an excessively formal approach had been adopted, albeit unintentionally, by the staff as it dealt with the public. It was decided therefore to brighten up the library, to develop simplified methods of providing cards and charging books, and to foster a positive and welcoming approach toward the patrons.

(5) What will provide the best trial and error evidence to guide future development? The Centerville staff was not sure that with its limited resources it wished to provide discussion groups or other collective services to the community. Still, the library did have a boardroom and there seemed no very good reason why it should not be used more than once a month. The committee recommended therefore that the librarian most interested in group activity try to organize a book-based discussion program during the first year of operation under the new system. If it proved successful, other similar activities could be started in later years.

(6) What external demands should be satisfied? In Center-

ville, as elsewhere, the increasing enrollment in the high school and the junior college had caused heavy use of the library to be made by students. While the staff believed that these needs should be served primarily by the high school and junior college libraries and that the public library should concentrate on voluntary reading, some account had to be taken of the needs expressed by students. The committee decided that perhaps the best way to do so and still to preserve a balanced program would be to shift parts of the collection so that those volumes most frequently used by students could be collected into a single reading and study room, leaving the rest of the library more accessible to voluntary readers.

(7) What will most contribute to staff morale? The collective spirit of the librarians at Centerville had already improved substantially as a result of their common effort on the survey and on the development of objectives. Further improvement would probably occur as a by-product of the achievement of other goals, such as the brightening-up of the library. But the committee thought that even more might be done in this respect. Therefore it recommended monthly professional meetings, at each session of which somebody would be brought in from outside to discuss a topic which had some bearing on the work of the library. The chief librarian was also asked to devote some attention to studying several points of friction in the library's operational procedures to see what could be done to make them less tension-provoking.

Finally, the entire group discusses and adopts the specific objectives to be sought during the first year of the program. Here again, a full and free discussion needs to be undertaken, focused sharply upon the goals to be sought during the coming year and aimed at the achievement of consensus concerning their desirability. In Centerville, it was necessary at this point to have only two discussions, since the board proved to be ready to accept all the recommendations made by the staff.

Local circumstances of timing, organization, and preference need to be considered in the ordering of the above procedures. For example, the distinction between accomplishments and principles may be made at the initial meeting and the members of the group asked to cast their original suggestions in the dual form or, alternatively, the idea of a separate list of principles may be abandoned if it does not seem important. The committee may incorporate the eighth step into the tenth. Broad and specific goals may be worked out together in the tenth step and presented simultaneously for discussion and adoption. All such changes are matters of tactics and should be made wherever they are thought desirable. The series of steps which has been proposed suggests a general strategy, not a fixed and invariable system.

Redesigning Program

In designing or redesigning the programs by which new institutional objectives are to be achieved, the persons responsible must in some cases consider all of the components in an educational framework and in other cases focus on only one or more of them. Thus in Centerville, the establishment of bookmobile service, the planning for branches, the staff's study of nonusers, its seminar program, and the creation of a book-based discussion group required the planning and execution of separate but comprehensive educational designs. But the strengthening of the public relations program, the enhancement of the attractiveness of the physical facilities, the revision of library procedures, and the development of a different way of serving school and college readers meant that in each case only one component of the total institutional program was being dealt with.

In both comprehensive planning and that directed toward the improvement of some component, it is often necessary to consider not merely those matters which have traditionally been considered to be within the province of education but also those in which the basic expertise lies outside that field. This fact has been referred to earlier at various places but it has particular relevance in the reconstruction of programs in institutions, particularly large and complex ones. In such cases the change from current practice to a new system may require a period of specialized attention either by the staff itself if it has the necessary competence or by some outside expert. Educational matters may require the help of specialists in curriculum, materials, guidance, and evaluation. Other elements require other forms of professional help. The redesigning of a building may call for the services of an architect, the reorganization of a large staff may require an institutional analyst or personnel expert, and the shift from one system of budgeting to another may need the guidance of an accountant. In such cases, whether the basic expertise is drawn from education or from some other field, there often occurs a relatively brief subcycle of planning while present practices are analyzed and a new procedure is perfected.

For while established habits of work influence and often control the program undertaken in any situational category, they have a particularly marked influence on one provided by an institution. The service actually provided to the clients is the product of both organizational and personality factors. The definition and allocation of functions, the lines of authority and responsibility, and the assignment of duties have all been developed, shaped, and reshaped by the past record of success and failure, by the influence of individuals who have held various roles, and by the development of a network of personal relationships, some formal and visible, others unseen but powerful. A subculture has grown up and become a continuing force in the lives of those who are part of it. Any change, therefore, requires some understanding of the existing system and careful planning of the best way to bring a new educational program into being or to effect some change in an element of institutional design.

Effecting the Plan

Continuing care for effective reconstruction is also required when a new plan is put into effect. Great effort may have been taken to involve the staff, define objectives, and design changes, yet the old ways of doing things may persist because of the influence of habit, the encountering of unexpected difficulties, or the actions of people who seem to be intellectually convinced of the value of a new order but are so emotionally tied to the past that their will to change is soon eroded. Sometimes a new way of doing things is tried for a while, only to be followed by a reversion to old routines.

Both the formal and the informal social structures of institutions give them special ways of preventing such reversions. In other situational categories such reinforcements are not so readily available. A self-guided learner, a tutor or leader, or a teacher must depend upon his own will, and the people involved in a C-6 or C-10 situation have no coordinated system of authority to keep them moving forward. But the hierarchical system of institutional control exercised by its board and its administrators, establishes responsibility for carrying out new policies and requires both groups and individuals to account for their actions. Informal systems of authority can also reinforce innovation. Some individuals have urged the changes and therefore feel especially involved in the effort to carry them out, even to the extent that they believe their own careers are at stake. It is sometimes true, of course, that neither hierarchical nor personal authority is sufficient to bring a new program fully into being. If difficulties are so substantial as to require an abandonment of objectives, the systems of authority may even organize and direct the retreat to the past. But in the normal order of events, reconstruction of the program is facilitated because it can be fostered by institutional leaders who feel they have a special mandate to bring a new order into being.

Measuring and Appraising Results

The measurement or appraisal of the results of a reconstructed program are often similar to those which occur in a new or continuing one. In Centerville the success of the book-based discussion group or of the bookmobile were judged on the same bases as any other kinds of educational activity would be. In at least two respects, however, the evaluation of a revised framework of operation may be different from that of a new or continuing program.

One difference arises from the fact noted above that an objective defined in a reconstructed program may concentrate on one component of design, thus requiring a kind of procedural measurement and appraisal which is not immediately concerned with learning outcomes though presumably related to them in some fashion. In Centerville an intensified publicity campaign, a refurbishing of the building, and a revision of library procedures were proposed, the results of which could be measured in quantitative terms. For example, the success of the public relations effort could be linked to the number of newspaper stories, mentions on radio or television, and staff appearances at voluntary associations. Appraisal could be made as to whether the results achieved seemed adequate for the effort expended. However, the influence of those results on the total institutional program or on the nature or quality of learning achieved would be much harder to estimate since the objective whose accomplishment is being measured deals with but one component in a total design.

Concentration of this sort on a single aspect of the program is not unknown in new or continuing programs; for example, a teacher may grow so interested in the use of a new instructional technique that he thinks about it almost to the exclusion of any other element in the format he is using. In reconstructed programs, a narrowness of approach is common. Most components in a design have been judged to be satisfactory and are retained; only one or a few remain to be dealt with. In institutions, the differentiated specialization of the staff may lead to the separation of a component from the rest of the program of which it is theoretically an integral part. The advancement of public relations, for example, may become so much a focus of special attention that its integration with the other elements of the program are ignored or forgotten. Unless care is taken, the same thing may also happen with other components. In such cases, means finally dominate ends and the ultimate purpose of the program and the institution are forgotten.

A second distinctive attribute of the evaluation of reconstructed programs lies in the fact that it permits both measurement and appraisal to be directly related to what has occurred since the survey was made and the new objectives were formulated. Benchmarks were then established; now a new set of circumstances is in existence. How much of a change has occurred and what is the meaning of that change? In Centerville, the survey showed how many people had been served by the library in recent years, what kinds of people they were, and how many books they had borrowed. At the end of a year of special effort, the new measurements of such matters should presumably be different in significant ways from the former ones and some judgment about the success of the new effort should be based in part on such changes. This kind of comparison is occasionally possible in new programs and more frequently possible in continuing ones (particularly those which have been reconstructed at some time in the past), but it is common in those which have been carefully reconstructed.

Continuing Cycle of Change

As the period of time established for the accomplishment of the initial set of goals draws to a close and both formal and informal processes of evaluation occur, it is necessary to set up new specific objectives. Sometimes the time schedule of the program makes possible the completion of evaluation before new goals are defined. For example, the staff of a summer school can use the other nine months of the year for appraisal and planning. It is much more common, however, for the operation of a program and its revision to overlap in time, because the institution must remain in continuous operation. In such a case, the process of program review and projection must be like that customary in the analysis and planning of budgets. Forecasts for the new year need to be made before the record of the current year is complete.

The committee on objectives in Centerville had been asked to remain on a standby basis to be reactivated at the beginning of the tenth month of the new program. The group made an analysis of what had happened in the library as a result of the new orientation and then its members conducted interviews with each of their colleagues asking for an assessment of how well present objectives were being achieved and what new goals should be set for the coming year. The committee then talked over matters at length with the chief librarian. On the basis of this information, a report was prepared and submitted to the staff, recommending that all major objectives be retained, that some specific goals be continued unchanged, that others be dropped or revised, and that new ones be added. The committee statement, revised by discussions with the staff, the chief librarian, and the board, was declared in effect for the second year. Thus the cycle of program development continued.

Centerville may have been unusual in maintaining this system of recurrent and independent program review on an all-institutional basis. Some institutions never look back at their reconstructed statement of objectives and others reexamine them only occasionally on a desultory basis. More frequently, perhaps, the review is continued but it is attached to the budget-making process, a practice which helps establish program planning on a recurrent systematic basis and which ties it realistically to the allocation of resources. But in practice the linkage between program planning and money allocation sometimes leads to disadvantages. It elevates one important component of design to a paramount position, making it so much the arbiter of all the others that they cannot be viewed independently. The competition for money may lead to a spirit of divisiveness rather than collaboration among the staff and help turn senior administrators into judges and arbitrators rather than creative program leaders. But while these difficulties often appear in practice, they are not inherent in the basic theory of budgeting, particularly that based on the measurement of performance.

As the cycle of program review and planning continues year after year, the continuity of development and adjustment to changing needs and times can be maintained. The major effort at reconstruction which the institution once made recedes into the background not merely because of the attrition of time but also because the accomplishment of new objectives makes old ways of work obsolete. This fact indicates the success, not the failure, of the major effort to reform. But that very success may eventually lead to the need for another fundamental reconstruction. After a few years, despite a careful annual revision, thought-resisting rigidities and orthodoxies may again grow dominant, the external environment may change in fundamental ways, the institution may achieve its existing aims and require new ones, or control may pass into new hands. The analysis and direction-setting possible in an annual review become insufficient to chart the course for the future. When that happens, a reconstruction of the program seems necessary and a major new cycle needs to begin.

Reconstructing Complex Institutions

The reconstruction of a large, complex, and geographically dispersed institution is always more difficult than that of a relatively simple one, such as the Centerville Public Library. Size and geographic distance, both separately or in combination, create problems of communication and decision making. Examples of such institutions are a citywide public school system; a national voluntary association with local, state, and regional chapters; and a complex, multifunctional university extension division. The difficulties presented in such situations usually require modification to be on a gradualist basis, first one component being changed, then another. If root and branch reform is necessary, outside surveyors are called in. They collaborate with the internal administrative and collective power systems as much as seems appropriate or possible, but the recommendations produced come essentially from outside the institution.

If program reconstruction is to follow the general pattern suggested in this chapter, some schedule of phasing is necessary. Each of the logically separable parts of the institution is usually treated as a unit with the administrators of the component parts constituting a special supraunit of authority. Thus a statewide agricultural extension service might begin the revision process by considering the total program undertaken by the administrative and supervisory staff at the university; then a reconstruction of activities might occur in a few pilot counties; and eventuallly a pattern of program analysis and development for every county staff might be set up on a five-year cycle which would involve the whole service in a recurrent pattern of reconstruction. The result would be a double cycle of program development with minor revisions occurring annually and major ones each half-decade.

The reason for identifying and working with relatively small units is that the number of people directly related to one another in a reconstruction effort of the sort contemplated here should never grow so large that the possibility of full collaboration is lost. The problems which lead to a need for complete redesigning of a program usually involve all who are concerned with it and no solutions can be wholly satisfactory which do not include them in the processes of deliberation and decision making. An effort to involve a hundred people in simultaneous face to face discussion and planning on an extended basis will lead to confusion, frustration, and a worsening of the problems for which a solution is sought.

No general system of reconstruction can be recommended for all large complex agencies; a special pattern must be devised for each one in terms of the requirements of its situation. Two organizations may have essentially the same overall structure and yet differ greatly in important ways. For example, it may be crucial to be aware of the major seat of authority for the program. If the branches or other subunits carry out the will of a central office, the process of reconstruction should probably begin at the center. However, if the central office serves chiefly as a facilitating unit to encourage and support the work of the branches, the major reconstruction should probably begin (perhaps on a pilot basis) in the units which provide the basic service.

Conclusion

This chapter has been so centrally concerned with institutions that perhaps at its end the focus of attention should again be broadened to include the other situational categories. In each of them, a complete reconstruction of program is a familiar phenomenon. Many men and women have grown dissatisfied with their independent study programs and have created new designs for learning which are drastically different from those to which they were accustomed. Tutors, groups, teachers, program committees, coordinative assemblies, and mass communicators all feel an occasional need to reconsider and reorient their educational activities. In doing so, each follows a pattern of action which is strongly influenced by its category and, indeed, its situation, but the fundamentals of all such patterns remain basically the same as they do in the creation of new programs or in the continuing revision of existing ones.

CHAPTER VII

The System
in Perspective

He who lets the world or his own portion of it, choose his plan of life for him has no need of any other faculty than the apelike one of imitation. He who chooses his plan for himself employs all his faculties. He must use observation to see, reasoning and judgment to foresee, activity to gather materials for decision, discrimination to decide, and when he has decided, firmness and self-control to hold to his deliberate decision.

John Stuart Mill, *On Liberty*

The skeletal form of a system has now been exposed and, by the use of illustrations and cases, has been shown to provide a structure which gives shape to seemingly varied programs of adult education. Now it is appropriate to place this system within the historical and analytical perspective suggested in Chapter One.

Andragogy and Pedagogy

Is education a single fundamental human process or are the learning activities of men and women essentially different from those of boys and girls? The whole content of this book reinforces the first alternative. If there were a separate science of andragogy, as many have argued, it would have to be based, at least at present, on the credos and systems summarized in Chapter One. A review of these credos shows that each has been argued by at least some modern leaders of childhood education. As far as systems are concerned, both Dewey and Tyler concentrated on the work of schools for the young, but both were also fully aware of adult education and intended to suggest processes which would be universal in their application. Community development and the systems evolved from Lewin's theories were first applied to the learning activities of adults but have subsequently been found to have relevance to those of children. Systems analysis is a generalized conception which has been adopted simultaneously by educational institutions at both age levels. Schools and colleges can as readily misapply systems useful for public relations, welfare, service, recreation, and other functions as can the agencies of adult education. And the system advanced in this book, though based on the examination of how men and women learn, has been reinforced at almost every point by that great body of research on the education of children which has been produced in the present century. If this debt is not clear in the book itself, the Bibliographic Essay amply demonstrates it.

Even one who turns away from theory and looks only at specific processes and forms of education notes a marked parallelism between those intended for adults and those intended for young people, partly because there has been much borrowing back and forth between institutions at the two levels. Literacy classes, evening schools and colleges, and university extension courses and centers all

bear clear evidence of the influence of childhood and youth education, and museums and public libraries are prone to count as educational only those activities which resemble the work of schools.
Borrowing in the reverse direction is also well established. Many of
the practices now regarded as innovative in the teaching of children
and youth originated in adult education or were simultaneously
evolved at both levels. Among them are the emphases on independent study and discussion, group dynamics and encounter sessions,
work experience credit, and the creation of new and less formal
institutional settings for learning. In some cities, demonstration
secondary schools are not contained within their own buildings but
are flexible arrangements in which learning occurs in a variety of
community settings; they look very much like patterns of institutionally dispersed adult education which have been common for
more than a hundred years.

   If pedagogy and andragogy are distinguishable, it is not
because they are essentially different from one another but because
they represent the working out of the same fundamental processes
at different stages of life. Aristotle and others have argued that
children are superior to adults in mastering exact knowledge and
that adults are superior to children in learning subtle and complex
relationships. Other differences have been suggested by theorists and
have been investigated by research workers. While they are all
matters of emphasis, not absolute distinctions, they do influence the
conduct of education in countless ways and, in particular instances,
usually determine the degree of success achieved.

   It seems reasonable to hope therefore that the proposed system, though based on the learning activities of men and women, also
has relevance for those of boys and girls. The definition of adult
education with which Chapter Two begins could easily be rephrased
to apply to young people or indeed to all mankind, but, if so, it
would encompass the full range of educative experiences in the
earlier as well as in the later years of life. Attention could not be
centered (as it so largely is) on the classroom setting of the school,
college, or university, with only occasional glances at all the other
learning and teaching activities undertaken in individual, group, or
institutional settings. Children study independently; they have
tutors; they form study groups and clubs; they engage in committee-

planned activities; their clubs work together for common ends; many local, state, and national institutions serve their educational needs; these institutions often collaborate with one another; and children and youth benefit from the purposeful teachings of the mass media. In all such settings, the model of planning and analysis (with its objectives, its format elements, its adjustments, and its evaluation) seems capable of application to the learning activities of children. But if the system is used in childhood and youth education for either analysis or planning, it must be applied in ways which are appropriate to the immaturity of the learners, even as, in other situations, the educator of adults who adopts a system devised for children has to adjust it to fit the requirements of men and women.

Comparison Among Systems

No adequate comparison can yet be made between the proposed system and those already avowed and practiced. Surface resemblances and differences are clear enough, but deeper study would require an analysis not merely of the processes but also of their underlying assumptions, a task which would be tediously time-consuming. It would also be suspect if attempted here, for the framer of one system can never be wholly objective in describing others. (For an illustration of this point, note Dewey's analysis of the views of his opponents.) Most important, however, comparisons should be based on practice as well as on theory, and the system here proposed has not yet been widely used.

However, all systems, including this one, have some characteristics in common. (1) No system can itself automatically guarantee success. Its ultimate nature is to establish a series of choice points, each of which requires both an analysis of a complex situation and a selection among alternative courses of action. The outcome of any particular program therefore depends in large measure upon the wisdom and competence of the person making the choices. (2) Skill in the use of a system requires practice which is critically examined. A knowledge of the nature of a model is merely the beginning of competence in its use. Education takes place in complex situations where there is difficulty in perceiving all the different components and the ways in which they mesh together. Lengthy, varied, and introspectively examined experience is the only basis for the mastery of any system. (3) Since the practice of education is always an art, every learner or teacher who uses a system must consciously develop his distinctive style of application. If he subordinates himself to what he regards as immutable laws and treats as ultimate authority the dicta of those who formulated them, the result is a classicism in which form is paramount, not life itself. However willing he may be to let himself be mastered by a system, he can never do so; his own personality influences its use at every point. (4) Every system which is enduringly successful must be capable of theoretical change or amplification as it is applied. If it is not improved and modified with use, it becomes fossilized.

Adult education will emerge as a full-fledged field only when its master practitioners achieve the ability to apply alternative processes, choosing, in each case, the one which best meets the requirements of the situation. Professionalizing occupations seem to move through successive phases in which early credos are followed by later dogmatic systems; but those who practice a vocation achieve maturity only when they are able to use many different ways of going about their work. Earlier, medicine was dominated by beliefs about blood-letting, purging, or the prescription of nostrums, and then by such theoretical approaches as allopathy or homeopathy, but the modern physician does not let his practice be controlled by any single remedy or system. He determines his diagnosis, remediation, and preventive treatment by the nature of each patient. If adult education is to move toward professionalization, its practitioners must follow a similar approach.

The system proposed in this book allows marked flexibility to anyone who uses it, but its very breadth and comprehensiveness may make some people regard it as too elaborate for easy and ready use. If so, they may prefer to devise their own ways of work or, alternatively, to use any credo or system which appears most useful for each of the situations with which they deal. In a remedial program, an educator may adapt for a mature audience a course of instruction usually intended for children. In human relations training, he may use change theory. In the redirection of urban life, he may use community development. Whatever the course of action (a comprehensive system or of any of a variety of specific models), successful program design is enhanced if the learner or the educator understands the need for proficient use of the various approaches chosen.

The Future

The need for a large number of people to build professional careers in adult education has been created by the astonishingly rapid spread of participation in learning by men and women throughout the world. Until fairly recently it was taken for granted that most people were condemned by their own inability or apathy to lead lives little better than those of savages, in which, said Thomas Hobbes, there are "no arts, no letters, no society, and, which is worst of all, continual fear and danger of violent death; and the life of man, solitary, poor, nasty, brutish, and short."[1] The egalitarian movement designed to carry the benefits of culture to all men, which had its slow beginnings after the development of printing, has constantly accelerated. The idea that education should enrich life throughout its whole duration is not new, but only in this century has it been seriously believed that such a life was possible for most people and perhaps eventually for all mankind. This ideal no longer seems impossible to achieve because so many men and women already take part in educational activities which they find rewarding. When the opportunity to participate has broadened to include everyone, the need for educators who can plan and conduct effective programs will be enormous.

Such a result, however easy to conceptualize, will not be readily achieved. The average span of adulthood in a nation is from thirty to fifty-five years, depending on its level of advancement. In each of these years, almost everyone alive would find it possible to realize some of his potential through education, thereby making his life more rewarding than it would be otherwise. But even the most highly developed societies are still far from reaching this ideal of universal involvement, and the less well developed ones are even further behind. Meanwhile many ills of society can be remedied only by widespread or universal education, and it takes disciplined intelligence of a very high order to devise the programs required to deal with them. In the future, even more than in the past, the meeting of needs and the satisfaction of desires will require creativeness, the expenditure of great individual and social effort, and the use of sophisticated thought about the design of education.

---

[1] *Leviathan,* Part I, Chapter 13.

Glossary

This glossary will be presented in two forms. The first is a summary of the book's content in which key terms (which are italicized when first mentioned) are in context. The second is a listing and definition of the same terms in alphabetical order. To avoid excessive elaboration, only one form of a word is given, the variant forms being implied. Thus the term *measurement* is given but not such terms as *measure* (as a noun or a verb), *measured,* or *measuring*. Some words (such as *objective, resource,* or *schedule*) which have many general meanings are defined only as used in educational terminology. The definitions are not intended to reflect or to provide standard meanings but to indicate how terms are used in this book.

226

Adult education has now reached the stage in which its leaders are much concerned with clarifying terms and establishing a proper relationship among them. It is hoped that this glossary will be useful in advancing this effort to achieve precision.

Summary

Adult education (and perhaps all *education*) is considered to be a *cooperative* (not an *operative*) art designed to increase *skill* (or *ability*), *knowledge* (or *information*), or *sensitiveness*. As a *process*, it becomes operationalized when some segment of human experience which is lived within a complex personal or social *milieu* (or *setting*) is separated out for examination by a *learner*, an *educator*, or an *analyst*. This segment is called a *situation*. Situations are always unique, but they can be classified into eleven *categories* (here designated numerically from C-1 to C-11). These categories may be broadly divided into those which occur on an *individual*, a *group*, an *institutional*, or a *mass* basis. Two basic institutional forms are identified, the *association* and the *organization*.

In a situation, an educational *activity* may be planned but not come to fruition, or it may actually occur either by chance or by intent. Both planning and analysis usually occur in terms of a time *period* (*act*, *episode*, *series* of episodes, or *aggregate* of simultaneous episodes) or a combination of such periods. The planning or analysis requires two reciprocal actions, which, taken together, make up the total *system* suggested here. The first one of these actions is the determination of the category in which the situation falls. The second action is the application to this situation of a *framework* (or *model*) of planning or analysis which includes a number of interrelated *components* of which the chief groups are:

(a) The *objectives* (or *aims*, *ends*, *goals*, or *purposes*). The factors which determine objectives are the milieu, the nature of the learners, the *aspirations*, the *motives*, the *content*, and the framework itself. Objectives may be stated either as *accomplishments* or as *principles*.

(b) The *elements* which combine together into an educational *format*. These elements include *resources*, *leaders*, *methods* (or *techniques*), *schedule*, *sequence*, *social reinforcement*, *individualiza-*

tion, roles and *relationships, criteria of evaluation,* and *clarity of design.*

(c) The *adjustments* required in fitting the format into the milieu. These adjustments include *guidance,* introduction of the program into the *life style* of the participants, *finance,* and *interpretation.*

(d) The *measurement* and *appraisal* of results which, taken together, are called *evaluation.*

The actual application of this framework to a situation, often as a result of a *need* or an *interest,* results in a *design* (or *program*) which takes account of all the components which are relevant to the situational category involved. The process of application is always unique to the situation because the components are not related to one another in any invariable order. A design may begin with any of them and proceed in any fashion. In both planning and analysis, however, it is often useful to review the components as they occur logically in a time-flow, requiring the use of several *decision-points* from the time when a possible educational activity is identified until its results are evaluated.

If there is a series of episodes, the experience gained in each should be used to improve the subsequent ones in a steady process of *revision* of the design. In addition, a complete *reconstruction* of it may sometimes be necessary. This latter process can be guided by any of a number of *strategies* but the one here described and illustrated lays heavy emphasis on the making of a *survey* and the careful and collaborative selection of objectives.

The proposed system is compared with a number of other approaches to process which have evolved during the recent history of organized *adult* education. Some of these are simple *credos.* Others are complex systems based on the thought of John Dewey, Ralph W. Tyler, and Kurt Lewin. Lewin's followers have devised two systems, *sensitivity training* and *change theory.* Other complex approaches are those based on *community development* and on *systems analysis.* In some cases, *functions* related to but different from adult education have been the source for systems which have been misapplied to it; among such functions are *public relations, service, recreation, aesthetic appreciation, fraternization, welfare,* and *therapy.*

ability See *skill.*

accomplishment A discernible achievement, here used to indicate one of the two major ways of stating objectives, the other being *principle.*

act A specific and relatively brief learning or teaching event.

activity A specific educational action or succession of actions occurring in a situation.

adjustment A way of harmonizing an educational format with the milieu in which it is to occur or with the lives of the learners or educators involved; usually requires some change in either the format or the milieu.

adult A person (man or women) who has achieved full physical development and who expects to have the right to participate as a responsible homemaker, worker, and member of society.

adult education The process by which men and women (alone, in groups, or in institutional settings) seek to improve themselves or their society by increasing their skill, their knowledge, or their sensitiveness. Any process by which individuals, groups, or institutions try to help men and women improve in these ways.

aggregate A cluster of educational activities (either related or unrelated to one another) occurring in the same span of time in the life of an individual, a group, or an institution.

aim See *objective.*

analyst One who tries to understand the nature of an educational activity by examining its parts or basic principles. An analyst may be a learner, an educator, or an independent observer. The term is most frequently used here to signify the observer.

appraisal A subjective judgment of how well educational objectives have been achieved, often based in part on the results of measurement and akin to measurement as a part of evaluation.

aspiration A desired perfection or excellence based on an ideal. It can exist in the absence of a plan of activity or it can establish the broad value inherent in an objective.

association A structured body of members who join together, more or less freely, because of a shared interest, activity, or purpose, and who, by the act of joining, assume the same basic powers and responsibilities held by other members. The collective membership elects its officers, giving them temporary authority. An association usually has its own members as its beneficiaries. It is distinguished from a group largely by size and complexity and may, in fact, be a constellation of groups.

category　A set of similar situations in which educational activities occur.

change theory　A system of individual, group, institutional, or community improvement. It involves a relationship in which a change agent enters into a helping role with a client or client system and by various means (some of them educational) seeks to alter performance and stabilize it at a new level.

clarity of design　The degree of understanding of an activity by those taking part in it or analyzing it.

community development　Any organized effort by which those who share a defined territorial area as a base for carrying out a major share of their activities can work collectively to try to solve a common problem.

component　An essential constituent part of the educational framework; includes objectives, elements of the format, adjustments, and measurement and appraisal of results.

content　Anything taught or learned in an educational activity, including knowledge, skill, or sensitiveness.

cooperative art　A system of principles and methods used to create a product or a performance when such an outcome is achieved by guiding and directing a natural entity or process. See also *operative art*.

credo　A statement of belief which is not part of any larger system of ideas or conceptions.

criteria of evaluation　Standards, rules, or tests used for measurement and on which an appraisal can be based.

decision-point　One of the places in the application of a system at which a program planner or analyst uses his judgment in creating a design.

design　The plan developed to guide educational activity in a situation or the plan which can be inferred by an analyst of that activity. Synonym: *program*.

education   The process by which human beings (alone, in groups, or in institutional settings) seek to improve themselves or their society by increasing their skill, their knowledge, or their sensitiveness. Any process by which individuals, groups, or institutions try to help human beings improve in these ways.

educator   One who seeks to improve other individuals or society by increasing their skill, their knowledge, or their sensitiveness. The term implies that the educator exerts purposeful effort to achieve such objectives though the people influenced may or may not intend to achieve them.

element   An essential and separately definable part of an educational format.

end   See *objective.*

episode   A related succession of acts making up a coherent educational whole.

esthetic appreciation   The enjoyment of the beautiful in any of its varied forms.

evaluation   The determination of the extent to which an educational objective has been accomplished. Evaluation includes the two closely related processes of measurement and appraisal.

finance   The direct and indirect cost of an educational activity.

format   The pattern of interrelated elements used in an educational design as an immediate and direct way of achieving objectives.

framework   The fundamental theoretical construct used in a situation to plan or analyze an educational design. Synonym: *model.*

fraternization   Association with other people in a brotherly or congenial way.

function   A generalized form of human activity differentiated from others by the intended result. Education, recreation, welfare, and therapy are distinguishable human functions.

goal   See *objective.*

group   A collection of human beings which has a common purpose and among whom interaction occurs.

guidance   The direction, advice, or assistance which one individual provides to another, usually by reason of the former's greater experience or knowledge. Often used here specifically to mean the special assistance given to those who are deciding whether or not to undertake a given educational activity or who need help in adjusting it to its milieu.

individual   A single human being.

individualization   The adaptation of a process to meet the requirements of each of the persons which it is intended to serve.

information   See *knowledge.*

institution   A comparatively stable, formally, and often intricately, structured body of persons which carries out common purposes or advances common causes and whose members share a standardized and complex system of habits, attitudes, and material facilities. Institutions tend to be either associations or organizations, though each of these two forms usually incorporates certain of the elements of the other.

interest   A feeling of curiosity, fascination, or absorption in an object or activity often leading to experiences with it which give rise to satisfaction and enjoyment.

interpretation   The clarification of meaning, often with the intent of winning acceptance. Usually used here to signify the interpretation of an educational activity to some person or public external to it.

knowledge   A cognitive or intellective mental component acquired and retained through education or experience. Here taken to be one of the three major kinds of interrelated educational accomplishments, the others being sensitiveness and skill. Synonym: *information.*

leader   A person who guides or directs another or others toward the achievement of objectives. Here usually used to refer to a person who exercises his influence because of his mastery of either content or process, but who may also be chosen because of his personality or status.

learner   One who increases his skill, his knowledge, or his sensitiveness. This result may be brought about as a result of purposefully educational effort on his part, purposefully educational effort on the part of an educator, or as a by-product of a random activity or one designed to achieve essentially noneducational purposes.

life style   The general pattern of behavior of an individual, a group, or some other body of people.

mass   A large number of persons who share an educational experience but who are so numerous or so dispersed that the individuals and groups included can be treated only in general and nonspecific ways.

measurement   The determination by objective means of the extent to which learners have achieved the criteria of evaluation. Closely related to appraisal as part of evaluation.

method   An established and systematic way of learning or teaching. Examples are: reading, discussion, or laboratory work. Synonym: *technique.*

milieu   Broadly speaking, the total social and physical environment surrounding a situation at a given time and place. More specifically (and with defining adjectives), some set of circumstances which is related to the situation in a meaningful way, for instance the institutional milieu (the pattern of structure and action in the institution of which the situation is a part) or the social milieu (the pattern of culture in which the situation occurs). Synonym: *setting.*

model   See *framework.*

motive   An inciting cause which helps to determine an individual's choice of an objective and his behavior in seeking it. A motive may be comprehended or unconscious.

need   A condition or situation in which something necessary or desirable is required or wanted. Often used to express the deficiencies of an individual or some category of people either generally or in some set of circumstances. A need may be perceived by the person or persons possessing it (when it may be called a felt need) or by some observer (when it may be called an ascribed need).

objective   An intended result of an educational activity or a guiding policy which is intended to achieve such a result. Objectives may be stated either as desired accomplishments or as principles. An objective may be known prior to the activity, emerge while it is occurring, or be perceived subsequently. Synonyms: *aim, end, goal,* and *purpose.*

operative art   A system of principles and methods used to create a product or a performance when such an outcome is controlled by the person using the system. Compare *cooperative art.*

organization   A body of people who work together to achieve a common purpose and whose internal structure is characterized by a hierarchical flow of authority and responsibility from the top downward with relatively permanent (rather than periodically rotating) occupants of the seats of power who, when replaced, are ordinarily designated from above rather than from below. Organizations ordinarily exist to benefit their owners, a defined clientele outside their own membership, or the public at large.

period   An interval chosen by an educator, a learner, or an analyst as a time boundary for the planning or analysis of an educational activity.

principle   A basic policy or mode of action. Here used to indicate one of the two major ways of stating objectives, the other being *accomplishment.*

process   A series of related actions undertaken to bring about an educational result.

program   See *design.*

public relations   The methods or activities employed to promote a favorable relationship with the general population or with some part or parts of it.

purpose   See *objective.*

reconstruction   A fundamental rethinking and restructuring of a design.

recreation   A pleasurable or diverting activity of either mind or body.

relationship   The formal or informal interaction of two or more people. See also *role.*

resource   Any object, person, or other aspect of the environment which can be used for support or help in an educational activity.

revision A change or modification of a design. Here used chiefly to mean the normal process of altering the design of an episode when it is repeated. Such alteration usually arises from the appraisal of past accomplishment. Contrasted with reconstruction.

role The characteristic behavior expected of an individual in a situation as perceived by himself or by others. The definition of roles and the establishment of relationships are here considered two aspects of the same element in the format of an educational program.

schedule The timetable of an educational activity.

sensitiveness A capacity to feel or perceive, to make discriminations, or to have insight into some aspect of life, often accompanied by some ethical value. Here taken to be one of the three major kinds of interrelated educational accomplishments, the others being knowledge and skill.

sensitivity training An effort to deepen the awareness of individuals concerning their own natures and their relationships with other people, usually by the use of a group process in which the members simultaneously or intermittently interact with one another and analyze that interaction.

sequence The order in which content is presented in an educational activity.

series A succession of related educational episodes.

service The provision of assistance or benefit to another or others.

setting See *milieu*.

situation The specific and unique combination of circumstances in which an educational activity occurs.

skill The capacity to perform some mental or physical act, whether it be easy and simple or hard and complex. Here taken to be one of the three major kinds of interrelated educational accomplishments, the others being knowledge and sensitiveness. Synonym: *ability*.

social reinforcement The facilitation of the educational process in a collective activity by the creation or maintenance of an emotional tone which may be characterized either by positive and supportive feeling or by a sense of challenge.

strategy A plan of maneuvers designed to bring about a complex result. Here given the specific meaning of a way of achieving the reconstruction of an institutional program.

survey A comprehensive examination of a situation.

system A body of interdependent factors which form a collective entity. Here most commonly used in two senses: as the way of planning or analyzing educational designs proposed in this book, or as the way of achieving the same end proposed by someone else.

systems analysis The conceptualization of a general process, usually in a diagram, by which the making of judgments and the taking of actions can be put into an orderly and established flow of work.

technique See *method*.

therapy The treatment of illness or disability.

welfare The provision of help or comfort for people who have been deprived of the goods or services thought to be essential in the society in which they live.

Bibliographic Essay

The literature of adult education is enormous. In 1971, the Library of Adult Education at Syracuse University, which owns the largest American collection of materials, had approximately a half million publications and maintained a file of about 700 periodicals and newsletters. As with any rapidly expanding field of inquiry, much of this material has been issued in the form of pamphlets, reports, occasional papers, doctoral theses (of which there are about one thousand, almost all produced in the United States), and other fugitive sources. Much of this literature focuses on the work in some particular format (such as the lecture, the discussion group, or the conference), institution (such as the public library, the community college, or the labor union), or goal-defined area (such as vocational education, world affairs education, or family life education). Also a very great deal of the literature deals with the shadowy zones between adult educational practice and such other fields of inquiry or application as anthropology, economics, history, philosophy, psychology, social work, librarianship, social psychology, sociology, human development, and physiology.

The purposes of this bibliographic essay are to indicate the chief published sources out of which the system presented in this book has been developed, to supplement the rather general statements of the book by indicating where fuller information on various topics may be found, particularly the detailed practices and techniques required in designing programs, and to illustrate various points of view suggested but not fully developed in the book. The bibliography is intended for use, not for comprehensiveness of listing. After an opening section designed for those who seek a general understanding of the field of adult education, attention is devoted entirely to the literature concerned with process. Some general references on this subject are given; after that, the structure of the book is followed to give a brief listing of works which are relevant to each of the topics dealt with. Wherever possible, widely available resources are suggested in preference to those which are obscure or hard to locate. Virtually all of the references cited are in English and there is an especially heavy reliance on American sources and practices.

After the identity of various institutions and journals has been established later in the essay, they will be referred to by the following abbreviations:

> AAAE—American Association for Adult Education
> AE—*Adult Education,* a journal published by the Adult Education Association of the United States
> AEA—Adult Education Association of the United States
> AE[B]—*Adult Education* [British], a journal published by the National Institute of Adult Education (England and Wales)
> AL—*Adult Leadership,* a journal published by the Adult Education Association of the United States

CSLEA—Center for the Study of Liberal Education for Adults
JAE—*Journal of Adult Education,* a journal published by the American Association for Adult Education
JCE—*Journal of Cooperative Extension,* published by Extension Journal, Inc.
NSSE—National Society for the Study of Education

The Field

The basic concept of adult education is an ancient one, as old as civilization itself, and the term has often been used in the past. For example, W. H. Hudson published *History of Adult Education* in England in 1851; it was reissued by the Woburn Press of London in 1969. In *American Ideas about Adult Education, 1710–1951* (Bureau of Publications, Teachers College, Columbia University, New York, 1959), C. Hartley Grattan assembled a number of early writings. But the concept and the term first came fully into focus in the *Final Report* of the Adult Education Committee of the British Ministry of Reconstruction issued in London in 1919. While this original document is now rare, essential portions of it, with an interpretive preface by R. D. Waller, were issued in 1956 in England, Canada, and the United States (where it was published by Association Press, New York) under the title *A Design for Democracy.*

Many monographic accounts of particular episodes of adult education exist, but there are few generalized histories, and no adequate comprehensive account has been published. The best general essay on the subject is *In Quest of Knowledge* by C. Hartley Grattan (Association Press, New York, 1955). The best account of the American experience is *The Adult Education Movement in the United States by* Malcolm Knowles (Holt, Rinehart, and Winston, New York, 1962). A generalized summary and interpretation is given in "An Overview and History of the Field" published in two issues of the journal *Adult Education, 7, 8* (Summer 1957 and Autumn 1957). The English literature is richer than the American in both monographic and general histories. The most comprehensive general account is provided by the second edition of *A History of Adult Education in Great Britain* by Thomas Kelly (Liverpool University Press, Liverpool, 1970). Another informative treatment

of the subject is J. F. C. Harrison's book *Learning and Living,
1790–1960* (Routledge and Kegan Paul, London, 1961).

Comprehensive descriptions of the field began to appear in
England in the 1920s and in the United States in the 1930s, following the substantial public attention devoted in both countries to the
British Ministry of Reconstruction Report. At present, the best
one-volume source of information on American programs is the
Handbook of Adult Education edited by Robert M. Smith, George
F. Aker, and J. R. Kidd (Macmillan, New York, 1970). Earlier
editions, undertaken by various editors and publishers, were issued
in 1936, 1950, and 1960. The first one-volume treatment by a single
author was Lyman Bryson's *Adult Education* (American Book,
New York, 1936). The major subsequent one-volume works dealing
with American practice have been

PAUL H. SHEATS, CLARENCE D. JAYNE, AND RALPH B. SPENCE,
Adult Education, the Community Approach (Holt,
Rinehart, and Winston, New York, 1953)

HOMER KEMPFER, *Adult Education* (McGraw-Hill, New York,
1955)

JOHN WALKER POWELL, *Learning Comes of Age* (Association
Press, New York, 1956)

COOLIE VERNER AND ALAN BOOTH, *Adult Education* (Center
for Applied Research in Education, New York, 1964)

ROGER AXFORD, *Adult Education: The Open Door* (Intext,
New York, 1969)

Comparative studies dealing with practice in various countries have
been written by Robert Peers in *Adult Education: A Comparative
Study* (Humanities Press, New York, 1959) and by Mary Ulich in
Patterns of Adult Education (Pageant Press, New York, 1965). The
most recent comprehensive book on English practice is *Adult Education in England and Wales* by John Lowe (Michael Joseph,
London, 1970). Many descriptions of the programs in other countries are also available in English.

Many authors have tried to assess the essential nature of the
field of adult education. Two excellent examples of such efforts are:
Malcolm Knowles, "What Do We Know about the Field of Adult
Education?" in *Adult Education, 14* (Winter 1964); and Jack

London and Robert Wenkert, "American Adult Education: An Approach to a Definition of the Field" in *Adult Leadership, 13* (December 1964).

The first major American periodical in the field was the *Journal of Adult Education,* issued by the American Association for Adult Education beginning in 1929. Two other peroidicals, the *Adult Education Journal* and the *Adult Education Bulletin,* grew out of the *Journal* and flourished in the 1940s. Both were supplanted in 1951, when the Adult Education Association of the United States was formed. Since then, the two major American journals have been *Adult Education* and *Adult Leadership,* both issued by the AEA. During the 1950s and 1960s, the Center for the Study of Liberal Education for Adults issued many reports. This publication program has now been incorporated into that of Syracuse University, which issues various periodicals and studies. The annual yearbooks for the National Society for the Study of Education sometimes deal with various aspects of adult education. Many journals or series of publications are focused chiefly or entirely on the programs of specific institutions; thus the *Extension Service Review* deals with the work of the Cooperative Extension Service, as does the *Journal of Cooperative Extension* (now the *Journal of Extension*).

Many other countries also have adult educational periodicals. The leading journal in Great Britain, for example, is *Adult Education,* which is here distinguished from its American counterpart by being referred to as *Adult Education* [British]. UNESCO has issued many publications in the field and has had two journals, *Fundamental and Adult Education* and *International Journal of Adult and Youth Education.* The major international publication in the field is now *Convergence,* which is published in Canada with articles or abstracts in four languages. An *International Yearbook of Adult Education,* published in Germany, was established in 1969.

Andragogy

From the beginning of the major American interest in adult education in the 1920s, attention has been given to the difference between it and the education of young people. Various approaches to the subject have been taken, the most frequent distinguishing between the characteristics of young and adult learners. See, for example, Robert Boyd, "A Psychological Definition of Adult Education," AL, *13* (November, 1966); and Jane C. Zahn, "Differences Between Adults and Youth Affecting Learning," AE, *17* (Winter, 1967). Other distinctions have arisen from an effort to distinguish between maturity and immaturity; see, for example, Edgar Z. Friedenberg, "The Mature Attitude," AL, *5* (February, 1957). Still other distinctions have been made on the difference between the goals of children and those of adults, on methods or institutions of instruction, on the directness of relevance of the learning to the affairs of life, on the distinction between full-time and part-time study, on the degree and kind of motivation, and on the extent to which study is voluntary.

The difference between the two broad ages of learning is symbolized in continental and European practice and in that of French-speaking Canada by using the term *andragogy* or one of its variant forms to contrast with the more familiar term *pedagogy*. The first term is taken to indicate the practice of adult education, the theory of adult education, or both. The major current exponent of the term is Dusan Savicevic, Professor of Education at the University of Belgrade. (Yugoslavia is the only European country which offers the doctorate in adult education.) Savicevic insists that andragogy can only be used to designate "the discipline which studies the adult education process." He also calls it "the science of adult education." (Dusan Savicevic, *The System of Adult Education in Yugoslavia,* Syracuse University Publications Program in Continuing Education, Syracuse, N.Y., 1969)

An excellent survey of the history and usages of the term has been prepared by G. van Enckevort of The Netherlands. His paper, entitled "Andragology: A New Science," is scheduled for publication in a new Irish journal of adult education. He believes that the word was first coined by a German educator, Alexander Kapp, in 1833, but says it was also invented (in variant forms) by other German, Swiss, and Venezuelan authors. The two best-known works in German on the subject are Heinrich Hanselmann, *Andragogik,* (Rotapfel, Zurich, 1961); and Franz Pöggeler, *Einführung in die Andragogik,* (Düsseldorf, 1957). The major Yugoslav statement on the subject is *Osnovi Andragogije* (Zavod Za Ixdavanje Udzbenika, Sarajevo, 1966). This work, *Bases of Andragogy*, is written in Serbo-Croatian, but has a brief and inadequate English summary.

Various American and British writers have attempted without great success to establish *andragogy* as a term in English. The best statement for Great Britain is J. A. Simpson, "Andragogy," AE [B], *37* (November, 1964). The term has also been adopted by Malcolm S. Knowles, whose first statement of it was in "Androgogy, Not Pedagogy!" AL, *16* (April, 1968). He also made it a central theme in his book *The Modern Practice of Adult Education* (Association Press, New York, 1970).

In Europe the conception of a lifelong education which deals with learning at every age has been developed in terms of what is called (in English rather awkwardly) permanent education. The central idea is that there should be a harmonious working-out of a plan of life in which each age would be devoted to the acquisition of that knowledge, skill, or understanding which can best be learned then. The most comprehensive treatment of this subject is a symposium written by authors from many countries and entitled *Permanent Education* (Council of Europe, Strasbourg, 1970).

Program Development: General

The system of program design suggested in the present work is based on the belief that the education of adults is but one part of the whole theory and practice of education. That part can be differentiated from the others—infant, child, adolescent, and immediate-post-adolescent education—by all the distinctions which have been used to separate andragogy from pedagogy, but learning and teaching seem to most to be essentially the same processes however young or old the learners may be. As noted in the text, additional support for this position would be produced if the educators of infants, children, and youth found the model here proposed to be useful for their purposes.

A more immediate and evident demonstration is provided by the extent to which this book rests on the literature of education, particularly that of the last half century. Much of this literaure has grown out of the work of schools and colleges and most of the illustrations provided by writers on education deal with the activities of children in classrooms, but anyone who looks beneath the surface can often distinguish principles and practices which have general application for learning at all ages.

The literature on program development in education is so enormous that no mind can fully encompass its scope and ramifications. Throughout the text itself and in this bibliographic essay (particularly in the comparison of program-planning systems) many references are cited. At this point, however, it may be useful to the reader to be reminded of the existence of certain comprehensive works which summarize much of the scientific knowledge of education and which collectively provide a background for all of the more specialized works mentioned later:

> N. L. GAGE, ed., *Handbook of Research on Teaching* (Rand McNally, Chicago, 1963)
>
> ROBERT L. EBEL, ed. *Encyclopedia of Educational Research* (Macmillan, New York, 1969)
>
> "Curriculum," *Review of Educational Research, 39* (June, 1969)
>
> DWIGHT W. ALLEN AND ELI SEIFMAN, eds., *The Teacher's Handbook* (Scott, Foresman, Glenview, Ill., 1971)
>
> *Encyclopedia of Education* (Macmillan-Free Press, New York, 1971)

Other less comprehensive but very useful sources are:

> *Theories of Learning and Instruction,* NSSE Yearbook (University of Chicago Press, Chicago, 1964)
>
> MAURITZ JOHNSON, JR., "Definitions and Models in Curriculum Theory," *Educational Theory, 17* (April, 1967)
>
> JOSEPH J. SCHWAB, "The Practical: A Language for Curriculum," *School Review, 77* (November, 1969)
>
> *The Curriculum: Retrospect and Prospect,* NSSE Yearbook (University of Chicago Press, Chicago, 1971)
>
> IAN WESTBURY AND WILLIAM STEIMER, "Curriculum: A Discipline in Search of Its Problems," *School Review, 79* (February, 1971)
>
> JOSEPH J. SCHWAB, "The Practical: Arts of Eclectics," *School Review, 79* (August, 1971)

Program Development: Adult Education

The books which deal generally with program development in adult education are highly practical. They may describe several or many formats or they may be restricted in some way, perhaps to a single category of activity, such as the discussion group or the conference, or to a single type of setting or sponsor, such as the industrial concern or the hospital. If such books deal with theory, it is often by the assertion of values or beliefs, thus offering a philosophy in the common man's use of that term, but they are essentially how-to-do-it manuals, achieving their major value by describing processes and procedures which have proved to be useful in practice.

Probably the best of these manuals is *The Modern Practice of Adult Education* by Malcolm Knowles (Association Press, New York, 1970), a completely rewritten version of his still useful *Informal Adult Education* (Association Press, New York, 1950). A more tightly knit and theoretically based book is *Teaching and Learning in Adult Education* by Harry L. Miller (Macmillan, New York, 1964). The program planning issue of AL, *1* (May, 1952) provided a number of integrated papers on the entire nature of the program planning process. *Adult Education: Outlines of an Emerging Field of University Study,* edited by Gale Jensen, A. A. Liveright, and Wilbur Hallenbeck (AEA, 1964) presents the views of a group of professors of adult education on the program-planning process. The other most generally available manuals of practice are

J. R. KIDD, *How Adults Learn* (Association Press, New York, 1959)

THOMAS F. STATON, *How to Instruct Successfully: Modern Teaching Methods in Adult Education* (McGraw-Hill, New York, 1960)

M. F. CLEUGH, *Educating Older People* (Tavistock Publications, London, 1962)

PAUL BERGEVIN, DWIGHT MORRIS, AND ROBERT M. SMITH, *Adult Education Procedures* (Seabury Press, Greenwich, Conn., 1963)

BARTON E. MORGAN, GLENN E. HOLMES AND CLARENCE E.

BUNDY, *Methods in Adult Education*. Second edition.
(Interstate, Danville, Ill., 1963)

ROGER W. AXFORD, *Adult Education: The Open Door* (International Textbook Company, Scranton, Pa., 1969)

EDWIN TOWNSEND COLES, *Adult Education in Developing Countries* (Pergamon Press, Oxford, 1969)

JENNIFER ROGERS, *Adults Learning* (Penguin, New York, 1971)

Training and management development have become important functions in modern industrial and commercial life. As a result, a large number of books dealing with the program processes used in such settings has been produced. Among the best-known are the following:

WILLARD E. BENNETT, *Manager Selection, Education, and Training* (McGraw-Hill, New York, 1959)

R. J. HACON, *Management Training: Aims and Methods* (English Universities Press, London, 1961)

WILLIAM MC GEHEE AND PAUL W. THAYER, *Training in Business and Industry* (Wiley, New York, 1961)

JOHN H. PROCTOR AND WILLIAM M. THORNTON, *Training: A Handbook for Line Managers* (American Management Association, New York, 1961)

ROGER BELLOWS, THOMAS Q. GIBSON, AND GEORGE S. ODIORNE, *Executive Skills: Their Dynamics and Development* (Prentice-Hall, Englewood Cliffs, N.J., 1962)

DAVID KING, *Training Within the Organization* (Tavistock Publications, London, 1964)

HOMER C. ROSE, *The Development and Supervision of Training Programs* (American Technical Society, Chicago, 1964)

ALLEN T. ZOLL, *Dynamic Management Education* (Management Education Associates, Seattle, 1966)

ROBERT L. CRAIG AND LESTER R. BITTEL, editors, *Training and Development Handbook* (McGraw-Hill, New York, 1967)

ROLF P. LYNTON AND UDAI PAREEK, *Training for Development* (Irwin, Homewood, Ill., 1967)

BERNARD J. BIENVENU, *New Priorities in Training* (American Management Association, 1969)

JOHN W. HUMBLE, *Management by Objectives in Action* (McGraw-Hill, New York, 1970)

WILLIAM R. TRACEY, *Designing Training and Development Systems* (American Management Association, New York, 1971).

Many other books deal with general program development in particular settings. For example, *Training and Continuing Education: A Handbook for Health Care Institutions* by (Hospital Research and Educational Trust, Chicago, 1970) is a complex and highly developed handbook for hospital administrators and training directors. *Administration of Continuing Education,* edited by Nathan C. Shaw (National Association of Public School Adult Education, Washington, D.C., 1969) deals chiefly, though not exclusively with adult education in the public schools. *Union Leadership Training* by A. A. Liveright (Harper, New York, 1951) describes the process of planning and carrying out programs in labor unions. *The Cooperative Extension Service,* edited by H. C. Sanders (Prentice-Hall, Englewood Cliffs, N.J., 1966), while dealing descriptively with all aspects of the work of agricultural and home demonstration extension, also provides a full-scale treatment of the program-development process of such work, with particular attention to methods. *Employee Training and Development in the Public Service,* edited by Kenneth T. Byers (Public Personnel Association, Chicago, 1970) is a manual of theories and techniques for the training of public employees.

Comparative reviews of these many books on program development are rare. Perhaps the most analytical is that by Watson Dickerman entitled "Books about Methods in Adult Education," *AE, 15* (Winter, 1965).

Growth of Systematic Thought

The first part of this essay has listed general sources on the history and status of the practice of adult education in the United States. This section will supplement that list by identifying a few of the references which deal with the growth of systematic thought in the field.

The transitional book between the English and the American experience was *Education for Adults* by Frederick Paul Keppel (Columbia University Press, New York, 1926). The best source of points of view during the early evangelistic era of adult education is the JAE; they are usefully summarized by a book of readings drawn from that journal, *Adult Education in Action,* edited by Mary Ely (AAAE, New York, 1936).

A constantly recurring theme in the early literature had to do with whether or not direct unguided experience was more influential in the life of the individual than planned educative programs. This issue was sharpened by the fact that the existing offering was scanty and ill-attended, particularly when measured against the lofty dreams of visionary leaders of the field. Allan Nevins made an eloquent statement supporting raw experience as against contrived education in "The Schoolmaster, Events," JAE, *12* (October, 1940). One of the early leaders of adult education, Nathaniel Peffer, turned against it in a brilliant essay, "Recantation," JAE, *7* (April, 1935), to which an equally powerful response was made by Alvin Johnson in "A Reaffirmation," JAE, *7* (June, 1935), in which he argued that adults can use education to change the nature of their culture.

Two accounts of the growth of thought in adult education by an analysis of the literature have been provided by Webster E. Cotton, "The Challenge Confronting American Adult Education," AE, *14* (Winter, 1964); and *On Behalf of Adult Education* (CSLEA, Boston, 1968).

The effort to find the "right" definition of adult education has continued in this country for more than a half-century. A spectrum of points of view on the subject is given by nine authors in "What is Adult Education? Nine 'Working' Definitions," AE, *5* (Spring, 1955). A useful effort to clear away some of the terminological confusion was made by Watson Dickerman in "What is This 'Continuing Education'?" AE, *15* (Autumn, 1964). An attempt to categorize all education into three basic forms (the family-educational, the sequential-unit, and the complementary-functional) was made by Paul L. Essert and Ralph B. Spence in "Continuous Learning Through the Educative Community," AE, *18* (Summer, 1968); of these three, the third is considered to be essentially adult educational. Orville G. Brim, Jr. and Stanton Wheeler, in *Socialization After Childhood: Two Essays* (Wiley, New York, 1966) provide an excellent example of the tendency of social psychologists to consider not education alone but all socialization, by which is meant the influence of the culture on the individual. An effort to distinguish between adult education as a profession and as a field of study is made by Mohammed A. Douglah and Gwenna M. Moss in "Adult Education as a Field of Study and Its Implications for the Preparation of Adult Educators," AE, *19* (Spring, 1969). An exploration of the implications for adult education of other established and emerging disciplines is presented by Burton W. Kreitlow in *Relating Adult Education to Other Disciplines* (published privately).

Efforts to lay a detailed philosophical base for adult education have been abundant, and many will be mentioned in subsequent sections. Among the most useful general approaches to this topic are the following:

GALE JENSEN, "Principles and Content for Developing a Theory of Learning," AE, *8* (Spring, 1958)

GALE JENSEN, "Guideposts for Adult Instruction," AE, *9* (Spring, 1959)

KENNETH D. BENNE, "Some Philosophic Issues in Adult Education," AE, *7* (Winter, 1957)

JOHN WALKER POWELL AND KENNETH D. BENNE, "Philosophies of Adult Education," *Handbook of Adult Education in the United States,* Malcolm S. Knowles, ed. (AEA, Chicago, 1960)

GEORGE E. BARTON, JR. *Ordered Pluralism: A Philosophic Plan of Action for Teaching* (CSLEA, Chicago, 1964)

Among the other generalized systems of program planning for adult education (which somewhat parallel that presented in this book) are the following:

GEORGE M. BEAL AND OTHERS, *Social Action and Interaction in Program planning* (Iowa State University Press, Ames, Iowa, 1966)

MALCOLM S. KNOWLES, "Program Planning for Adults as Learners," AL, *15* (February, 1967)

JACK LONDON, "A Perspective on Programming in Adult Education: A Critical Challenge," AL, *15* (February, 1967)

GERALD J. PINE AND PETER J. HORNE, "Principles and Conditions for Learning in Adult Education," AL, *18* (October, 1969)

Except as noted at other parts of this essay, the program-planning theories in the general field of the curriculum have only limited usefulness for adult education since they are largely based on the specific practices of schools and colleges. This narrowness of focus is now being attacked on many sides in such papers as that by Bruce R. Joyce, "The Curriculum Worker of the Future," *The Curriculum: Retrospect and Prospect* NSSE Yearbook (University of Chicago Press, Chicago, 1971).

Centering on a Goal

In *A History of Adult Education in Great Britain,* Second Edition (Liverpool University Press, Liverpool, 1970), Thomas Kelly gives an account of how in his nation's history first one theme and then another has been dominant so far as adult education is concerned. Among such themes were religious salvation, the understanding of science, and liberal education. Such large goals as these tend to be only retrospectively seen as unifying forces, however, and except for the last, did not exercise a strong coordinating effect among those engaged in a variety of services. The most powerful modern statement of the significance of liberal education as a focus for adult education is Sir Richard Livingstone's "The Future in Education" in *On Education* (Macmillan, New York, 1945). Some evidence exists that the British viewpoint as to the centrality of liberal studies is now changing. In "Impressions of Adult Education in the United States," AE, *12* (Spring, 1962), John Lowe defined the field in England as being "a branch of education designed for adults who are interested primarily in cultivating their minds and only secondarily, if at all, in obtaining vocational skills and qualifications." Eight years later, however, his book *Adult Education in England and Wales* (Michael Joseph, London, 1970) argued that the British reliance on liberal education had become too narrow and constricting. In a volume issued in 1970 by the leading British group in higher adult education, the Universities Council for Adult Education, it is asserted, "It is in the integration of the liberal and vocational elements in adult education that universities have an essential contribution to make: there is no antithesis between the two terms" (*University Adult Education in the Later Twentieth Century*, privately published).

Many Americans have urged that adult education be centered on one or more major goals. In one of the first two doctoral dissertations in the field, William H. Stacy argued that adult education should be integrated in terms of certain major themes he called "the seven great arts." (*Integration of Adult Education*, Bureau of Publications, Teachers College, Columbia University, New York, 1935). Thirty years later, in "Lifelong Challenge," AE, *16* (Spring, 1966), he maintained the same position. In "Adult Education's Great Purpose," AL, *7* (June, 1958), Glen Burch asserted that the unifying goal of the movement is "the cultivation of the human mind." R. J. Blakely in "Adult Education Needs a Philosophy and a Goal," AE, *3* (November, 1952) expounded the theme suggested by his title and gave other expressions of the same idea in *Adult Education in a Free Society* (Guardian Bird Publications, Toronto, 1958). In "Some Observations on the Status of Adult Education in the U. S. Today," AE, *16* (Summer, 1966), A. A. Liveright presented the gloomy belief that adult education is "fragmented, lopsided and lacks a sense of direction." Two years later, in "Adult Education—for What?" AL, *17* (December, 1968), he argued that there is a "crucial need for a philosophy and a sense of direction."

Adult education is, of course, but one of many social movements which feel the need for unifying themes. Those who seek to gain perspective by viewing the field more broadly will find it useful to read *The Social Psychology of Social Movements* by Hans Toch (Bobbs-Merrill, Indianapolis, Ind., 1965).

Meeting Needs and Interests

The belief that all adult education should be based on the felt needs and interests of learners has been expressed or assumed since the beginning of the American movement, underlying, for example, the early study by Douglas Waples on "What Do Adults Want to Learn?" JAE, 2 (October, 1930). Jeffrey Fleece in "Adult Followership," AL, 7 (January, 1959) says that felt needs are the true source of goals for adult education; the same point is made by Ralph C. Dobbs in "Self-Perceived Educational Needs of Adults," AE, 16 (Winter, 1966). A survey of British radio listeners made by John Robinson implies that the serving of their interests is the chief requirement of adult education: "Exploring Adult Education," AE [B], 38 (May, 1965). In Book Selection and Censorship (University of California Press, Berkeley, 1960), Marjorie Fiske highlights the fact that most public librarians believe that they should choose books in terms of the desires of their readers. The entire educational program development process in the hospital is treated from the same point of view in Training and Continuing Education: A Handbook for Health Care Institutions (Hospital Research and Educational Trust, Chicago, 1970). Jack London presents a broad social background for adult education largely in terms of community needs in "The Social Setting for Adult Education," Handbook of Adult Education (Macmillan, New York, 1970).

Analytical approaches to the study of felt needs and interests are taken by several authors. In Identifying Educational Needs of Adults (U. S. Office of Education Circular No. 330, Government Printing Office, Washington, D.C., 1951), Homer Kempfer identifies the ways by which public schools and community colleges can identify needs. A useful categorization of various approaches to the subject is given by H. Mason Atwood and Joe Ellis in "The Concept of Need: An Analysis for Adult Education," AL, 19 (January, 1971). An equally useful account is provided by J. Paul Leagans, "A Concept of Needs," JCE, 2 (Summer, 1964). An analysis and extended annotated bibliography on the topic is provided by Ernest E. McMahon in Needs—of People and Their Communities—and the Adult Educator (AEA, Washington, D.C. 1970). A sharp attack on the adequacy of the needs approach is made by Bernard

J. James in "Can 'Needs' Define Educational Goals?" AE, 7 (Autumn, 1956).

Adapting Schooling

Much adult education is conducted by schools, colleges, and universities which aim to provide elementary, secondary, and higher education to men and women. The administrators of many such institutions believe that their chief task is to make such study conform as closely as possible to the patterns established for young people. In fact, in *School-teachers and the Education of Adults* (UNESCO, Paris, 1966), A. S. M. Hely points out that throughout the world teachers often treat adult students as though they were children. The entire literature of basic and fundamental education deals, in one way or another, with the ways by which child-based standards should be accepted or, alternatively, with the methods by which an adult oriented program can be developed. Four representative sources drawn from this literature are

RUTH KOTINSKY, *Elementary Education of Adults,* (AAAE, New York, 1941)

MARY AGNEW MC LEAN, "Remodeling Elementary Adult Education," JAE, *13* (April, 1941)

ANGELICA W. CASS, *Adult Elementary Education* (Noble and Noble, New York, 1956)

FRANK W. LANNING AND WESLEY A. MANY, eds., *Basic Education for the Disadvantaged Adult: Theory and Practice* (Houghton Mifflin, Boston, 1966)

In higher education, degree programs for adults still mirror the curricular patterns evolved for young people. *Policies and Practices in Evening Colleges 1969* (Scarecrow Press, Metuchen, N.J., 1969), edited by William A. Hoppe, shows in great detail just how evening colleges adapt the formal patterns of their universities. In *Ivory Towers in the Market Place* (Bobbs-Merrill, Indianapolis, Ind., 1956), John P. Dyer provides a broad discussion of the evening college as an adaptation of the university's culture to white collar workers. In *The Emerging Evening College* (Bureau of Publications, Teachers College, Columbia University, New York, 1960),

Ernest E. McMahon firmly establishes the evening college as an adaptation of the traditional pattern of securing degrees.

Many people believe that such adaptation cannot be a sufficient guide to adult education. In "Designing Courses for Adults," AE, 8 (Summer, 1958), James Wilber Harrison presented data which show distinctive differences between the education which is merely an adaptation of schooling and that which grows out of a direct effort to serve the educational needs of adults. Myrtle S. Jacobson presented a study in depth of the conflict between an evening college and its university as the former tried to create new ideas and programs, thus going against the desire of the latter to maintain traditional means of schooling. *Night and Day* (Scarecrow Press, Metuchen, N.J., 1970). In two papers, Paul A. McGhee strongly attacked the formalism of the usual university approach to adult education: "Higher Education and Adult Education: Four Questions," AE, 4 (November, 1953); and "Three Dimensions of Adult Education," *Educational Record, 35* (April, 1954). In "Back to New Francisco," AL, 15 (February, 1967), Cyril O. Houle distinguished school-centered and other theories of adult educational programming. Bernard H. Stern and Ellsworth Missall, *Adult Experience and College Degrees* (Western Reserve University Press, Cleveland, 1960), described how a program at Brooklyn College was adapted to take account of life experience.

Many efforts are now being made to establish new ways to award certificates and credits. For example, the high school equivalency credential is suggested as a basis for planning a secondary school adult educational program by Fred D. Carver, "A Re-entry Route for Yesterday's Dropouts," AL, 15 (April, 1967). Keith E. Glancy, in "A New Tool for Adult Educators," AL, 20 (May, 1971) describes the development of a new quantitative unit, the "continuing education unit" as a measurement of less formal kinds of instruction than traditional courses. The concept of the degree (usually the baccalaureate) especially for adults is now being widely considered but no substantive treatments of it have yet appeared.

Strengthening Leadership

The belief that leadership (as variously conceived) is the central concern of program planning has long been an important theme in the literature. In "Tools and the Teacher," JAE, 7 (October, 1935), Gustav Francis Beck asserted the primacy of the teacher as the major element in any instructional program. Paul Essert focussed his broadly based book *Creative Leadership of Adult Education* (Prentice-Hall, Englewood Cliffs, N.J., (1951) on the fostering of leadership. J. Kenneth Wishart, in *Techniques of Leadership* (Vantage Press, New York, 1965), develops the argument that leadership development is a process of adult education. *Leadership for Action* by Burton W. Kreitlow, E. W. Aiton, and Andrew P. Torrence (Interstate, Danville, Ill., 1965) deals with the development of leaders in rural communities. Much attention has also been paid to the best means of developing leadership. A. K. Rice, in *Learning for Leadership* (Tavistock, London, 1965) argues for the conference process as being a central method, whereas Martin Tarcher in *Leadership and the Power of Ideas* (Harper and Row, New York, 1966) stresses the need for content in any effort to develop leaders for adult education.

Improving Institutions

The shoptalk of adult education and the literature which arises from that shoptalk tend to focus on institutional practice and improvement. Ordinarily the focus is sharp and clear on the church, the hospital, the industrial training department, the specific voluntary association, or some other well-established structure of service. Many of the works cited earlier have a central focus of this sort. A second much less substantial body of references has to do with the interaction of institutions; this theme is dealt with in the sections of this essay having to do with C-6 and C-10 situations. Occasionally an author will lay claim to supremacy for one institutional form; for example, Alvin Johnson does so in *The Public Library—A People's University* (AAAE, New York, 1938). The institutional approach to adult education is itself sometimes studied; one example is: Robert M. Smith and John McKinley, "An Institutional Approach to Adult Education in the Community," AE, 6 (Autumn, 1955).

Subverting Formalism

Many educators of adults conceive of themselves as enemies of systematization, particularly as it is manifested in childhood-youth education. More than a few such people have raised their opposition to the status of a guiding principle, or, in a few cases, a dedicated obstructionism. Some well-reasoned statements have been put forward expounding the virtues of informality or reform. Thomas H. Nelson, in *Ventures in Informal Adult Education* (Association Press, New York, 1933) stresses the fact that good adult education must be informal. R. H. Tawney in *Education: The Task Before Us* (Workers' Educational Association, London, 1943) argues that the task of adult education is to reform all education. J. Macalister Brew in *Informal Education* (Faber and Faber, London, 1948) describes various approaches to education, such as "through the stomach," "through the feet," and "through the work of the hands." John W. Herring in "Adult Education: Senior Partner to Democracy," AE, *3* (November, 1952) insists that educators of adults must break through formalism and professionalism and deal directly with the community's problems.

Systems Based on Dewey's Thought

Dewey's thought pervades so much of the field of adult education that it is now virtually taken for granted. His works which have had the greatest influence on the field are *How We Think* (Heath, Boston, 1910); *Democracy and Education* (Macmillan, New York, 1916); and *Experience and Education* (Macmillan, New York, 1938). Two early interpretations of his ideas for adult education were made in: Eduard C. Lindeman, *The Meaning of Adult Education* (New Republic, New York, 1926); and Ruth Kotinsky, *Adult Education and the Social Scene* (Appleton-Century-Crofts 1933). An example of a program development system based on Dewey's thought is *Conference Methods in Industry* by Henry M. Busch (Harper, New York, 1949).

Systems Based on Tyler's Thought

The basic books in which Ralph W. Tyler explained his rationale are: *Principles of Curriculum and Instruction* (University of Chicago Press, Chicago, 1950); and with E. R. Smith *Appraising and Recording Student Progress* (Harper, New York, 1942). However, his chief influence has been exerted personally with the groups and individuals with whom he has worked during a long lifetime and who have extended and applied his ideas in myriad ways, such

as by the development of taxonomies of objectives. Robert M. Mc-
Clure observed in 1971 that "Scarcely a curriculum committee at
work in a local school district can be found which does not have, at
least in a 'knowledge' sense, the 'taxonomy' built into its curricular
ideas." "The Reforms of the Fifties and Sixties: A Historical Look
at the Near Past," *The Curriculum: Retrospect and Prospect,* NSSE
Yearbook (University of Chicago Press, Chicago, 1971). Efforts to
enlarge the original Tylerian conceptions are now being made by
Tyler himself and by others; one such book is *Handbook on Formative and Summative Evaluation of Student Learning* by Benjamin
Bloom, J. Thomas Hastings, and George F. Madaus (McGraw-
Hill, New York, 1971). Another is *Designing Training and Development Systems* by William H. Tracey (American Management
Association, New York, 1971). Meanwhile attacks are now being
made. Herbert M. Kliebard in "The Tyler Rationale," *School Review, 78* (February, 1970) observes that the rationale "has been
raised almost to the status of revealed doctrine" but nonetheless he
finds many flaws in it. Elliott W. Eisner has attacked the whole
Tylerian conception of objectives in "Educational Objectives: Help
or Hindrance," *School Review, 75* (Autumn, 1967, pp. 250–60).
A somewhat similar view is expressed by K. H. Lawson in "The
Concept of 'Purpose' ", AE[B], *43,* (November, 1968). A wholly
new approach to curriculum development is urged by Decker F.
Walker in "A Naturalistic Model for Curriculum Development,"
School Review, 80, (November, 1971).

Most of the general books on program development in adult
education or the treatments of specific components of that process
bear the influence of Tyler's thought; such works are noted elsewhere in this essay. Several further illustrations of the point may
also be useful. One adaptation of the Tylerian system to adult education is made by Patrick G. Boyle in "Planning With Principle,"
AE, *9* (Autumn, 1958). Another is *Curriculum Development in
Adult Basic Education* by Edgar J. Boone and Emily H. Quinn
(Follett, Chicago, 1967). Darcie Byrn, editor, *Evaluation in Extension* (H. M. Ives, Topeka, Kans., 1959) shows how completely
the rationale has been adopted by the Cooperative Extension Service. And certainly the system suggested in the present book owes a
great deal to Tyler's thought.

Systems Based on Lewin's Thought

Lewin's influence was exerted by the whole body of his writings and his personal charisma, not by any single work. In *The Practical Theorist: The Life and Works of Kurt Lewin* (Basic Books, New York, 1969), Alfred J. Marrow has presented a full account of Lewin's life and thought, with passages which show how directly influential he was on sensitivity training and indirectly on change theory.

Sensitivity Training

The study of small groups and their behavior has long been closely allied to the field of adult education, many writers and investigators being influential in both theoretical analysis and practical application. Sensitivity training in its various forms has usually been conducted for mature people, not children. An excellent brief account of such training is provided by Malcolm and Huldah Knowles in *Introduction to Group Dynamics* (Association Press, New York, 1959). Another survey of the topic is given by Arthur Blumberg, *Sensitivity Training: Processes, Problems, and Applications* (Syracuse University Publications in Continuing Education, Syracuse, N.Y., 1971). The monographs issued in the *Selected Readings Series* of the National Training Laboratories of the National Education Association provide a wealth of information on various aspects of the group learning process. Other general treatments of the topic are:

WILLIAM FOOTE WHYTE, *Leadership and Group Participation* (New York State School of Industrial and Labor Relations, Cornell University, Ithaca, N.Y., 1952)

HERBERT A. THELEN, *The Dynamics of Groups at Work* (University of Chicago Press, Chicago, 1954)

LELAND BRADFORD, JACK R. GIBB, AND KENNETH D. BENNE, *T-Group Theory and Laboratory Method* (Wiley, New York, 1964)

EDGAR SCHEIN AND WARREN G. BENNIS, *Personal and Organizational Change Through Group Methods* (Wiley, New York, 1965)

DORWIN CARTWRIGHT AND ALVIN ZANDER, *Group Dynamics,*
Third Edition (Harper, New York, 1968)
ARTHUR BURTON, editor. *Encounter* (Jossey-Bass, San Francisco, 1969)

More detailed accounts of the specific application of group dynamics principles to adult education are also available. "Social Inventions for Learning" a special issue of AL, *2* (October, 1953) describes many techniques which emerged from the group dynamics movement. An effort to explain the nature of a brief experience in human relations training was made by Leland P. Bradford, Gordon L. Lippitt, and Jack R. Gibb in "Human Relations Training in Three Days," AL, *4* (April, 1956). Irving R. Weschler and others provided a relatively short summary of the application of group dynamics to adult education in "Yardsticks for Human Relations Training," AE, *7* (Spring, 1957). A broad philosophical statement was made by Kenneth D. Benne in "The Re-education of Adults in Their Human Relationships," AE, *8* (Spring, 1958). In *New Patterns of Management* (McGraw-Hill, New York, 1961), Rensis Likert deals with the employment of human relations training in the business organization. Albert W. Silver, "Transactional Group Dynamics in a Group Leadership Workshop," AL, *15* (April, 1967) offers a special theory of application in sensitivity training.

From the very beginning, the group dynamics movement has encountered a hard core of opposition. Kurt W. Back in "Group Addiction—Its Cause and Cure," AL, *3* (October, 1954) defines group dynamics in a much more restricted way than its proponents would accept. Edward Gross mounted a sharp attack in "Group Worship—the New Orthodoxy?", AL, *4* (April, 1956) and Robert B. Browne dealt with "groupiness" in "Winds of Doctrine," AE, *8* (Winter, 1958). An all-out indictment of group dynamics and other forms of "secular" education which pervert the purpose of true Christian education was made by John R. Fry in *A Hard Look at Adult Christian Education* (Westminster Press, Philadelphia, 1961).

Change Theory

Change theory is a loose and amorphous topic with no single structural work to give it coherence. Sometimes its key terms are used with precision in terms of a theory, but sometimes they have only a general and vague connotation. Of the general statements concerning change theory, three have been written or edited by educators of adults:

RONALD LIPPITT, JEANNE WATSON, AND BRUCE WESTLEY, *The Dynamics of Planned Change* (Harcourt, Brace, and World, New York, 1958)

LOWRY NELSON, CHARLES E. RAMSEY, AND COOLIE VERNER, *Community Structure and Change* (Macmillan, New York, 1960)

WARREN G. BENNIS, KENNETH D. BENNE, AND ROBERT CHIN, editors. *The Planning of Change* Second Edition (Holt, Rinehart, and Winston, New York, 1969)

An early effort to apply change theory, very broadly conceived, to the whole adult educational process was described by Leland P. Bradford in "The Teaching-Learning Transaction," AE, *8* (Spring, 1958). A more systematic effort to develop "a conceptual scheme for the identification and development of the processes of adult education" according to change theory was made by Coolie Verner in *Adult Education Theory and Method* (AEA, Chicago, 1962). An application of one familiar concept to the differential participation of adults in education was presented by Harry L. Miller, *Participation of Adults in Education: A Force-Field Analysis* (CSLEA, Boston, 1967). A system of change theory as applied to education was presented by Burton W. Kreitlow and Teresa MacNeil in *An Evaluation of the Model for Educational Improvement as an Analytical Tool for Describing the Change Process* (Wisconsin R. and D. Center for Cognitive Learning, Madison, 1969). Russell D. Robinson applied change theory to adult education in "Toward a Conceptualization of Leadership for Change," AE, *20* (Summer, 1970). In "Toward a Theory of Practice," AE, *21* (Spring, 1971), Jack Mezirow based a theory of adult education on the emerging sociological concept of "grounded theory," which is somewhat analogous to change theory.

A number of accounts have been given of the use of change theory in various forms of adult education. One is "Planned Change in a Netherlandic Rural Region" by William A. C. Zwanikken, AE,

12 (Autumn, 1961). The social scientific backgrounds of planned change in agriculture are explored in *Behavioral Change in Agriculture,* edited by J. Paul Leagans and Charles P. Loomis (Cornell University Press, Ithaca, N.Y., 1971). Everett M. Rogers has given an extended and graphic account of another example of application in *Modernization Among Peasants* (Holt, Rinehart, and Winston, New York, 1969), and Herbert F. Lionberger has dealt with the diffusion of innovative practices in agriculture in *Adoption of New Ideas and Practices* (Iowa State University Press, Ames, Iowa, 1960). Robert D. Boyd edited a series of papers which deal with the theme *Beyond the Four Walls: Adult Educators as Urban Change Agents* (University Extension, The University of Wisconsin, Madison, 1969). A combination of the Tylerian rationale and change theory is suggested in *Programming in the Cooperative Extension Service: A Conceptual Schema* by E. J. Boone, R. J. Dolan, and R. W. Shearon (North Carolina Agricultural Extension Service, Raleigh, 1971).

Community Development

While the boundaries of adult education are by no means identical with those of comunity development, the two overlap so substantially that their similarities are greater than their differences. Only a relatively few references which are squarely in both fields will be mentioned. A useful collection of readings on the interpretation of the concept of community by both social scientists and literary artists has been edited by David W. Minar and Scott Greer in *The Concept of Community* (Aldine-Atherton, Chicago, 1969). At least two periodicals are in existence—the *Community Development Journal* and the *Journal of the Community Development Society.* Influential works which state the general conception and theory of community development are

RICHARD W. POSTON, *Small Town Renaissance* (Harper, New York, 1950)

RICHARD W. POSTON, *Democracy is You* (Harper, New York, 1953)

OTTO G. HOIBERG, *Exploring the Small Community* (University of Nebraska Press, Lincoln, Neb., 1955)

T. R. BATTEN, *Communities and Their Development* (Oxford University Press, Oxford, 1957)

JESS OGDEN, "A Philosophy of Community Development," *AL, 6* (April, 1958)

WILLIAM W. BIDDLE AND LOUREIDE J. BIDDLE, *The Community Development Process* (Holt, Rinehart, and Winston, New York, 1965)

KEITH JACKSON, "Adult Education and Community Development," *Studies in Adult Education, 1970* (David and Charles, Devon, England, 1971)

Manuals of techniques for community development abound. Two special issues of AL have been concerned with the topic— "Initiating Social Action," AL, *1* (February, 1953); and "Building Better Communities," AL, *4* (May, 1955). Douglas Ensminger prepared *A Guide to Community Development* for India (Ministry of Community Development, Government of India, New Delhi, 1957). T. R. Batten has developed a critical study of method in *Training for Community Development* (Oxford University Press, Oxford, 1962). A general account has been given by James J. Shields, Jr. in *Education in Community Development* (Praeger, New York, 1967).

A number of efforts have been made to define adult education as a community development process. One such attempt was made by Richard Waverly Poston in "The Relation of Community Development to Adult Education," AE, *4* (May, 1954). This statement gave rise to a number of responses from other people, including Arthur Crabtree who said "My sole disagreement lies in his [Poston's] proposal to put all our adult education eggs in the one basket of community development. In my opinion, there are other eggs and other baskets." Varying points of view on this relationship were given by five authorities in "The Role of Adult Education in Community Development," AE, *6* (Autumn, 1955). Bertis L. Jones identifies community development as the essential process of adult education in "A Philosophical View of Community Development as an Adult Education Function," AL, *13* (February, 1965). An effort to combine community development and change theory has been made by Arthur F. Wileden in *Community Development: The Dynamics of Planned Change* (Bedminster Press, Totowa, N. J., 1970).

The literature abounds with case studies. A special journal, *The International Review on Community Development,* appeared for some years and is particularly rich in descriptive material. In addition to the general references given in the section of this essay which deals with case studies, the following sources may be useful:

> JAMES DAHIR, *Region Building: Community Development Lessons from the Tennessee Valley* (Harper, New York, 1955)
>
> PETER DU SAUTOY, *Community Development in Ghana* (Oxford University Press, Oxford, 1958)
>
> HOMER KEMPFER, "Community Development and Social Education in India," AL, *9* (September, 1960)

The institutional approach to community development is widely described and illustrated. In *The Community School and Community Self-Improvement* (Michigan State Superintendent of Public Instruction, Lansing, 1954), Maurice F. Seay and Ferris N. Crawford give an account of the public school as a center for community development and a somewhat comparable English point of view is expressed by Cyril Poster in *The School and the Community* (Macmillan, New York, 1971). In *The Campus and the Community* (Harvest House, Montreal, 1961), Alexander Fraser Laidlaw provides one of the most complete accounts of the work of St. Francis Xavier College at Antigonish, Nova Scotia, and the worldwide impact its program has had.

Community development has been viewed with skeptical eyes by many adult educators. Paul McGhee argues against the community action and development point of view in AE, *6* (Winter, 1956) and a somewhat similar criticism is provided by William Gruen in "A Pragmatic Criticism of Community-Centered Adult Education," AE, *6* (Winter, 1956). Charles B. Adrian in "The Folklore of Community Development," AL, *11* (April, 1963) suggests that many approaches to community development are far too simple to achieve any lasting effect.

Systems Analysis

The application of systems analysis to education has as yet occurred only in very general terms with little or no specific reference to adult education. Among the most useful works are

> ROBERT G. SMITH, JR., *An Annotated Bibliography of the Design of Instructional Systems* (George Washington University, Washington, D.C., 1967)
>
> LEONARD SILVERN, *Systems Engineering of Education* (Educational and Training Consultants, Los Angeles, 1968)
>
> HARRY J. HARTLEY, *Educational Planning, Programming, Budgeting: A Systems Approach* (Prentice-Hall, Englewood Cliffs, N.J., 1968)
>
> H. W. HANDY AND K. M. HUSSAIN, *Network Analysis for Educational Management* (Prentice-Hall, Englewood Cliffs, N.J., 1969)
>
> ROBERT F. ALIOTO AND J. A. JUNGHERR, *Operational PPBS for Education* (Harper and Row, New York, 1971).

A few detailed illustrations of the application of systems analysis to adult education have appeared. Two deal with industrial training: George S. Odiorne, "A Systems Approach to Training," *Training Directors Journal* (October, 1965); and Michael Toye, "Training Design: Algorithm," *Training in Business and Industry*, 7 (October, 1970). A case study of how PPBS works in the Oregon Division of Continuing Education is given by Dale E. Price and Dwight W. Fairbanks, "Extension Programming by Goal: A Progress Report," *NUEA Spectator, 36* (December, 1970–January, 1971). Several papers dealing with systems analysis in the Cooperative Extension Service have also appeared in JCE: James Solem and Herbert D. Warner, "PPBS: A Management Innovation", JCE 6, (Winter, 1968); Richard L. Stauber, "PPBS for Extension?", JCE, 6 (Winter, 1968); and George H. Axinn, "A Systems Approach to Extension", JCE, 7 (Summer, 1969).

Misapplied Systems

In some cases, as will be noted, authors have directly espoused some social function as being equivalent to adult education.

More often, perhaps, broadly knowledgeable authors have written articles which deal only with a special application of adult education to some such field of service as esthetic appreciation or the performing arts, not intending thereby to state their whole positions. It may happen, however, that readers of such pieces give them a universality of approach their authors never meant to convey. It also sometimes happens that those who seek a special goal (such as welfare or health) limit their thought on programming solely to the methods distinctively appropriate to it; they do not deny other methods but they do not suggest them. For these reasons, it is often hard to tell from any given piece just how universalistic an author might be if he chose to state his whole position.

Public Relations

While the view that public relations should be the guiding principle of adult education is widely held—and put into practice—by university presidents, superintendents of schools, and other administrators, no general defense of the position could be found in the literature. Even more surprising, no all-out attack on the point of view seems to have been made, though it has often been referred to with disfavor.

Service

A careful analysis of the relative claims of service and education was made by Richard N. Baisden in "How Far May a University Go in an Action Program?" AE, 7 (Autumn, 1956).

Recreation

A reciprocal relationship between recreation and education was stated in an early and influential book by Lawrence Pearsall Jacks, *Education Through Recreation* (Harper, New York, 1932), who asserted that "the education that is not also recreation is a maimed, incomplete, half-done thing. The recreation that is not also education has no recreative value." This position has often been restated. Thus Caswell M. Miles observed, "Ideally recreation is education in its truest sense" in *Play and Recreation for Children and Adults* (University of the State of New York, Albany, 1937). Bernard E. Thorn said, "The dividing line between education, particularly adult education, and recreation is as difficult to draw as it is unimportant." ("Adult Education or Recreation?," AL, 7 (January, 1959). And Walter L. Stone identified recreation closely with informal adult education in "Adult Recreation," AL, *10* (October, 1961).

Aesthetic Appreciation

In many works which relate esthetic appreciation to adult education, it is hard to tell where one topic begins and the other ends. Thus *The Drama in Adult Education* (His Majesty's Stationery Office, London, 1926) seems to take it for granted throughout that the drama is itself adult education. Frank L. McVey, in "Painting for Pleasure," JAE, *2* (June, 1930) celebrates the value which actual participation in painting has for the education of the individual who undertakes it. Philip Newell Youtz, "The New Arts and Education," JAE, *2* (January, 1930) implies that the process of esthetic enjoyment is itself an educative process. Two distinguished authors have dealt with the educative effect of reading which is done for pleasure and not for the conscious purpose of learning—Bonaro Wilkinson Overstreet, "Justification by Enjoyment," JAE, *6* (April, 1934); and Dorothy Canfield Fisher, "The Author as Educator," JAE, *12* (October, 1940). Two surveys of university adult education in the arts by Freda H. Goldman sometimes treat education as being distinct from enjoyment but sometimes tend to coalesce the two functions—*University Adult Education in the Arts* (CSLEA, Chicago, 1961); and *The Arts in Higher Adult Education: A Second Review of Programs* (CSLEA, Boston, 1966).

Fraternization

Perhaps the best-known statement that adult education should be governed by the function of fraternization was made by Jaime Torres-Bodet, Director-General of UNESCO, at the International Conference on Adult Education in Elsinore, 1949. In a lengthy passage, he said that what the educator of adults "should have in mind before all else is the spiritual loneliness in which each member of his audience is always living. . . . Adult education should be based on the idea that necessarily underlies every international institution—the brotherhood of human destiny." *Adult Education Journal, 8* (October, 1949). This basic theme has been developed in various ways in the literature. Kenneth D. Benne provided a philosophical exploration of the meaning of fraternity and its influence in practical situations in "The Uses of Fraternity," *Daedalus* (Spring, 1961). In "Sacrificed to Schooling," JAE, *5* (October, 1933), Beulah Amidon argued that shared participation and exploration is the essence of true adult education. A somewhat similar view was expressed in Vincent McHugh, "Toward a Theory of Approach in Adult Education," AE, *1* (June, 1951). The conscious stress of fraternization in group adult education was urged by two authors—Eduard C. Lindeman, "Democracy and the Friendship Pattern," *Adult Education Journal, 3* (January, 1944); and Bruno Lasker, "Social Education Through Happy Memories," AL, *6* (March, 1958). Fraternization was stressed as an aspect of religious education in the church by J. Dean Foley in "The Personal Experience of Caring," AL, *17* (November, 1968). Robert N. Dick studied "Gregariousness as a Factor in Adult Participation in University Non-Credit Evening Classes," AL, *12* (March, 1964).

Welfare

Adult education has long been considered by many people to be an activity intended exclusively or chiefly for underprivileged men and women and the success of programs with such goals has reinforced that point of view. This historical study by Edward George Hartmann, *The Movement to Americanize the Immigrant* (Columbia University Press, New York, 1948) defined that movement as essentially a welfare effort. *Twenty Years at Hull-House* by Jane Addams (Macmillan, New York, 1910) is the classic account of how adult education appears within a settlement house orientation and Louise C. Wade, "The Educational Dimension of the Early Chicago Settlements," AE, *17* (Spring, 1967) reinforces that point of view. More recent developments in settlements and social centers are described in Gaynell Hawkins, *Education for Social Understanding* (AAAE, New York, 1940); Arthur Hillman, *Neighborhood Centers Today* (National Federation of Settlements and Neighborhood Centers, New York, 1960); and Robert Perlman and David Jones, *Neighborhood Service Centers* (Government Printing Office,

Washington, D. C., 1967). Systematic explorations of the relationships between social group work (chiefly with a welfare orientation) and adult education are made in Louis Lowy, *Adult Education and Group Work* (Morrow, New York, 1955) and in *Social Group Work in Great Britain,* edited by Peter Kuenstler (Faber and Faber, London, 1955). Another effort to identify the two is Simon Slavin, "Common Denominators in Adult Education and Social Work," AE, *5* (Spring, 1955).

The welfare approach is stressed in many adult educational enterprises. R. L. Derbyshire has written an eloquent essay on "The Sociology of Exclusion: Implications for Teaching Adult Illiterates," AE, *17* (Autumn, 1966). Frederick E. Miller asserts that "There is Need for Militancy in Adult Basic Education," AL, *16* (June, 1968), treating that area of service largely as a welfare matter. Jane Berry deals with the "Effects of Poverty on Culturally Disadvantaged Women," AL, *18* (May, 1969). Home economics as a field for welfare-based services is discussed by Pauline G. Garrett and Uma Nag, "Educating Adults from Culturally and Economically Depressed Environments," AL, *14* (February, 1966). Darrell Anderson and John A. Niemi present an analytical view of the topic in *Adult Education and the Disadvantaged Adult* (ERIC Clearinghouse on Adult Education, Syracuse, N.Y., 1969). Glenn E. Holmes makes the case for the welfare approach as a continuing requirement in "Upgrading Through Education," AL, *14* (June, 1966), and Robert J. Blakely argues for a deep understanding of the welfare approach to adult education in "The Thistle," AL, *14* (April, 1966).

Therapy

Several bodies of literature are centered on this theme, particularly those of vocational rehabilitation, occupational therapy, and recreational therapy. Of particular interest recently has been the effort to build a bridge between psychotherapy and learning or even to identify the two as the same thing. Albert Bandura in "Psychotherapy as a Learning Process," *Psychological Bulletin, 58* (1961, pp. 143–59) surveyed the literature which attempts to answer the question "Can human behavior be modified through psychological means and if so, what are the learning mechanisms that mediate behavior change?" E. Lakin Phillips and Salah El-Batrawi, "Learning Therapy and Psychotherapy Revisited," *Psychotherapy* (Fall, 1964) tried to make a connection between the two topics considered. Thomas S. Szasz, *The Ethics of Psychoanalysis* (Basic Books, New York, 1965) treated psychoanalysis as a process of education. Ruth Porter edited a series of papers presented at an international conference on *The Role of Learning in Psychotherapy* (Little, Brown, Boston, 1968).

Communication

Erving Goffman once observed that ". . . although communication has often been offered as the medicine, it has seldom produced a cure." (*Strategic Interaction,* University of Pennsylvania Press, Philadelphia, 1969). Certainly the first part of that statement has been true so far as adult education has been concerned; many people have argued that the essential idea of learning or teaching is the process of communication between or among people. Thus *The Process of Communication* by David K. Berlo (Holt, Rinehart, and Winston, New York, 1960) treats learning as being virtually equivalent to communication, as does Len S. Powell in *Communication and Learning* (Pitman, New York, 1969). This point has been made in one way or another by many educators of adults. Among those who have advanced various positions, the following can serve as examples:

NORMAN N. ROYALL, JR., "Adult Education's Major Premise," AE, *4* (November, 1953)

JOHN WALKER POWELL, "Adult Education: A Philosophy of Communication," AL, *12* (January, 1964)

HENRY J. KENEALLY, JR., "Documentation of the Communication Process in Program Activities," AL, *13* (May, 1964)

HENRY J. KENEALLY, JR., "The Inter and Intra Agency Communication Process Used in a Community Development Program," AL, *14* (March, 1966)

WESLEY WIKSELL AND MILTON J. WIKSELL, "Improving Clarity in Interpersonal Communication," AL, *19* (February, 1971)

The study of the processes and effects of mass communication has also had many implications for adult education. Some of the more explicitly useful treatments are:

> WILBUR SCHRAMM, editor, *The Process and Effects of Mass Communication* (University of Illinois Press, Urbana, Ill., 1965)
>
> ALFRED G. SMITH, *Communication and Culture* (Holt, Rinehart, and Winston, New York, 1966)
>
> J. M. TRENAMAN, *Communication and Comprehension* (Longmans, London, 1967)

In *Personal Influence* (Free Press, New York, 1955), Elihu Katz and Paul F. Lazarsfeld advanced the idea of the two-step process by which mass communications are reinforced by actions of local influential people. While this work does not refer to adult education, the implications of its point of view on practice have been substantial. An interesting English study is *The Communication of Ideas* by T. Canter and J. S. Downham (Chatto and Windus, London, 1964) which traces out the major influences in the communication of thought in the city of Derby.

Performing Arts

The relationship of the performing arts to adult education has not been explored systematically at any depth but many references illustrate aspects of it. In "The Theater in Modern Education," JAE, 5 (April, 1933), Edith J. R. Isaacs considers the educative effect of the theater. A study of noncommercial theater treated as adult education was presented by Jean Carter and Jess Ogden in *Everyman's Drama* (AAAE, New York, 1938). A somewhat similar view of the "human relations potentials in drama" was given by Jack Simos in *Social Growth Through Play Production* (Association Press, New York, 1957).

Religion

In the point of view of some authorities, learning (being an aspect of man's realization of his own potential) is itself either religion or an important element of it. Thus J. Carson Pritchard points out that "our sacred literature admonishes us to learn and to teach." "The Divine Imperative to Learn and to Teach," AL, *11* (June, 1963). A full-scale study in depth of the relationship of religion to adult education is presented by Basil A. Yeaxlee in a two-volume work *Spiritual Values in Adult Education* (Oxford University Press, Oxford, 1925). Other authors consider religion as a subject-matter for learning or as part of the work of churches. Presenting the latter point of view are the following statements:

BLANCHE CARRIER, "Self-Reliance: The Educational Aim of the Liberal Church," JAE, *8* (January, 1936)

DON DEFFNER, "The Church and Adult Education," AL, *6* (December, 1957)

KENNETH STOKES, "The Creative Role of Interpersonal Groups in the Church Today," AL, *17* (November, 1968)

NATHAN D. THORP, "Programming for Adult Religious Education," AL, *17* (November, 1968)

The approaches of various denominations to adult education have often been described. Two symposia dealing with the views of Jews, Protestants, and Catholics so far as adult education are concerned are presented in "The Churches and the Gospel of Education," JAE, *3* (October, 1931), and "Where are We in Adult Religious Education?", AL, *7* (February, 1959). A statement concerning "Organizational Adult Jewish Education" was provided by Samuel I. Cohen in AL, *17* (May, 1968) and concerning "Religious Education Among Mormons" by William G. Dyer in AL, *17* (November, 1968). A review of the research on the church as a religious adult educational institution was presented by Lawrence C. Little in "Some Recent Research Contributions to Understanding Our Religious Adult Education," AL, *13* (March, 1965).

Participation

In "Training for Participation," AL, *13* (June, 1965), Ronald Lippitt approaches adult educational programing in terms of increasing participation and making it more meaningful. Alan B. Knox and Richard Videbeck have reported research which demonstrated that "The variations between status configurations in degree of participation in adult education were closely paralleled by variations in participation in voluntary associations." "Adult Education and Adult Life Cycle," AE, *13* (Winter, 1963). Mohammed Douglah in "Some Perspectives on the Phenomenon of Participation," AE, *20* (Winter, 1970) considers adult education as essentially a form of participative behavior. In these and other cases, the meaning of participation is not always clear but it generally has to do with the overt behavior of individuals or groups in taking part in general social activities.

Creativeness

Creativeness as a generalized human trait has often been related or even equated to adult education. The latter position was taken by Hughes Mearns in *The Creative Adult* (Doubleday, Doran, New York, 1940). L. R. Mobley emphasized that "healthy change in individuals and organizations results from creative acts of individuals." "Creative Leadership," AL, *9* (March, 1961). In "What Does an Organization Want—Creativity?", AL, *13* (January, 1965), A. R. Wright considers the creative elements in an institution which lead to the educative development of those who are part of it. Jane Zahn in *Creativity Research and Its Implications for Adult Education* (CSLEA, Boston, 1966) has made the connection between the two functions without implying that they are identical.

Health

The field of public health education (including that of adults) has grown up outside the academic study of education and has its own distinct literature and patterns of training and practice. Three references which describe this form of practice and indicate something of its general relevance to adult education are

> FRANK ERNEST HILL, *Educating for Health* (AAAE, New York, 1939)
>
> LOWELL S. LEVIN, "The Voluntary Health Agency in Planned Social Change," AL, *16* (October, 1967)
>
> DONALD C. KLEIN, *Community Dynamics and Mental Health* (Wiley, New York, 1968)

Case Studies

A fundamental assumption of this book is that program theory both arises from practice and is tested by it. For this reason, copious illustrations are provided for all general points and five extended case studies (four in Chapter Three and one in Chapter Six) are given. No generalized casebook of adult educational practice exists but a large sector of the literature is made up of descriptions of programs. Anyone who wishes, for either learning or teaching purposes, to find additional cases will be able to locate many book-length accounts of them. The chief sources for shorter cases are the periodicals of adult education, both American and foreign. The JAE was particularly rich in such accounts, a few of which were also included in Mary Ely's book *Adult Education in Action* (AAAE, New York, 1936). AE and AL also have a large number of case histories and surveys, as do AE [B] and the periodicals of the Canadian Association for Adult Education, *Food for Thought* and *Continuous Learning*. A book somewhat resembling Miss Ely's but based on Canadian experience is *Learning and Society,* edited by J. R. Kidd (Canadian Association for Adult Education, Toronto, 1963).

Most of the books which present case studies are related to some single agency of service or some method. The work of libraries has been amply illustrated by John Chancellor in *Helping Adults to Learn* (American Library Association, Chicago, 1939), by Margaret Monroe in *Library Adult Education* (Scarecrow, Metuchen, N.J., 1963), and by Eleanor Phinney in *Library Adult Education in Action* (American Library Association, Chicago, 1956). Cases on management education in industry are presented in *The Development of Management Talent* (American Management Association, New York, 1952) and in *Training by Objectives* by George S. Odiorne (Macmillan, New York, 1970). Community development, as broadly and variously conceived, is illustrated in *Community Education* NSSE Yearbook (University of Chicago Press, Chicago, 1959); two books by Clarence King, *Working with People in Community Action* (Association Press, New York, 1965) and *Working with People in Small Communities* (Harper, New York, 1958); and two especially useful books by Jean and Jess Ogden, *Small Communities in Action* (Harper, New York, 1946) and *These*

Things We Tried (University of Virginia Extension, Charlottesville, Va., 1947). The use of C-6 and C-10 situations by many different groups and agencies is illustrated in *Community Organizations in Action,* edited by Ernest B. Harper and Arthur Dunham (Association Press, New York, 1959). Several case studies of discussion and analyses of them are provided by Thomas Fansler in *Discussion Methods for Adult Groups* (AAAE, New York, 1934).

Analyses of Categories

The categories of program development and analysis used in this book are described and illustrated in many of the foregoing sources and the references which deal with each one will be given in the following sections. Formats have been taxonomized elsewhere in various ways, but, so far as could be discovered, no previous classification of the sort described in Chapter Four has been devised and systematically developed in the field of adult education. The categories presented here have been derived from an examination of actual practice but they parallel a number of forms of social organization studied by social psychologists. *Interpersonal Dynamics* by Warren G. Bennis, Edgar H. Schein, and David E. Berley (Dorsey Press, Homewood, Ill., 1964) offers an excellent and lively collection of readings dealing with such forms.

Independent Study

As suggested in the text, the chief source of accounts of independent study are to be found in the field of cultural history and particularly in biographies and autobiographies. A vast literature of both practical and evangelistic self-help books also exists; it has been analyzed in a profound but interesting fashion by John G. Cawelti in *Apostles of the Self-Made Man* (University of Chicago Press, Chicago, 1965). A briefer but more comprehensive account of this whole literature is provided by Jindra Kulich in "An Historical Overview of the Adult Self-Learner" in the *International Congress of University Adult Education Journal, 9* (September, 1970).

Some of the early developers of adult education in the United States were interested in independent study. Two of the essays on the subject are David Snedden, "Self-Education," JAE, 2 (January, 1930) and Samuel Cornelius, "Without Teacher: A Different

Learning", JAE, *13* (April, 1941). Generalized advice on personal plans for learning was offered by Leonard S. Stein in "Plan for Personal Learning," AL, *6* (October, 1957) and by R. Wayne Shute in *For Adults Only* (Deseret Book Company, Salt Lake City, 1968). Specific assistance of this sort for business managers was provided by William R. Dill and others in "Strategies for Self-Education," *Harvard Business Review, 43* (November-December, 1965). Advice on how to study both independently and in groups is given by Cyril O. Houle in *Continuing Your Education* (McGraw-Hill, New York, 1964).

Analytical studies of self-education are still rather rare. John W. C. Johnstone and Ramon J. Rivera made a nation-wide sampling study of the extent and nature of this phenomenon and furnished the results in their book *Volunteers for Learning* (Aldine-Atherton, Chicago, 1965). Allen Tough analyzed a number of examples of such activity and published two accounts of his findings, "The Assistance Obtained by Adult Self-Teachers," AE, *17* (Autumn, 1966) and *Learning Without a Teacher* (Ontario Institute for Studies in Education, Toronto, 1967). More recently he has reviewed the whole nature of independent study—alone, with a tutor, or in groups—in *The Adult's Learning Projects* (Ontario Institute for Studies in Education, Toronto, 1971).

Tutorial Teaching

The breadth of application of tutorial teaching in adult education and some of the theories related to its various forms are suggested by the references cited in the text. Additional sources which deal with various ways by which this form of dyadic learning occurs will be cited but they can merely illustrate the great profusion of literature available on this subject.

A psychologically oriented treatment of this relationship is given in *The Helping Interview* by Alfred Benjamin (Houghton Mifflin, Boston, 1969). The consultant-client relationship is also developed by several authors in "Effective Consultation" a special workshop feature of AL, *3* (April, 1955) and by an article by William H. Koch, Jr., "A Stance Toward Helping" in AL, *16* (December, 1967). A more informal approach is followed by Robert D. Boyd, "The Dynamics of Adult Education," AE, *14* (Spring,

1964) and by Lee Holder and Sitarama Subbiah, "The Informal Approach in Health Education Activities," AL, *10* (June, 1962).

More highly structured and cognitive-oriented approaches also exist. The role of the readers' adviser in the public library is described in two books—John Chancellor, Miriam D. Tompkins, and Hazel I. Medway, *Helping the Reader toward Self-Education* (American Library Association, Chicago, 1938); and Jennie M. Flexner and Byron C. Hopkins, *Readers' Advisers at Work* (AAAE, New York, 1941). The superviser-worker relationship is dealt with in "The Art of Supervision," a special workshop feature of AL, *4* (October, 1955) and special applications in nursing are described in *Developing the Supervisory Skills of the Nurse* by Adelma E. Mooth and Miriam M. Ritvo (Macmillan, New York, 1966). Arthur E. Durfee has published two papers on this relationship in the Cooperative Extension Service in "Changing Role of the Supervisor", JCE, *1* (Fall, 1963) and "Helping Others Improve Performance", *Journal of Extension, 8* (Summer, 1970). Two of the many books on this topic in business and industry are Aaron Q. Sartain and Alton W. Baker, *The Supervisor and His Job* (McGraw-Hill, New York, 1965); and Bill C. Lowin and Emery Reber Casstenens, *Coaching, Learning, and Action* (American Management Association, New York, 1971). In the early 1960s much attention was devoted to programed learning. Wilbur Schramm has edited a useful guide to the research on this subject in *The Research on Programmed Instruction: An Annotated Bibligraphy,* U. S. Office of Education Bulletin No. 35 (Government Printing Office, Washington Printing Office, Washington, D.C., 1964). Two useful books which deal with various aspects of this subject are Jerome P. Lysaught and Clarence Williams, *A Guide to Programmed Instruction* (Wiley, New York, 1963); and *Programmed Instruction* NSSE Yearbook (University of Chicago Press, Chicago, 1967).

Correspondence instruction is an old and widespread form of tutorial teaching. Leonard S. Stein has argued in "Design of a Correspondence Course," AE, *10* (Spring, 1960) that designing such teaching is basically similar to designing a course. Charles A. Wedemeyer edited *The Brandenburg Memorial Essays on Correspondence Instruction* (University Extension Division, University of Wisconsin, Madison, Wis., 1963), and a series of essays on correspondence education with particular reference to its use in African countries is to be found in *Mass Education* edited by Lars-Olof Edström, Renée Erdos, and Roy Prosser (The Dag Hammarskjöld Foundation, Stockholm, 1970). The potential importance of correspondence teaching in the Cooperative Extension Service is suggested by Ralph C. Dobbs and Richard M. Markoff in "Is Independent Study an Answer?", *Journal of Extension, 9* (Spring, 1971). A survey of all aspects of correspondence study is provided in *Teaching by Correspondence* by Renée P. Erdos (Longmans and UNESCO, London, 1967) and its use as a method of preparing for degrees and other advanced qualifications is described by Ron Glatter and others in *Study by Correspondence* (Longmans, London, 1971).

Learning Group

The learning group has long been a center of attention in adult education, either on its own terms or as the major format which uses the process of discussion. An early essay by Jessie Allen Charters, "The Training of Leaders for Adult Study Groups," JAE, *2* (January, 1930) made a sharp distinction between the teacher and the group leader. In *Education for Maturity,* John Walker Powell reported on group processes in adult education and in "Study Circles in Sweden," AE, *14* (Spring, 1964), Robert E. Belding described a national pattern of activity. The use of sociometric techniques to form instructional groups in an institutional setting is described by James W. Longest "Group Formation for Teaching," JCE, *2* (Fall, 1964). James A. Davis, *Great Books and Small Groups* (Glencoe, Beverly Hills, 1961) gives the results of a survey of the activities of groups sponsored by the Great Books Foundation. An exploration of many of the aspects of group development in learning situations (with particular reference to the British experience) is undertaken by A. K. C. Ottaway in *Learning Through Group Experience* (Routledge and Kegan Paul, London, 1966). Derek J. de Solla Price and Donald deB. Beaver studied the way by which a group of advanced scientists keep up on developments in their field in "Collaboration in an Invisible College," *American Psychologist, 21* (November, 1966).

Because discussion is the chief means for pooling experiences, it has often been thought to be the chief method of adult education and has been the subject of much attention in the field, including many references cited elsewhere in this essay. Three sources illustrate the general nature of such treatments—"Leading Discussion," a special issue of AL, *1* (March, 1953) has a number of essays dealing with this subject. Two useful manuals are Halbert E. Gulley, *Discussion, Conference, and Group Process* (Holt, Rinehart, and Winston, New York, 1961), and Russell H. Wagner and Carroll C. Arnold, *Handbook of Group Discussion* (Houghton Mifflin, Boston, 1965).

Autonomous groups, which spring up without any conscious external influence and which may have many purposes in addition to education, have been extensively studied by a number of investigators, particularly a circle centered around Maria Rogers. Her own brief statement concerning such groups is "Come and Be Educated!", JAE, *10* (October, 1938), and a more extended account, under her editorship, is given in "Autonomous Groups: A New Field for Adult Education," a special issue of the *Journal of Educational Sociology*, *19* (May, 1946). A research report on such groups was made by Hurley H. Doddy in *Informal Groups and the Community* (Bureau of Publications, Teachers College, Columbia University, New York, 1952). Learning as a by-product of work-oriented groups was dealt with in "Effective Committees and Work-groups," a special workshop feature of AL, *5* (September, 1956).

The educational effect of group processes has long been a concern of the field of social work and efforts to relate that line of investigation to adult education are to be found in *Adult Education and Group Work* by Louis Lowy (William Morrow, New York, 1955) and in Irving Spergel, "Elements of Social Group Work Service," AL, *12* (September, 1963).

The study of the nature and operation of groups has been a major concern of social psychology and much of this work has been created by investigators who regarded themselves as educators of adults. References to the group dynamics movement will be found elsewhere in this essay. An overview of the developing research on small groups is provided in a number of sources of which the following are representative:

MATTHEW B. MILES, *Learning to Work in Groups* (Bureau of Publications, Teachers College, Columbia University, New York, 1959)

A. PAUL HARE, *Handbook of Small Group Research* (Glencoe, Beverly Hills, 1962)

A. PAUL HARE, EDGAR F. BORGATTA, AND ROBERT F. BALES, editors, *Small Groups.* Revised edition. (Knopf, New York, 1965)

GERARD EGAN, *Encounter: Group Processes for Interpersonal Growth* (Wadsworth, Belmont, Ca., 1970)

Teacher-Directed Group Instruction

Teacher-directed group instruction is the chief format category dealt with in the references given in the two sections of this essay on the general literature of education on program development and on program development in adult education. In addition, many of the specialized references given elsewhere deal specifically or by implication with this form of learning. At this point, therefore, only a few sources will be mentioned, all of which are restricted to the C-4 situation. It is dealt with at all educational levels in *The Dynamics of Instructional Groups* NSSE Yearbook (University of Chicago Press, Chicago, 1960). "Teaching Adults," a special workshop feature of AL, *3* (March, 1955), provides a treatment of this subject by several authors. *The Adult Class* by A. J. J. Ratcliff (Thomas Nelson, Camden, N.J., 1938) offers an early English view, and *Teaching on Equal Terms,* edited by Jennifer Rogers (British Broadcasting Corporation, London, 1969) presents a more recent survey of the topic. In "Community Adult Education—the Role of the Professional," AE [B], *44* (September, 1971), Keith Jackson argues that the class should have many more of the characteristics of the voluntary group or association than it does at present.

Committee-Guided Group Learning

While C-5 situations have many forms, they have generally been considered in terms of conferences or of large scale meetings, conducted singly or in series. On the latter topic, useful sources are

LELAND P. BRADFORD AND STEPHEN M. COREY, "Improving Large Group Meetings," AE, *1* (April, 1951)

"Improving Large Meetings," a special issue of AL, *1* (December, 1952)

"The Single-Shot Meeting," a special workshop feature of AL, *3* (June, 1954)

A theoretical statement which provides valuable groundwork for conferences, institutes, and workshops is the chapter entitled "On Temporary Systems" of *Innovation in Education*, edited by Matthew Miles (Columbia University Press, New York, 1966). Practical treatments of the subject are given in

"Conferences that Work," a special issue of AL, *2* (May, 1953)

"Workshops and Institutes," a special workshop feature of AL, *4* (January, 1956)

RICHARD BECKHARD, *How to Plan and Conduct Workshops and Conferences* (Association Press, New York, 1956)

MARY CAPES, ed., *Communication or Conflict* (Association Press, New York, 1960)

HERBERT S. KINDLER, *Organizing the Technical Conference* (Reinhold, New York, 1960)

MARGARET MEAD AND PAUL BYERS, *The Small Conference: An Innovation in Communication* (Mouton, Paris, 1968)

HARRY P. ZELKO, *The Business Conference* (McGraw-Hill, New York, 1969)

The development of residential centers throughout the world, beginning in Denmark in the first half of the nineteenth century, has given rise to a special field of interest and concentration which is often called residential adult education. Cyril O. Houle has provided a brief history and interpretation of this work in *Residential Continuing Education* (Syracuse University Publications in Continuing Education, Syracuse, N.Y., 1971). In *Continuing Education in Action*, (Wiley, New York, 1968), Harold Alford describes the work of a number of American centers which work chiefly in terms of the C-5 category.

Collaborative Group Education

The literature on collaborative group education tends to fall into two clusters, that which is based on an agency and that which is based on a community, however defined. Most sources deal with some practical situation and offer relatively little general theoretical treatment. Among the useful items are

BERTRAND L. SMITH, "Coordinated Community Group Action: Functional Adult Education," *Adult Education Bulletin,* 7 (April, 1943)

"The Group in the Community," AL, *1* (October, 1952)

O. ROSS MC DONALD, "Community Development Through Interclub Councils," AL, 7 (September, 1958)

ISABEL B. HAGLIN AND MABEL SWANSON, "An Experiment in Coordination," AL, *9* (September, 1960)

VINCENT J. AMANNA, "Planned Coordination for Study-Discussion," AE, *13* (Autumn, 1962)

BEULAH M. EDGETT AND ANNE K. STENZEL, "An Inter-Agency Approach in Training Volunteers," AL, *12* (December, 1963)

Institutions

A substantial literature on institutional structure and operation has been developed in the academic disciplines of political science and sociology as well as in such fields of application as business, education, and welfare. The following general works are not related specifically to adult education but have proved useful to those who seek a deeper understanding of how institutions operate:

THEODORE CAPLOW, *Principles of Organization* (Harcourt, Brace, and World, New York, 1964)

JAMES G. MARCH, ed., *Handbook of Organizations* (Rand, McNally, Skokie, Ill., 1965)

DANIEL KATZ AND ROBERT KAHN, *The Social Psychology of Organizations* (Wiley, New York, 1966)

WILLIAM A. GLASER AND DAVID L. SILLS, eds., *The Government of Associations* (Bedminster Press, Totawa, N.J., 1966)

BERTRAM M. GROSS, *Organizations and their Managing* (Free Press, New York, 1968)

JOSEPH A. LITTERER, *Organizations: Structure and Behavior.* Second edition. (Wiley, New York, 1969)

OSCAR GRUSKY AND GEORGE A. MILLER, editors, *The Sociology of Organizations* (Free Press, New York, 1970)

As yet the serious study of adult educational institutions has been limited primarily to descriptions of specific organizations or associations. The early general treatments of the subject were highly practical but later ones are more theoretical. Three issues of AL were devoted to "Committees, Boards, and Officers," AL, *2* (September, 1953), to "Locals and Their Nationals," AL, *2* (January, 1954), and to "The Larger Organization," AL, *3* (September, 1954). John E. Tsouderos developed a general statement of the major aspects of voluntary associations in his article "Voluntary Associations," AL, *6* (April, 1958). In various places, analyses of the institutional structure of adult education have been given; one such reference is a chapter by Malcolm Knowles "The Field of Operations in Adult Education" in *Adult Education: Outlines of an Emerging Field of University Study*, edited by Gale Jensen, A. A. Liveright, and Wilbur Hallenbeck (AEA, Chicago, 1964). A creative piece of research outlining the stages of growth of adult educational institutions was described by William S. Griffith in "Implications for Administrators in the Changing Adult Education Agency," AE, *15* (Spring, 1965). An effort to develop an adequate model to describe adult educational institutions was presented by Roy J. Ingham in "A Comparative Study of Administrative Principles and Practices in Adult Education Units," AE, *19* Autumn, 1968).

The three intrainstitutional categories of program planning (C-7, C-8, and C-9) suggested in this book appear to be consistent with both the general and the adult educational literature but apparently they have not been previously defined in the present form. No references could be found which dealt with them separately or collectively as they are analyzed here.

Collaborative Institutional Planning

The need to coordinate the programs of adult educational institutions has been a concern of leaders in the field since it first emerged on the American scene. At first it was thought that the chief instrument to achieve the purpose would be a general adult educational council, one of which might emerge in every community. Jacques Ozanne, in "Counsel for Councils," JAE, 6 (April, 1934) gave advice concerning their proper operation, and Ruth Kotinsky, in *Adult Education Councils* (AAAE, New York, 1940), gave a thoughtful appraisal of their practices and theory. On a broader basis, Lyman Bryson presented *A State Plan for Adult Education* (AAAE, New York, 1934).

While the need for generalized councils has not declined and some of them continue to exist, most of the attention in the field is now directed toward the development of more specific kinds of bilateral and multilateral operations. Three issues of AL were largely devoted to that topic—"Improving Communication Among Local Organizations," AL, 4 (November, 1955), "Working Together for Adult Education," AL, 4 (December, 1955), and "Representative Councils in Action," AL, 5 (May, 1956). Other useful references on C-10 situations are

> PER STENSLAND AND CAROL STENSLAND, "Community Education for International Understanding. Part I—State and Local UNESCO Councils," AE, 2 (October, 1951)
>
> LESLIE THIS, "Relationship Between Agencies," AL, 5 (October, 1956)
>
> NATHAN HURVITZ, "A Cooperative Inter-Agency Adult Education Program," AE, 8 (Autumn, 1957)
>
> J. D. MEZIROW, "The Coordinating Council in Community Development—an Evaluation," AE, 8 (Summer, 1958)
>
> JOHN L. GABLE, "An Advisory Council for Adult Education," AL, 12 (February, 1964)
>
> *Inter-Association Cooperation Reconsidered* (CSLEA, Boston, 1965)
>
> J. DANIEL HILL, "Can Cooperative Extension and Community College Work Together?" *Journal of Extension, 8* (Winter, 1970).

In addition, Arthur Dunham provides a description of C-10 situations in the field of social welfare (which often overlaps adult educational practice) in *Community Welfare Organization: Principles and Practices* (Crowell, New York, 1958).

Mass Education

Mass education, as considered in this book, includes many methods and media such as lecturing, exhibits, and museum displays, as well as the instruments of widespread communications (such as the press, radio, motion pictures and television) which are commonly referred to as the mass media. Each aspect of this broad field has its own extensive literature and in many cases the writings reach back to antiquity; for example, rhetoric and oratory were arts well known to the ancient Greeks. Much of the writing specifically in the field of adult education is an adaptation of ideas originally advanced in other fields. Some of it applies generally to all mass communication; AL, *1* (March, 1953) was given over to this subject. Most of it, however, deals with some form of mass education. The handling of a large audience, for example, was described by Harry Hollingworth in *Psychology of the Audience* (American Book Company, New York, 1935) and Bert and Frances Strauss presented a somewhat broader approach in *New Ways to Better Meetings* (Viking, New York, 1951). Reading was dealt with in *Adult Reading*, NSSE Yearbook (University of Chicago Press, Chicago, 1956).

Much modern writing has dealt with one or more of the mass media. Background works on this subject have been widely used, among them *People, Society, and Mass Communication*, edited by Lewis Anthony Dexter and David Manning White (Free Press, New York, 1964) and *Mass Media and National Development* by Wilbur Schramm (Stanford University Press, Stanford, Ca., 1964). Other works, specifically in the field of adult education have been plentiful. Among the most useful are

"Using Television for Adult Education," A special workshop feature of AL, *5* (October, 1956)

BRIAN GROOMBRIDGE, editor, *Adult Education and Television* (National Institute of Adult Education, England and Wales, London, 1966)

JOHN OHLIGER, *Listening Groups: Mass Media in Adult Education* (CSLEA, Boston, 1967)

JOHN OHLIGER, *The Mass Media in Adult Education, A Review of the Recent Literature* (ERIC, Syracuse, N.Y., 1968)

HENRY C. ALTER, *Of Messages and Media* (CSLEA, Boston, 1968)

JOHN A. NIEMI, editor. *Mass Media and Adult Education* Educational Technology Publications, Englewood Cliffs, N.J., 1971)

Identification of New Educational Activities

Numerous publications tell educators of adults how to discover the needs and interests of present or potential learners. Many such sources are listed elsewhere in this essay, but it may be useful at this point to mention two works which provide inventories of need-locating techniques. *Identifying Educational Needs of Adults* by Homer Kempfer (Office of Education Circular No. 330, Government Printing Office, Washington, D.C., 1951) classifies the ways by which public schools and community colleges identify needs. A somewhat broader approach and an extended annotated bibliography are provided by Ernest E. McMahon in *Needs—of People and Their Communities—and the Adult Educator* (AEA, Washington, D.C., 1970).

Many accounts provide descriptions of new and original program approaches; the evident intent is to stimulate their borrowing or adaptation elsewhere. A good example of this kind of work is *New Directions in Programming for University Adult Education* by Peter E. Siegle and James B. Whipple (CSLEA, Chicago, 1957).

Deciding to Proceed

Little attention has been given to the decision-making process by which potential adult educational programs are either accepted or abandoned. Countless statements of objectives or policies which might be used to help select or reject activities have been made, but little or no consideration has been given as to how these statements are actually used for this purpose. However, the formal techniques used by staffs to select the best programs among various alternatives are sometimes described or analyzed. One such reference is J. L. Matthews, *National Inventory of Extension Methods of Program Determination* (U. S. Department of Agriculture, Washington, D.C., 1952).

Identifying and Refining the Objectives

Virtually all works which describe adult education or deal with program planning devote some attention to objectives, and the general educational literature on program development provides a rich background for the consideration of the topic. Furthermore, the various systems of program planning and analysis described elsewhere all deal with aims or goals in some fashion. In this section, therefore, only a few general references which relate specifically to the identification and refinement of objectives will be listed.

"Working Toward Goals," a special issue of AL, *1* (September, 1952) provides both theoretical exposition and practical advice on the selection and use of goals in adult education. Malcolm Knowles, in "Philosophical Issues that Confront Adult Education," AE, 7 (Summer, 1957), reviews the major starting points or sources of objectives. Horace M. Kallen, in *Philosophical Issues in Adult Education* (Charles C Thomas, Springfield, Ill., 1962) explores the essentially humanistic values which govern and may be achieved by adult education.

Each of the six factors which (it is here suggested) mesh to create objectives has been considered separately and in depth. In analyzing learners, it is possible to use the rich psychological literature describing the change of individuals throughout the lifespan. While the following books which deal with this subject do not deal specifically with adult education, they provide valuable background material for a consideration of specific categories of learners:

SIDNEY L. PRESSEY AND RAYMOND G. KUHLEN, *Psychological Development Through the Life Span* (Harper and Row, New York, 1957)

JUSTIN PIKUNAS, *Human Development: A Science of Growth* (McGraw-Hill, New York, 1969)

L. R. GOULET AND PAUL B. BALTES, eds. *Life-Span Developmental Psychology* (Academic Press, New York, 1970)

In the adult educational literature which applies psychological concepts to practice in the field, the following references are typical and useful:

> JOHN B. SCHWERTMAN, "I Am a Slippery Subject" in *I Want Many Lodestars* (CSLEA, Chicago, 1952)
>
> GARDNER MURPHY AND RAYMOND KUHLEN, *Psychological Needs of Adults* (CSLEA, Chicago, 1955)
>
> ROBERT J. HAVIGHURST AND BETTY ORR, *Adult Education and Adult Needs* (CSLEA, Chicago, 1956)
>
> JOHN C. WHITEHORN, "The Development of Mature Individuals," AL, 5 (January, 1957)
>
> JESS BURKETT, "Comprehensive Programming for Life-long Learning," AE, *10* (Winter, 1960)
>
> RAYMOND KUHLEN, editor. *Psychological Backgrounds of Adult Education* (CSLEA, Boston, 1963)

In the analysis of the influence of the milieu on educational objectives, the most general work is *Sociological Backgrounds of Adult Education,* edited by Hobart W. Burns (CSLEA, Boston, 1964). Robert H. Snow, in *Community Adult Education* (Putnam's, New York, 1955) and Wilbur C. Hallenbeck and others, in *Community and Adult Education* (AEA, Chicago, 1962), suggest the ways by which the aims of adult education should grow out of community needs. In dealing with content, Arthur H. Compton, in "Science and Man's Destiny," *The Key Reporter* (February, 1952), argued the need for scientific knowledge and content as an important aspect of adult educational objectives, and Howard R. Neville, in "An Interdisciplinary Approach to Continuing Education," AE, *10* (Winter, 1960), stressed the importance of cutting across recognized fields of knowledge in establishing the goals of programs. Relatively few authors treat the design of a program as being a determinant of its goals, but many of them imply it; thus, works on television programing assume that the method will determine what is done, and works on the processes of group dynamics imply the significance of human relations training. The richest exploration of aspiration so far as adult education is concerned is to be found in JAE; in it many American and European leaders explored the potential values which the field might achieve. Much of that literature is summarized

in Mary Ely, *Adult Education in Action* (AAAE, New York, 1936).
An unusually valuable essay on how value systems become incorporated into adult educational practice was offered by R. W. K.
Paterson in "Values in Adult Education," *Rewley House Papers*
(Oxford 1964–1965). One treatment of motives is given by Max
Birnbaum in "Mind and Emotion in Adult Education," AE, *7*
(Spring, 1957).

The literature on the statement of adult educational objectives has been almost entirely based on the general educational
literature on that subject. A thoughtful analysis of the range of
objectives that sometimes occur in adult education is provided by
Alan Knox in "Conference Objectives: Prelude to Evaluation,"
AL, *12* (February, 1962). The significance of a clear awareness
of objectives for subsequent learning was demonstrated by John P.
Blaney and Douglas McKie in "Knowledge of Conference Objectives and Effect upon Learning," AE, *19* (Winter, 1969). One
controversial issue has to do with whether objectives should be stated
in behavioral terms so that their accomplishment can readily be
measured. During much of the recent history of education, it has
usually been thought that statement in this fashion represents enlightened practice. A comprehensive treatment of the topic is presented by Miriam B. Kapfer in *Behavioral Objectives in Curriculum
Development* (Educational Technology Publications, Englewood
Cliffs, N.J., 1971). Recent attacks have been made upon behavioral
objectives. Two articles in this vein are J. Myron Atkin, "Behavior
Objectives in Curriculum Design: A Cautionary Note," *Science
Teacher, 35* (May, 1968); and Harry S. Broudy, "Can Research
Escape the Dogma of Behavioral Objectives?," *School Review, 79*
(November, 1970). A rejoinder to such attacks and a thoroughgoing defense of behavioral objectives was made by W. James
Popham in "Probing the Validity of Arguments Against Behavioral
Goals" in *Current Research on Instruction,* edited by Richard C.
Anderson and others (Prentice-Hall, Englewood Cliffs, N.J., 1969).

Developing Format

The matter of format as defined here is generally dealt with
in the books on program design in adult education which have

already been cited or in the works on educational methods which will be included in a subsequent section.

Selecting Learning Resources

Adult educational programs are so diverse in character that they draw upon many kinds of learning resources. Jacques Ozanne, in "Material Consideration," JAE, *11* (January, 1939), suggested a number of principles which might be used in choosing materials; while some of his comments are still relevant, others demonstrate how much more fortunate modern adult educational leaders are than their predecessors of Ozanne's day. "Using Resources," a special issue of AL, *1* (July-August, 1952) provides a great deal of practical information on adult educational resources and their uses.

The location of appropriate reading material for adult groups has long been a problem. A. E. Heath, in "Books and Adult Education," JAE, *1* (October, 1929), dealt with this subject, as did Margaret Charters Lyon in *The Selection of Books for Adult Study Groups* (Bureau of Publications, Teachers College, Columbia University, New York, 1937) and Angelica Cass in "Reading Materials for Adults," AE, *1* (October, 1950).

The special preparation of reading materials, particularly at elementary levels of comprehension and skill, has had much attention. Gustav Francis Beck, in "Pitfalls of Popularization," JAE, *1* (April, 1929), dealt with the question of adapting content and materials to the level of the learners to be reached. The study of readability was pioneered by Rudolf F. Flesch in *Marks of a Readable Style* (Bureau of Publications, Teachers College, Columbia University, New York, 1943) and an outstanding demonstration of the application of readability indices to mass publications was described by L. E. Sarbaugh in "Improving Readability of U.S. D. A. Popular Publications," AL, 6, (March, 1958). Two manuals on the preparation of elementary materials for adults have been issued by UNESCO—*Simple Reading Material for Adults: Its Preparation and Use* (UNESCO, Paris, 1953); and *Literacy Primers: Construction, Evaluation, and Use* (UNESCO, Paris, 1961).

The impact on adult education of the newer media and the content they provide has also had substantial attention. One general work prepared by Wilbur Schramm and others, *The New Media: Memo to Educational Planners* (UNESCO, Paris, 1967) provided a general survey for all forms of education. Peter H. Rossi and Bruce J. Biddle edited a book on *The New Media and Education* (Aldine-Atherton, New York, 1966), with a chapter by Malcolm S. Knowles on "Adult Education." *Educational Media* by Raymond V. Wiman and Wesley C. Meierhenry deals with the application of communication theory to education (Charles E. Merrill, Columbus, Ohio, 1969).

The influence of the total environment of the physical plant as an educational resource has been stated by Robert H. Anderson in "The School as an Organic Teaching Aid" in *The Curriculum: Retrospect and Prospect* NSSE Yearbook (University of Chicago Press, Chicago, 1971). While he focuses on children and schools, his comments have relevance to adult education as well. Works which deal more specifically with that field are

> N. L. ENGELHARDT AND N. L. ENGELHARDT, JR. *Planning the Community School* (American Book, New York, 1940)
> *Creating a Climate for Adult Learning.* Report of a National Conference on Architecture for Adult Education. (Division of Adult Education, Purdue University, Lafayette, Ind., 1959)
> *Architecture for Adult Education* (AEA, Chicago, undated)

Leaders

The location, selection, training, and employment of leaders has long been a major problem in adult education because it has been well understood from the very beginnings of the field that none of its formats other than self-directed study could succeed without the guidance and direction of competent people. An early effort to explore this whole topic was undertaken by Harry A. and Bonaro W. Overstreet in *Leaders for Adult Education* (AAAE, New York, 1941). Another effort to look broadly at leadership was made by Cyril O. Houle in "Professional Education for Educators of Adults," AE, 6 (Spring, 1956), an analysis which was amplified and somewhat altered in the same author's chapters on the subject in the 1960 and the 1970 *Handbook of Adult Education* the latter published by Macmillan, New York, 1970.

Most of the major periodicals in adult education have devoted one or more issues to various aspects of leadership selection and training. AL, *1* (June, 1952); AL, *2* (June, 1953); AL, *3* (November, 1954); and AL, *5* (June, 1956) were devoted to the topic. The entire issue of AE, *2* (June, 1952) was devoted to the in-service training of educators of adults in various agencies. A special issue of AE [B], *38* (March, 1966) dealt with the recruitment and training of staff for adult educational agencies. The first issue of *Convergence, 1* (March, 1968) was also centered on this topic.

The nature of leadership in adult education has also been studied objectively by various investigators. A. A. Liveright, in *Strategies of Leadership in Conducting Adult Education Programs* (Harper, New York, 1959), described various approaches and techniques, as did Richard Solomon and others in *Teaching Styles and Learning* (CSLEA, Chicago, 1963). In two papers, Burton W. Kreitlow dealt theoretically with leadership education—*Educating the Adult Educator. Part 1. Concepts for the Curriculum* (Government Printing Office, Washington, D.C., 1965); and *Educating the Adult Educator. Part 2. Taxonomy of Needed Research* (Wisconsin R. and D. Center for Cognitive Learning, Madison, 1968). Thurman White, in "Some Common Interests of Adult Education Leaders," AE, *6* (Spring, 1956) analyzed what leaders in four widely varied occupational clusters felt that they needed to know. A somewhat similar study was made by Martin Chamberlain, in "The Competencies of Adult Educators," AE, *11* (Autumn, 1960). Other works of value are

JOHN S. DIEKHOFF, *The Domain of the Faculty* (Harper, New York, 1956)

HARRY L. MILLER, "What's Your Line?" AL, *6* (September, 1957)

MARILYN V. MILLER, editor, *On Teaching Adults: An Anthoogy* (CSLEA, Chicago, 1960)

ALTON C. JOHNSON AND ROBERT W. MC CORMICK, *Staffing Decisions in the Cooperative Extension Service* (National Agricultural Extension Center for Advanced Study, University of Wisconsin, Madison, 1962).

ANNE K. STENZEL AND HELEN M. FEENEY, *Volunteer Training and Development* (Seabury Press, New York, 1968)

JOHN T. WOESTE, "Staffing Patterns in Extension," JCE, 7 (Spring, 1969)

Methods

The writers on adult education in the United States have been preoccupied with method, usually basing their approach on some technique, such as discussion, or some cluster of techniques, such as audio-visual instruction. George Aker has provided an extensive bibliography of such treatments in *Adult Education Procedures, Methods and Techniques* (Library of Continuing Education, Syracuse University, Syracuse, N.Y., 1965), and Coolie Verner has analyzed the literature on the subject in "Instructional Methods in Adult Education," *Review of Educational Research, 29* (June, 1959). Virtually all of the works listed under the heading "Program Development in Adult Education" include extended treatments of methods. Additional volumes which focus directly on the topic are

A. D. MUELLER, *Principles and Methods in Adult Education* (Prentice-Hall, Englewood Cliffs, N.J., 1937)

EARLE S. HANNAFORD, *Conference Leadership in Business and Industry* (McGraw-Hill, New York, 1945)

MEREDITH C. WILSON AND GLADYS GALLUP, *Extension Teaching Methods,* Extension Service Circular No. 495 (Government Printing Office, Washington, D.C., 1955)

PAUL BERGEVIN AND DWIGHT MORRIS, *Group Processes for Adult Education* (Community Services in Adult Education, University of Indiana, Bloomington, 1954)

GEORGE M. BEAL, JOE M. BOHLEN, AND J. NEIL RAUDABAUGH, *Leadership and Dynamic Group Action* (Iowa State University Press, Ames, Iowa, 1962)

MARTHA M. LEYPOLDT, *Forty Ways to Teach in Groups* (Judson Press, Valley Forge, Pa., 1967)

An interesting contrast to the American approach to method is provided in a book edited by Norman Dees, *Approaches to Adult Teaching* (Pergamon Press, Oxford, 1965) which is a series of essays on how to teach various content fields to adults in classrooms. Other English works which emphasize C-4 situations but treat methodology directly rather than as an aspect of content are John Robinson and Neil Barnes, editors, *New Media and Methods in Industrial Training* (British Broadcasting Corporation, London, 1967); and Michael D. Stephens and Gordon W. Roderick, *Teaching Techniques in Adult Education* (David and Charles, Devon, England, 1971). Essays on teaching adults are provided by Herbert Schueler, "The Method of Adult Education," AL, *5* (April, 1957) and by James B. Whipple, *Especially for Adults* (CSLEA, Chicago, 1957). A discussion of the potential use and effect on education of new instruments of communication which have not yet been fully developed is provided by Ben H. Bagdikian, *The Information Machines* (Harper and Row, New York, 1971).

Time Schedule

While scheduling is often mentioned in general treatments of program in adult education, no special studies of it could be located.

Sequence

The literature on sequence has been concerned almost entirely with its application in C-2, C-4, C-5, and C-11 situations and has been included in the sections of this essay which deal with these topics.

Social Reinforcement

Much of the literature of sensitivity training, mentioned elsewhere, has to do with the theme of social reinforcement. Also essays and studies on residential continuing education included earlier in the treatment of C-5 situations are also concerned with it. More general works are

JACK R. GIBB, "A Climate for Learning," AE, *9* (Autumn, 1958)

HELMUT J. GOLATZ, "Probing the Institute 'Glow'," AE, *12* (Winter, 1962)

DELL LEBO, "Setting and Maintaining an Effective Emotional Atmosphere," AL, *11* (June, 1962)

KING M. WIENTGE AND JAMES K. LAHR, *The Influence of Social Climate on Adult Achievement* (University College Research Publications, Washington University, St. Louis, 1966)

ROBERT L. BRUCE AND G. L. CARTER, JR. "Administrative Climate," JCE, *5* (Spring, 1967).

Individualization

The need to individualize instruction has been a central theme in the general literature of education for many years and countless ways of doing so—such as the Winnetka plan, the contract plan, and the Morrison mastery concept—have been created. In recent years a heightened concern with this need has been manifested by new formulations, such as the mastery concept put forward by Benjamin Bloom and others and the learning strategies proposed by Philip G. Kapfer in "An Instructional Management Strategy for Individualized Learning," *Phi Delta Kappan, 49* (January, 1968). The general theory and practice of individualizing instruction was presented in *The Individual and the System: Personalizing Higher Education* (Western Interstate Commission for Higher Education, Boulder, Colo., 1967). A summary and review of the literature on how groups work to influence their members in various ways and situations is given in Margaret E. Bennett, *Guidance and Counseling in Groups,* Second Edition, (McGraw-Hill, New York, 1963).

Much of the work on individualization in adult education has been related to sensitivity training, whose literature is cited elsewhere in this essay. Two general sources may be mentioned here, however. "Personal Growth Through Group Experience" was the topic of one issue of AL, *2* (February, 1954), and Armand L. Hunter in "The University, Adult Education, and the Individual," AL, *15* (December, 1966) dealt with the crucial importance of reaching the individual student by the institutional program.

Roles and Relationships

The application of social psychological concepts to the structure and processes of adult education attracted much attention to the roles and relationships of learners and educators in all categories of program planning and execution. Two influential papers in the general field of education were J. W. Getzels, "A Psycho-Sociological Framework for the Study of Educational Administration," *Harvard Educational Review, 22* (Fall, 1952) and J. W. Getzels and E. G. Guba, "Social Behavior and the Administrative Process," *School Review, 65* (Winter, 1957). Among the treatments of the subject in the field of adult education, two of the most general approaches are to be found in two issues of AL which were largely given over to the topic: "Spotlight on Member Roles," AL, *1* (January, 1953) and "Making Leadership Fit Your Program," AL, *5* (November, 1956). Russell Robinson has dealt with the roles which university personnel can appropriately play in their community relationships in "University Roles in Adult Education," AL, *14* (June, 1966) and Gordon L. Lippitt has dealt with a variety of situations in "Multiple Roles of the Meeting Planner," AL, *17* (October, 1968). A number of studies on this topic have been made in the Cooperative Extension Service; among them are Art Gallaher, Jr., "The Agent as an Analyst," JCE, *5* (Winter, 1967); Art Gallaher, Jr. and Frank A. Santopolo, "Perspectives on Agent Roles," JCE, *5* (Winter, 1967); and Hoyt M. Warren, "Working Relationships," JCE, *5* (Fall, 1967).

Criteria for Evaluation

The establishment of criteria for evaluation is intimately tied to the processes of measurement and appraisal which will be dealt with later. The choice of forms of measurement, the central theme of the present section, is dealt with in a general fashion by Robert L. Ebel in *Measuring Educational Achievement* (Prentice-Hall, Englewood Cliffs, N.J., 1965); though this book deals entirely with school and college situations, the techniques suggested are applicable to adult classes. "Evaluating Program and Performance," a special issue of AL, *1* (April, 1953) presents various theories and processes of criteria-setting, measurement, and appraisal. C. O. Banta, "Sources of Data for Program Evaluation," AE, *5* (Summer, 1955) describes some of the special approaches and data sources which give rise to criteria.

A theoretical discussion of criterion-referenced measurement can be found in a pair of articles in the *School Review, 79* (February, 1971). Robert L. Ebel states one side of the issue with a paper on "Criterion-Referenced Measurements: Limitation" to which James H. Block responds with a paper entitled "Criterion-Referenced Measurements: Potential." The two authors are concerned chiefly with childhood education and their use of the term *criterion* is not identical with the meaning given to it in this book, but the issues which they explore are well-expressed and relevant to adult education.

Clarity of Design

The task of making a program design clear to all participants is crucially important but seems to be so obvious a process that it has not been dealt with, in any substantial fashion, in the literature. Perhaps the closest approximations are program checklists or systems analysis patterns which, by making the total program clearer to the planner presumably help him to make it clearer to the participants. One such checklist is offered by Frank C. Goodell in "A Program Planning Checklist for the Meeting Planner," AL, *18* (December, 1969).

Fitting Program into Life Patterns

In the general literature of education, the elements of format are assigned to the field of curriculum while the adjustments required to fit the format into the milieu are assigned to the fields of counseling and administration. This division is not sharply observed when adult educational programs are under consideration since format is often so intricately related to counseling and interpretation that no separation can be undertaken. Many general works on programing mentioned both earlier and later in this essay combine elements and adjustments into a single treatment. Even the few works which deal specifically with the administration of adult education usually include discussions of format. One such book is *Administration of Adult Education* by Frank M. Debatin (American Book Company, New York, 1938).

Guidance and Counseling

The literature on the guidance and counseling of adults takes two approaches—the general (which deals largely with theory) and the institutional (which considers how the needs of adults for such

services can be met in the C-7 through C-10 categories). Eugene
M. DeGabriele took a broad approach to the subject in *Guidance
Services for Adults* (California State Department of Education,
Sacramento, 1961), as does E. C. Thoroman in *The Vocational
Counseling of Adults and Young Adults* (Houghton Mifflin, Boston,
1968). An approach which is similar to that suggested in the present
book is made by Louis J. Cantoni and Lucile E. Cantoni in "Counseling—A Larger Concept" AL, *16* (October, 1967). Edward V.
Hurlbut urges the importance of constant counseling by educators
in "Adult Teachers are Counselors," AL, *10* (March, 1962). A
simply written book on counseling adults in all kinds of situations
is provided in *The Art of Helping People Effectively* by Stanley C.
Mahoney (Association Press, New York, 1967). The distinctiveness
of adult requirements for assistance is suggested by Lee Porter in
"Adults Have Special Counseling Needs," AL, *18* (March, 1970).

An early institution-based approach was described by Anne
Evans in "Adjustment and the Dispossessed," JAE, *5* (June, 1933).
In "Development of a Counseling Program in a School of Adult
Education," AE, *10* (Autumn, 1959), Helen E. Williams describes
the program of the New School of Social Research in New York
but also makes applications of principles to other settings. The services offered by universities are described by Martha L. Farmer in
Student Personnel Services for Adults in Higher Education (Scarecrow Press, Metuchen, N.J., 1967).

The Modification of Lifestyles

The clearest evidence of the importance of the modification
of lifestyles is found in the literature on the retention or dropout of
students. A serious problem of adult education is its low retention
rate and the research on its causes makes clear the fact that many
of them are related to the inability of students to adjust their
patterns of life to incorporate learning as a continuing process. Two
studies which suggest this conclusion among others are

COOLIE VERNER AND GEORGE S. DAVID, JR., "Completion and
    Drop Outs: A Review of Research," AE, *14* (Spring,
    1964)

CYRIL O. HOULE, "Who Stays—and Why?", AE, *14* (Summer,
    1964)

Financing

An early consideration of the financing of adult education was presented by A. Caswell Ellis, "Can we Afford Not to Afford It?" JAE, 5 (April, 1933). The broadest approach was made by J. R. Kidd in *Financing Adult Education* (Scarecrow Press, Metuchen, N.J., 1962) while another book of the same title by Edward B. Olds (AEA, Chicago, 1964) surveyed the financial provisions made for public schools and community councils. A recent effort to make a comprehensive financial analysis of adult educational practice was described by J. Alan Thomas, William S. Griffith and others in *Adult and Continuing Education* (National Education Finance Project, Chicago, 1970). A cost-benefit study of various kinds of programs is presented in *Continuing Education* by Melvin R. Levin and Joseph S. Slavet (Heath Lexington Books, Lexington, Mass., 1970).

Interpretation

The more subtle aspects of interpretation, as a part of intimate interpersonal relationships, is treated in the literature of adult education either as a task to be taken care of by counseling or as a product of one or more of the elements of the format such as the exercise of leadership. Most works which deal directly with the subject treat it as part of the public relations effort of an institution. A general text, broadly conceived but useful for adult educational programs is *Effective Public Relations* by Scott M. Cutlip and Allen H. Center (Prentice-Hall, Englewood Cliffs, N.J., 1964). A graphic account of how an entire institutional form can suffer from poor interpretation is *Adult Education in Transition: A Study of Institutional Insecurity* by Burton Clark (University of California Press, Berkeley, 1968). Russell Becker in "Promotion Through Service," AE (June, 1951) deals with some important ways of promoting and explaining adult education. The special public relations tasks of associations are dealt with in two sources—"Getting and Keeping Members," a special issue of AE (November, 1952); and Lawrence K. Frank, "What Influences People to Join Organizations?", AL (February, 1958). Other useful sources on public relations in adult education are

"Your Public Relations" a special workshop feature of AL
(March, 1954)

PAUL MC GHEE, "Merchandising Adult Education," AE
(Spring, 1955)

Effective Public Relations (AEA, Chicago, 1957)

MILTON R. STERN, "New Ideas in Promotion and the Recruitment of Adult Students," AE (Winter, 1959)

THOMAS F. DAMON, "Publicizing Local Programs of Adult
Education," AE (Spring, 1960)

MILTON R. STERN, *People, Programs, and Persuasion* (CSLEA,
Chicago, 1961)

T. C. BLALOCK, MARY NELL GREENWOOD, AND ROLAND H. ABRA-
HAM, "What the Public Thinks of Extension", JCE
(Spring, 1963)

EVA L. GOBLE, "Young Homemakers and Extension," JCE
(Fall, 1964)

Measurement and Appraisal of Results

Most educators of adults who have considered measurement
and appraisal have borrowed heavily from the general educational
literature and particularly from the work of Ralph W. Tyler and
his followers. This influence has been particularly strongly felt in
the work of the Cooperative Extension Service and is seen, for example, in *Evaluation in Extension*, Darcie Byrn, editor (Ives, Topeka,
Kans., 1959), in *Six Keys to Evaluating Extension Work* by Laurel
K. Sabrosky (Federal Extension Service, U.S. Department of Agriculture, PA-371, Government Printing Office, Washington, D.C.,
1958), and in "Measuring Extension's Impact" by Dan D. M.
Ragle, Roger G. Barker, and Arthur Johnson, JCE, 5 (Fall, 1967).
In *Evaluating Liberal Adult Education*, Harry L. Miller and Chris-
tine McGuire (CSLEA, Chicago, 1961) have used in depth a
straightforward Tylerian approach. *The Assessment of Change in
Training and Therapy* by James A. Belasco and Harrison M. Trice
(McGraw-Hill, New York, 1969) deals with the evaluation of
changes brought about in large organizations. *Evaluation of Management Training* by Peter Warr, Michael Bird, and Neil Rackham
(Gower Press, London, 1970) is an English work which suggests a
practical framework, with cases, for evaluating training needs and

results. One of the few available generalized measuring instruments yet developed in adult education is described in "An Attitude Scale Technique for Evaluating Meetings" by Russell P. Kropp and Coolie Verner, AE, 7 (Summer, 1957). The importance of unplanned consequences in the appraisal of a conference is illustrated by Jeffrey Fleece, "A Conference Communications Model," AL, *20* (October, 1971).

New approaches to measurement and appraisal are now being made in the education of children and young people and will probably be influential in the education of adults. Two comprehensive sources which describe these conceptions are *Educational Evaluation: New Roles, New Means*. NSSE Yearbook (University of Chicago Press, Chicago, 1969); and *Handbook on Formative and Summative Evaluation of Student Learning* by Benjamin S. Bloom, J. Thomas Hastings, and George F. Madaus (McGraw-Hill, New York, 1971).

Repeating Educational Cycle

The influence of measurement and appraisal on subsequent practice is usually considered (if at all) as one aspect of evaluation. The only reference which could be found which deals directly with the subject is Lee J. Cronbach, "Evaluation for Course Improvement," *Teachers College Record, 64,* 672–683.

Major Program Reconstruction

A surprisingly small amount of generalized literature could be found which focused directly on this topic, important though it is. Countless efforts to reconstruct adult educational programs have been made, but few have been fully described. Many surveys of practice are in existence but they are usually either typewritten or inexpensively duplicated, so that it would be pointless to include them in a general bibliography. The detailed analyses presented in Chapter Six arise from an examination of many of these fugitive sources as well as from the lengthy experience of the author. The following references deal with only a few of the topics touched upon in the chapter.

The question of how institutions can remain innovative is a central concern of the literature dealing with organizations and institutions, which was referred to in an earlier section of this essay. The following volumes drawn from the literature of business administration, education, political science, and social psychology deal directly with this theme:

R. L. KAHN AND OTHERS. *Organizational Stress* (Wiley, New York, 1964)

ROBERT N. LEHRER, *The Management of Improvement* (Reinhold, New York, 1965)

CHRIS ARGYRIS, *Organization and Innovation* (Dorsey, Homewood, Ill., 1965)

WARREN G. BENNIS, *Changing Organizations* (McGraw-Hill, New York, 1966)

FREDERICK C. MOSHER, editor, *Governmental Reorganizations* (Bobbs-Merrill, Indianapolis, Ind., 1967)

VICTOR A. THOMPSON, *Bureaucracy and Innovation* (University of Alabama Press, University, Ala., 1969)

FREMONT E. KAST, "Planning the Strategies in Complex Organizations," in *Education, Administration and Change* (Harper and Row, New York, 1970)

The problems of change encountered in university adult education are considered in *Institutional Backgrounds of Adult Education,* edited by R. J. Ingham (CSLEA, Boston, 1966). The proper use of outside consultants by adult educational agencies is suggested by models developed by Richard E. Byrd in "Planning with Volunteers," AL, *14* (May, 1965). Sources which suggest how to make a community survey are

Studying the Community: A Basis for Planning Library Adult Education Services (American Library Association, Chicago, 1960)

ROLAND L. WARREN, *Studying Your Community* (Free Press, New York, 1965)

PAUL R. MICO, "Community Self-Study," AL, *13* (March, 1965)

Of the available case studies, by far the most detailed is *Social Action and Interaction in Program Planning* by George M. Beal and others (Iowa State University Press, Ames, Iowa, 1966).

A study of a state-wide effort is given in *Kentucky on the March* by Harry W. Schacter (Harper, New York, 1949). A brief account of the self-study of a collegiate program is "Self-Study of Adult Education Division of Drury College" by Adelaide H. Jones, AE, *14* (Autumn, 1963).

Bibliographies

The British literature on adult education is much more carefully canvassed than the American. The most recent comprehensive bibliography in the former country was edited by Thomas Kelly, *A Selected Bibliography of Adult Education in Great Britain* (National Institute of Adult Education, London, 1962). In *Adult Education in Continental Europe,* Jindra Kulich has provided a valuable bibliography of sources in English covering the period from 1945 to 1969. (Ontario Institute for Studies in Education, Toronto, 1971). In the United States, the best general resources are the occasional issues of the *Review of Educational Research,* which summarize the literature of the field during the preceding period of years. The ERIC Clearinghouse for Adult Education at Syracuse University provides a wide variety of bibliographic resources, including reports on specific topics. Many of the books, particularly the general references cited elsewhere in this essay also have general or specialized bibliographies. Most of the general bibliographies in the field are so hard to find that it is virtually useless to list them, but the following three are somewhat more widely available:

RALPH A. BEALS AND LEON BRODY, *The Literature of Adult Education* (AAAE, New York, 1941)

J. D. MEZIROW AND DOROTHEA BERRY, *The Literature of Liberal Adult Education 1945–1957* (Scarecrow Press, Metuchen, N.J., 1960)

GEORGE F. AKER, *Adult Education Procedures, Methods and Techniques; A Classified and Annotated Bibliography, 1953–1963* (Syracuse University Library of Continuing Education, Syracuse, N.Y., 1965)

Name Index

303

Subject Index

A

Abbreviations, 238–239

Accomplishment, 227, 234; defined, 229; in program design, 147–148, 169; in program reconstruction, 203–204, 206, 207, 208, 209, 211. *See also* Behavioral objectives, Principle

Accrediting associations, 193

Act, 227; defined, 37; implemented, 182; in mass education, 127; in repeating educational cycle, 184; scheduling of, 160–161; in teacher-directed group instruction, 106

Activity, educational, 227; bibliography for, 285–300; as component, 47, 48; defined, 229; in program design, 133–134; in program reconstruction, 187–188; scheduling of, 9

Adaptation of means: bibliography for, 253–254; credo of, 7–8

Adjustment, 228; defined, 229; in life pattern, 173–180

Administration: institutional, 115; systems analysis in, 24

Administrator: as analyst, 38; as leader, 155; power of, defined, 191

Adult, defined, 227, 229

Adult education: agencies for, 45; assumptions of, 32–40; bibliographies for, 302; cases in, 59–89, 187–217, 263, 264, 273–274, 301–302; categories of,

310

B

relationships of, 167–168. *See also* Agricultural extension service

Creating an educational institution (C-7), 49–50, 54, 282; analysis of, 116–118; in Army prevocational instruction, 81; decision to proceed in, 135–136; in educational farm program, 68; examples of, 44; individualization of, 166–167; leadership training in, 157; in master planning, 87; roles and relationships in, 168; and social reinforcement, 165

Creative planning in new activity design, 121–123

Creative release of energy credo, 9

Creativeness: bibliography for, 272; not adult education function, 29

Credos, 7–9, 228; adaptation of means in, 7–8; as base for andragogy, 221; contradictions in, 9; and creative release of energy, 9; defined, 6, 230; and institutional processes improved, 8–9; and leader's importance, 8; mission-oriented, 7; need fulfillment in, 7

Criteria of evaluation, 228; in adult education, 170–171; in Army prevocational instruction, 83; bibliography for, 295–296; defined, 230; in format design, 47, 52, 169–171; in hobo school, 64; inferential, 170–171; and measurement and appraisal, 183; in program reconstruction, 193, 207

Curriculum: analysis of, 141; building, 13; specialist in, as analyst, 38, in future, 250; as leader, 155

Cycle: bibliography for, 300; and examination for new activities, 55–56; in program reconstruction, 215–217; repeating revision in, 184–185, 187

D

Decision-making: bibliography for, 285–286; in collaborative group education, 111; in committee-guided group learning, 109; in institutional growth model, 114; in learning group, 104; as process in selecting objectives, 200–201

Decision point, 228, 296; checklist of, 110, 122; defined, 230; nature of a system of, 224; order of, 47, 132; in program reconstruction, 187

Decision to proceed: bibliography for, 285–286; as component, 47, 48; in program design, 134–136; in program reconstruction, 191–200; strategies for, 192–194, 200

Demonstration method, 4, 159

Department of Agriculture and educational farm program, 65

Design, 228; defined, 230; in refinement of objectives, 143, 146. *See also* Clarity of design

Designing new activities in established formats (C-9), 48, 53, 129, 282; analysis of, 120–123; educational activity identified in, 133; in educational farm program, 68; examples of, 44–45; individualization of, 166–167; leadership training in, 157; in master planning, 87; roles and relationships in, 168; and social reinforcement, 165

Designing new institutional format (C-8), 49, 50, 54, 129, 282; analysis of, 118–120; in Army prevocational instruction, 81; and decision to proceed, 135, 136; in educational farm program, 68; examples of, 44; individualization of, 166–167; and interpretation, 180; in master planning, 87; roles and

education, 128; role of, 155;
and sequencing, 163; and
social reinforcement, 165;
sources of influence of, 155–
156; in teacher-directed
group instruction, 105
Leadership, 151; in adult education,
156; in balance among components, 56; in independent
study, 95; in learning group,
104; as resource, 152;
strengthening, 254–255; in tutorial teaching, 101
Learner, 227; defined, 232–233; refinement of objectives for,
143, 145; role of defined, 38
Learning: experiences in, 14; process
of, 2; resources for, 9; sequence structuring for, 24
Learning group (C-3), analysis of,
101–105; bibliography for,
277–279; and committee-
guided group learning, 110;
criteria for, 170; and decision
to proceed, 135; in educational farm program, 67; examples of, 43, 44; in format
design, 151; implementation
of, 213; individualization of,
166; in master planning, 87;
reconstruction of, 219; and social reinforcement, 165
Library. *See* Public library
Life pattern. *See* Format fit to life
patterns
Lifestyles, 228; of adults, 107–108; in
Army prevocational instruc-
tion, 82; bibliography for,
297; defined, 233; in fitting
format to life, 47, 53, 176–
177; of hobo school, 64; in
mass education, 128
Literacy courses, 28; as influenced
by pedagogy, 221–222; se-
quencing of, 163
Literary club: as adult education,
28; as learning group, 102

M

Mass education (C-11), 50, 51, 57,

129, 293; analysis of, 126–128;
bibliography for, 284–285;
category of, 44, 45, 221; criteria for, 170; in educational
farm program, 68; examples
of, 44, 45; individualization
of, 167; in master planning,
87; objectives for, 148–149;
reconstruction of, 219; sequencing of, 163; and social
reinforcement, 165
Master plan for city: as adult education program, 84–88; analysis
of, 87–88
Measurement of results, 151, 228; in
Army prevocational instruction, 82; as balanced among
components, 56; bibliography
for, 299–300; as component,
47, 54–55; defined, 54, 182–
183, 233; in development of
program design, 182–184; in
educational farm program, 68;
in hobo school, 65; in institutional administration, 115; in
mass education, 128; in master
planning, 88; neglect of, 187;
in program reconstruction,
214–215
Methods, 227; ability to use, 158–
159; in Army prevocational
training, 82, 83; bibliography
for, 292–293; defined, 158,
233; in format design, 47, 50,
158–160; of hobo school, 64;
need for several, 159; and resources, 152–153
Milieu, 227; bibliography for, 287;
defined, 233; refinement of objectives in, 143, 145
Ministry of Reconstruction, 7, 239,
240
Misapplied systems, 25–30; and andragogy and pedagogy, 221;
bibliography for, 264–272
Mission-oriented credo, 7
Motive, 227; bibliography for, 288;
defined, 138–139, 233; in refinement of objectives, 143,
146

design, 47, 52, 167–169; of hobo school, 64; in independent study, 95; in learning group, 104; in tutorial teaching, 97, 100–101

S

St. Francis Xavier University, 22, 263

Schedule and scheduling, 151, 152, 227; of activities, 9; of aggregate, 160; in Army prevocational instruction, 82, 83; aspects of, 160; component balance in, 56–57; defined, 235; in format design, 47, 50–51, 160–161; of hobo school, 64; in mass education, 128; no bibliography for, 293; studies on, scarce, 160–161

Sensitiveness, 227; defined, 235

Sensitivity training, 4, 103, 228; bibliography for, 258–259, 294; defined, 235; and group dynamics, 17, 18; implementation of, 181; as learning group, 102; resources for, 152; sequence of, 51; workshop objectives of, 144

Sequence of events, 151, 152, 227; in adult education, 162–163; in Army prevocational instruction, 82, 83; defined, 161–162, 235; in format design, 47, 51, 161–163; of hobo school, 64; no bibliography for, 293

Series, educational, 227, 228; defined, 37, 235; implementation of, 182; in mass education, 127; scheduling of, 160–161

Service: bibliography for, 265; defined, 235; not adult education function, 26, 29, 228

Settlement house, 4; bibliography for, 267; and clubs, 43, 111; focus of, 136; leadership training, in, 157; objectives of refined, 145

Situation, 227; as approach to adult education, 12, 32–40, 228; defined, 235; factors in category selection for, 129; and nature of learning, 32

Skill, 227; defined, 235

Social reinforcement, 18, 35, 151, 227; in Army prevocational instruction, 82, 84; in balance among components, 56, 57; bibliography for, 293–294; defined, 235; ethos of, 164; in format design, 47, 51, 163–166; fraternization as, 29–30; of hobo school, 64; in independent study, 95–96; and interpretation, 179; in learning group, 104; in mass education, 128; in master planning, 87; as motive, 138–139; in teacher-directed group instruction, 105; ways to foster, 165

Socialization, 249

Socialized learning situation, 16–18

Stages of survey: data collection, 197–199, 208; data examination, 199; emphases in, 196–197; framework and scope of, 195–196

Statements of objectives, 146–150; as abstractions, 147; accomplishment of, 147–148, 169, 203–204, 206, 207, 208, 209, 211, 227, 229, 234; as clearly stated, 149; cooperative, 148–149; as facilitative, 149–150; principle in, 148, 169–170, 203–204, 206, 207, 208, 209, 211, 227, 229, 234; as reality conforming, 147

Strategy, 227; defined, 236

Study groups: as committee-guided group learning, 43; as learning group, 103; objectives of refined, 145

Supervisor: in Army prevocational instruction, 82; as educator, 11, 38; as leader, 155, 156;